PRACTICE
MAKES
PERFECT:

HOW ONE DOCTOR FOUND
THE MEANING OF LIVES

DAVID ROBERTS, M.D.

ISBN: 1481104810
ISBN-13: 9781481104814

DEDICATION

To my children: Charles, Robert and Lindsey,
who rarely saw their father during the time period of this book,
and have each grown into wonderfully delightful adults,
of whom any father would be immensely proud.

ACKNOWLEDGMENTS

This book is a labor of love. Mostly, it flows out of the love of those closest to me, Chantel and my parents and children. In addition, there were a number of close friends, family, and even patients that took the time to read various chapters and give important feedback, and given how busy they each are, they should each be named: Dennis Angellis, M.D., Gail Blackwell, Amor Brannin, Jim Bruce, M.D., Jason Caldwell, Mark Cowen, M.D., Sheila Delaney, Dick Elkins, Mike Henderson, Jim Kaehr, Jack Knight, Julie Lujan, Fran Roberts, Peter Snow, and David Wilbern, PhD, as well as my family: Chantel, Charles, Robert, Lindsey and, Martha. Equally important has been the encouragement of my closest friends Tracy, Michael, Jim and Cesar, as well as all of the men in my three literary groups: David V., Mark, Peter, Dick E., Dick R., Jim, Terry, Bob, David W., Frank, Jack, Joe, Ross, and Steve.

I owe to the real Mark Edwards, M.D., a lifelong debt of gratitude. He took me into his new private practice before he could afford it, taught me everything I needed to know to succeed as a physician, and provided the rich gifts of friendship, mentoring, humor, and unconditional acceptance despite, as you shall soon see, the many ups and downs of those first five years. His memory is better than mine, and his remembrance of those days brought a great deal of additional richness and humor to the creation of this book.

I had two excellent editors that provided me with very straightforward and constructive feedback, in exhaustive detail: Nina Cantanese and Beth

Skolny at LaunchPad Media. As it turned out, my initial draft of this book contained exactly the right number of commas, but were it not for Nina and Beth, none of them would have been correctly placed.

There are two authors to whom I am deeply indebted. Sir Arthur Conan Doyle, through his characterization of Sherlock Holmes, inspired me to pursue a career in medicine. Second, James Herriot, through his work *All Creatures Great and Small*, led me to decide thirty years ago to someday write the book you are now holding, containing the stories of human rather than veterinary patients.

Of course, the ultimate acknowledgement must go to each of those patients who provided their inspiring stories for these pages. Without them, there would be only my own story to tell, a far less interesting tale. I owe my deepest gratitude to each of you.

INTRODUCTION

"… then laugh, leaning back in my arms

for life's not a paragraph
And death i think is no parenthesis."

E. E. Cummings, (1894 – 1962), American poet,
painter, essayist, author, and playwright

If you ask a good friend to describe to you the most important turning points in her life, and you have the time and inclination to listen, you will likely hear rich and meaningful stories about those events that brought an important change in how she came to understand her own place in the world. These events often include births, like the birth of one's first child, or each child, or perhaps the third child, when parents must switch from the man-to-man to zone defense to create some illusion of control in the chaos of family life.

Of course, there will be other important, life-altering, and calendared moments she may choose to chronicle. First kisses, a first date, graduations, meeting the "right" person, and a wedding may be added to her list. Her first day on the job in a brand new career might have offered her an important "ah ha" moment, or her retirement from a long and successful career, along with the many new opportunities that came her way in the next chapter of her life.

Which alter our lives to the greater measure: pleasant or unpleasant events? It may be part of the human condition that we are inspired, or perhaps more likely, compelled, to seek greater self-understanding in life's most difficult moments. You may hear her story of the time she lost a job, that difficult move away from her friends and loved ones, her divorce from the man she thought was so right at one time, or her strained relationship with a rebellious teenage daughter.

Alas, I myself have made no noteworthy changes in my own life as a result of everything going well. So, like me, your friend may list the hardships she has faced at the top of her list of her most important life experiences. And, if we must acknowledge births, successes, and hardships, so too must we be reminded of the role of death in shaping our lives.

The passing of her seventy-eight-year-old grandmother when she was eight. The death of her mother, just after her own children left home. Or, if she had been forced to face one of the most difficult challenges life can bring, the death of one of her children.

In sum, the exhilarating and the devastating, all those wonderfully profound events bringing radical alterations to one's life can usually be counted on the fingers of one or both hands. Yet, as you listen to her list, or create your own, there are two more important stories that are missing, which will temporally, if not profoundly, frame each of your lives. On your own list, you will likely not mention your own birth or your own death.

In my work as a physician over the past thirty years, I have had the privilege of sitting with patients who have experienced all of these common milestones of life, and then some. The onset of crippling arthritis affecting a single mother with two young children, which prevents her from working. The senseless murder of a forty-year-old man's teenage daughter, from which I seriously doubt he will ever recover. The death of a passenger in a motor vehicle accident for which the driver was not at fault, but he carries his own deep guilt for decades.

When we hear of such events, we can't help but imagine how difficult and overwhelming, how severe the challenges must be for those affected. We reflexively focus on their pain and suffering, which seems so completely senseless. If we know the person well, we may ask, "Why did this happen to *her*?" And, if we are feeling especially brave that day, we may also append, "…and not to *me*?"

What strikes me most deeply is that many of these stories – as they have been told to me as a physician, behind the closed examination room door – usually begin with the phrase, "Doctor, I've never told anyone this before, but…" The ensuing deep and passionate stories describe major turning points in their lives, hero's quests, and yet why am I the first to hear them? Or, more importantly, why am I perhaps the only one to benefit from the deep learning these brave souls have discovered?

The poet Muriel Rukeyser once said, "The universe is made of stories, not atoms." It is always clear to me, as I hear my patients' stories in their telling, that the true substance of a patient's life is being revealed to me.

For years, I have thought to myself, *Someone really ought to tell their stories.*

Like your hypothetical friend, we may each count our number of truly life changing events to be five to ten – perhaps one every seven to twenty years of our life. But what if our criteria are too strict? What if some of the events that have altered the course of our lives by only five degrees are more important in the end than those ninety and even one hundred-eighty degree turns resulting from our deepest hurts?

The good news is that instead of having twenty opportunities to see ourselves differently per lifetime, we may have twenty such opportunities per day – or more. Every interaction we have with another person, or the beauty of nature, or ourselves in a quiet moment has the opportunity to transform us. As a physician, I am blessed with twenty such opportunities per day in my work with my patients. Because I have been so intimately involved with men and women at critical crossroads of their lives, I have been blessed with the wonderful opportunity to learn from their challenges, their triumphs, their sorrows, their mistakes. And, as an added blessing, I have the opportunity now to tell some of these wonderful tales of lives changed both by good fortune and misfortune. Stories of our own deaths are rarely written, for somewhat obvious reasons. Yet you may find, as I have, that such accounts may be the best of the lot. Although the death of a patient both begins and ends this book, I hope you will see, as E.E. Cummings wisely observed, that "death … is no parenthesis."

While it is certain the events described in the following pages changed each patient's life, if we are open to the possibility, they may also change *our* lives. *Practice Makes Perfect: How One Doctor Found the Meaning of Lives* is also about the changes that have taken place in my life as a result of serving as the physician for people with remarkable stories, tales that they have never told themselves but still want for the telling. Each may hold a clue to the meaning of our lives.

As a physician, the challenge in writing these stories is to make them as true as possible, while not providing so much information that individual privacy will be violated. Since twenty-five years have passed, many of the patients we will learn from in these chapters, and who survived the five-year time period of the book, will have since passed away themselves. Of course, I changed every name of every character, including my own. I have also necessarily changed some non-critical details in an effort to respect each patient's privacy. Nonetheless, it is my hope that the feeling and meaning of each story rings true and the lessons offered to me by each patient will pass through to the reader in their purest possible form.

As you read these tales, I hope you too will glean some of the same rich wisdom from these courageous souls who have faced fears and challenges far beyond anything they ever dreamed possible. Some of these patients profoundly inspired me, while others deeply frustrated me. I have laughed with some, cried with others, and silently blessed (or occasionally even cursed) each of them. But now, years later, I find they have all been my teachers. When the student is ready, the teacher will appear.

As individuals, we each bring a unique set of experiences and perspective into the world, which have never been and never will be duplicated in all the history of the universe. Who will tell *your* stories? What are the moments of your own life that most clearly changed your course in the world and brought you greater understanding of yourself and your place here?

It is my hope that you will be inspired by the teachings of these patients to tell your own stories as well.

CHAPTER 1

"Good judgment comes from experience.
Experience comes from bad judgment."

Rudolph Reichert, M.D. (1922 –), American cardiologist and mentor
(also attributed to many others)

Wednesday, July 8, 1981, 5:00 a.m.

This being my very first week of hospital rounds as a new attending physician fresh out of internal medicine residency training, I awoke extra early and arrived at the hospital at 5:00 a.m., determined to see Mr. Harandi, my sickest and most challenging patient, first.

On the closed door of his room, there was taped a note for me:

"Dr. Roberts: PLEASE do not
go into this room without
speaking to me first!
Sara Ryan, R.N."

I had not met Sara before, and I learned quickly she was a newly graduated nurse in her first week of inpatient work. Despite having been up all night, she looked bright and enthusiastic in her brand new white

1

nursing blouse and skirt, obviously as excited as I was to have just crossed the threshold of our new careers. If, as I had already been told several times, I looked too young to be an attending physician, then she looked too young to even be in high school, so we had two things in common thus far. Nevertheless, she looked very nervous about talking to me and began with an overly official tone.

"Can we go into the conference room for a few minutes?" she asked respectfully.

She had long, straight brown hair tied back with a barrette on each side and bright green eyes. I could see her hands were clenched in a way that made me think she was summoning all of her determination for what she was about to do.

After she closed the door and we both sat down, she began, "Mr. Harandi doesn't want to see you today."

I admired her direct approach and preferred it to the usual ten minutes of a conflict-averse and vague story unfolding, only to arrive at the same place.

"He says you deeply insulted him. I don't think you should go in to his room today." She sighed with relief, as if to say, "There. I've said it!" Her hands relaxed to the point that her nails were no longer digging into her palms.

Here was a brave young woman who was willing to challenge me, a supposed authority figure, in her first week on a new job. This was a rare event, and it should have made me quite curious. However, I have found through the years that defensiveness and curiosity are mutually exclusive emotions, at least inside of me. I was feeling defensive and unfortunately had no capacity to be curious.

"When I saw him yesterday, I knew he was very unhappy with me, but I didn't have the slightest idea why. Did he say what it was I had done to offend him?"

"No," she replied. "I asked him several times myself and never really got an explanation. He was quite clear he never wanted to see you again, though."

"At a minimum, Sara, I still need to go in there and talk to him about who he wants his new doctor to be. I suppose one of his pulmonary or cardiology doctors would be willing to take the responsibility for his care instead."

"I really don't think you should go into his room," she cautioned. "I've never seen a patient so angry."

I felt trapped between the horns of this dilemma, with an ominous certainty I would be gored either way.

"Legally, I believe I have to transfer his care to another doctor, and in order to do that, I need to speak with him, at least briefly. I'll only go in there for a minute and will just tell him Dr. Westerman, his pulmonary doctor, will follow him here in the hospital until he is discharged."

"Listen," she attempted again, her hands now returned to tight fists, "as I told you, this is my first week as a real nurse, and I don't understand all the legal requirements."

In retrospect, she was trying desperately to reach me, but unfortunately, in my mind, what seemed to me like a legal imperative tended to outweigh her good judgment regarding the gravity of the situation.

"This man made me promise I wouldn't let you in the room!"

I was completely unaware of how I was feeling about all of this, but looking back now, I realize I was overwhelmed with both embarrassment at being "fired" by a patient on my second day and an excessive sense of responsibility to make this situation better. I have since learned to recognize these two emotions, embarrassment and excessive responsibility, as a fatal combination. Excessive responsibility, in particular, is my lifelong strong suit. These days, I am sometimes able to hit the "abort" button before it is too late. But not on that day.

"Listen, Sara, I really appreciate all you are trying to do here. Let's go down to his room together, and I'll just stick my head in the door, let him know I'm happy to arrange for another doctor to take care of him, see who he wants, and then I'll leave and write an order to transfer his care."

I could tell she was not in agreement with this plan, but having been denied by me three times (before sunrise and the cock's crow, no less), she likely felt she had done everything she could do. We moved together down the hall to his room. I removed the sign she had written for me, knocked softly, and slowly opened the door.

Despite it being quite early, Mr. Harandi was sitting in his chair, slumped over and half asleep. But only for a moment. As he looked up at me, his face began turning a pale shade of purple, and in a single motion, he stood up quickly from his chair and threw his inhaler at me. While I dodged the projectile, he began to shout, "Get out! Get out!"

"Mr. Harandi, I know you want a new doctor. That is fine. I am…"

"You have insulted me. Get out! GET OUT!" His voice was getting progressively louder and I worried the patients in nearby rooms were being awakened.

"I'm going to ask Dr. Westerman to take over your care. I'm sorry for whatever I did to insult you. That was not my…"

Nothing I had to say had any beneficial effect. His face now a bright purple, Mr. Harandi tried an alternative plan and began rushing for the door.

"…intention, I assure you. I apologize."

He pushed himself between us and careened into the corridor.

"Mr. Harandi!" Sara cried. "Come back!"

We both rushed after him down the hall toward the nursing desk, deeply concerned about his running after suffering a massive heart attack, especially in this highly agitated and emotional state. He glanced back over his right shoulder and saw us following. He then made a sharp left turn into the alcove near the end of the hall, appeared to lose his footing, and fell forward to the floor with his head landing near the small shower in the back of the recess.

We looked down at him. He was motionless. Using the same level of clinical acumen I had exhibited thus far this morning, I suggested, "He looks like he's fainted."

Sara, using the same level of clinical acumen *she* had shown this morning, said, "Doctor, I think he may have had a cardiac arrest."

We were now both kneeling. He had no respirations, and neither of us could find a pulse.

"Call the code!" I yelled.

Ten seconds later, the hospital's ceiling-mounted loudspeakers blared on every floor, "Code Blue, 1100 Unit. Code Blue, 1100 Unit."

Sara and I performed CPR, she on respirations and I doing chest compressions, for about ninety seconds until the code team arrived. Despite the fact we had witnessed his cardiac arrest and CPR had been initiated within seconds, the code team was unsuccessful in our attempts to bring him back to life.

CHAPTER 2

"It is better to understand a little than to misunderstand a lot."

Anatole France (1844 - 1924), French poet, journalist, and novelist

Monday, July 6 (two days earlier), 1981, 7:30 a.m.

I hurried into the office on Monday morning. This was the day I started my first week on call for my new medical practice. I joined Mark Edwards, M.D., in the practice of Internal Medicine, five days earlier, on Wednesday, July 1, 1981. The culmination of twenty-three years of formal education, June 30th had been my last day of my three-year training in Internal Medicine. While I had the ability to act rather independently in my work as an intern and resident, every conversation with or examination of a patient, and every order I wrote, had been legally considered to be under the auspices of an attending physician, who was ultimately responsible for my actions. Our hospital had over six-hundred such "attendings" and each had finished their formal medical training and passed their certifying examination in their specialty.

So finally, I was a "real doctor."

Mark, ever generous, put himself on call over the Fourth of July weekend, and my turn came on Monday, July 6th. We each took the on-call rotation for a whole week, from one Monday morning at 8:00 a.m. to the next. Being on call involved seeing all of our own patients admitted to the hospital, performing consultations for other physicians, and then coming back to the office for six hours of patient care in our office. In addition, the on-call doc would carry the practice pager and answer all telephone calls from our patients outside of our regular office hours. The practice was quite busy even on the day I started, and so evening and particularly weekend calls were often abundant.

The sickest patient on our hospital service was the one whom Mark had saved for last, Amin Harandi. He was a sixty-four year-old Persian gentleman who had moved to the United States and, for the past three years, lived in our Midwestern town with his daughter and son-in-law. He smoked heavily, to the point of developing severe emphysema, had diabetes, very high cholesterol, and uncontrolled high blood pressure because he refused to take any medications for these problems. Apparently, his father and all three of his brothers had already died of coronary artery disease and resulting heart attacks.

"He's a walking chronicle of risk factors for coronary artery disease," Mark observed, as he explained the details of his hospital course.

He had been brought in by ambulance with a massive heart attack two weeks prior and then had a cardiac arrest shortly after admission to the coronary care unit. After his transfer out of the CCU to a step-down unit he had to be transferred back twice for episodes of rapid heart rate. An angry man with a short temper, both episodes occurred after emotional outbursts: one directed at a nurse and the other at his son-in-law. What both eruptions had in common was that no one really understood what he was upset about. It seemed as though he just started yelling for no apparent reason.

"He's lucky to be alive," Mark concluded, "and should be able to go home sometime this week if his lungs are clear and his wheezing is gone."

Mark then handed me the on-call beeper, in what was the final act of this Monday morning accountability transfer. He looked unusually exhausted.

"Was it a bad weekend?" I asked, somewhat apprehensive about the new responsibilities I was about to take on and looking mainly for my own reassurance.

"Not that bad," he replied. Mark was never one to complain. "It just occurred to me, though, that I have been on call for my practice for three

hundred seventy straight days! That's too long for anyone to be on duty."
After a short pause for reflection, he added with a smile of relief, "Boy, am
I ever glad to be handing this to you!"

With the word "you," I felt the beeper press into the palm of my hand.
For a moment, I had the impression this small 1.5 by 2.5 by 0.5 inch box
of electronics weighed fifty pounds. Perhaps it was pressure from Mark's
hand or simply a premonition of the incredible weight I would feel each
time I began my call duties for our two-physician Internal Medicine group.

Having finished our "check-out," we both began a full day of seeing
outpatients in the office. Miraculously, I had no phone calls on my very
first Monday night on call as an attending physician. When I awoke very
early Tuesday morning, I took the beeper's silence as a favorable omen
that perhaps my anxiety and fear about my new responsibilities were
unfounded.

The next morning, Tuesday, July 7, I arrived at the hospital at about
5:30 a.m. Needing to be back in the office to see patients at 9:00 a.m., I
had calculated I could see everyone in the hospital in just less than three
hours, which would give me thirty minutes of extra time before my first
office patient. Everything went according to plan, and I was able to see all
of our patients but Mr. Harandi by 8:15 a.m., including writing progress
notes in each chart and additional detailed notes for myself. I discharged
two patients who were ready to go home, and I wondered if Mr. Harandi
might be the third.

As I walked down the stairs to the first floor to see him, Dr. Westerman,
one of my favorite teachers and the pulmonary specialist who had been
following this patient and helping us to manage his lung disease, stopped
me. In his early forties, Chuck was a brilliant clinician with a wry sense
of humor that was one of the bright spots of my residency training. The
crisply starched white coat and the blue pinstripe shirt contrasted sharply
with his longish, curly brown hair, moustache off the cover of one of the
early Crosby, Stills & Nash album covers, and his psychedelic tie.

Chuck stopped me to let me know our mutual patient was not ready
for discharge yet. "Still wheezing this morning, but much better. We'll

stop his NMTs and IV and convert to PO medications." In medical shorthand, he was telling me he had discontinued Mr. Harandi's nebulized mist treatments, a form of lung therapy delivered by a small machine that was stronger than the hand-held inhaler he had ordered to replace them, and that our patient should now take all medications and fluids orally, rather than intravenously. "He'll be ready to go hopefully tomorrow, or Thursday at the latest."

"Thanks, Chuck," I replied and quickly glanced at my watch to ensure I wouldn't be late for my office patients. He continued up the stairs as I went down.

"Oh, by the way," he called after me, "congratulations on your first day of inpatient rounds as a new attending physician. Different, isn't it?"

Somewhat embarrassed at the fact this revelation had only come to me this week, I replied, "I had *no idea* how stressful it can be to be responsible for *everything*. When I was a resident, I really believed I was carrying the burden myself. It feels twenty times heavier just one week later."

"You'll get used to it," Chuck answered, smiling knowingly. "You might not believe this, and I certainly mean no offense, but there were a few times when I was nervous when *you* called me in the middle of the night."

Like most doctors, I have ready recall of every mistake I've ever made, and I could immediately remember at least two times I had called Dr. Westerman in the middle of the night about very sick patients in his medical intensive care unit. Both times, awaking from sleep, he had graciously pointed out other possible explanations for the patients' sharp turns for the worse than the ones I had theorized and already started to treat, and each time he was proven to be right on our rounds together the following morning.

"And you are, I mean *were*, one of the best residents I've ever worked with," he added hastily, likely misinterpreting the frown on my face.

"Well, it's humbling to realize my whole worldview for my three years of training was so insular, so one-sided, so immediately exposed after just one week as an attending physician," I sheepishly admitted.

"Like most of everyone's views on everything, I suspect," he concluded, now ascending the stairs again and disappearing from view.

On the first floor, I located Mr. Harandi's chart and made my way to his room. He was sitting in the chair next to his bed, intently watching a news story on the television regarding the anticipated nomination of the first female Supreme Court justice in history by Ronald Reagan later that day. He seemed to be upset about the television and was grumbling softly. I grabbed the remote control from his bed, and with a quick and cursory apology, I turned off the television so that we could talk.

He was a large man with a grave appearance and dark black hair that covered not only the usual territory of the human scalp but also at least half of his forehead. The gap between his hairline and his equally bushy eyebrows disappeared each time he wrinkled his forehead. His deep dark eyes seemed to radiate anger and foreboding. Every muscle in his body appeared tense, and I noticed mine beginning to tense as I introduced myself as I had done all morning.

"Hello, Mr. Harandi, my name is Dr. David Roberts. I'm Dr. Edwards' partner. I'm making hospital rounds this week, and I'll be…"

"Where is Dr. Edwards?" he interrupted in a thick accent, which was a bit difficult for me to understand initially.

Speaking a bit more slowly, I responded, "Well, Dr. Edwards is in the office seeing patients this week, and I'll be in the hospital. I'll be here each day until you go home…"

"I need to talk to Dr. Edwards about this inhaler," he asserted sharply, holding up the inhaler the nurse had given to him that morning as a result of Chuck Westerman's order.

"Well, I'd be happy to talk to you about the inhaler if you like." I remembered Mark's comment about being on call for three hundred seventy consecutive days, and I was not about to have him make a trip back to the hospital this week. I was also feeling the need to defend myself and not just my new practice partner. All of Mark's other hospitalized patients had seemed absolutely delighted to meet me this morning. Many of them were worried about how overly hard they believed Mark was working, and they were not only very accepting but overtly encouraging me as their new hospital physician. I had felt my confidence grow with each introduction. Apparently, though, I had not saved the best for last.

"I need to talk to Dr. Edwards about my inhaler. TODAY!" Without being certain I remembered what a gauntlet actually was, I could see a vague image of a rusty glove, made of armored material, lying at my feet.

"Dr. Edwards won't be at the hospital all week. He's busy seeing patients in the office. I'd be happy to talk to you about your inhaler."

Up to this point in my life, I had always thought the expression "His face turned beet red" was pure hyperbole. As I watched Mr. Harandi closely, though, I could see his face turn various shades of red, crimson, and finally the red-purple color of a beet. It was so disconcerting, I felt a panic well up inside of me. Here was a man with horrible heart disease turning purple right in front of me, and I had no idea what to do. He crossed his arms over his chest, grunted as if to emphasize his prior demand, and actually turned his back to me. As he turned, I had the sense the color might be receding a bit.

Maybe there is a language barrier here, I thought. *Maybe he thinks I've insulted him.* I looked at my watch: 8:35 a.m. *You have fifteen more minutes to spend in this room, maximum,* I calculated. *You can run to your car, drive quickly to the office building in five minutes, run into the practice office, and still be on time for your 9:00 a.m. patient.* Back in that period of my life, I used running and fast driving to attempt to what seemed to be the unreasonable limitation of possessing only twenty-four hours in any given day.

"Mr. Harandi, I'm just going to sit here and go over your chart in detail. When I'm done, we can talk more about your inhaler. Will this be all right with you?" I opened the chart and began to read it in detail.

Up to this point, he had been sitting with most of his back facing toward me, but at enough of an angle that I could see some of the left profile of his face. He dropped his elbows to the armrests of the chair, lifted up a bit, and began to move.

I looked up again, and just as I thought, *Perhaps we're making progress here,* he rotated his chair to his right, positioning himself carefully so his own back and that of his chair were perfectly facing me, any trace of a profile gone. I absentmindedly began counting the symmetric rolls of adipose tissue on the back of his neck. *…Three, four…* I gently reiterated my plan to study his chart and continued poring through it. It took ten minutes, reading quickly through the thick medical record.

"Mr. Harandi, I've reviewed your entire chart, and Dr. Edwards provided me with a very detailed summary of your hospital care yesterday. I'd like to listen to your lungs and heart now if I may."

No response. I walked around the bed and stood next to his chair, on his left.

"I'd just like to open your gown in the back and listen to your lungs. Okay?" He remained stiff. "Dr. Edwards asked me to be sure and check your lungs this morning," I tried. His shoulders relaxed, and I took this as his tacit approval to proceed. As Chuck had mentioned earlier, he still had very mild wheezing, but this was a dramatic improvement over what Mark's chart note and his verbal description to me the previous day had provided.

"Your lungs sound much better, Mr. Harandi. I'm going to listen to your heart now."

With neither his cooperation nor resistance, I was able to reach around and listen to his heart in a sitting position. He had a loud murmur that, according to his medical record, had been heard by others and a suggestion of an extra sound that implied the continued failure of his heart to pump effectively.

"I'd like to have you move over to the bed, if you don't mind, so I can really listen to your heart well with you lying down. Would you be willing to do that?"

No response again, which I took to be a clear, "No." *Maybe tomorrow*, I thought. *You probably should only invoke Dr. Edwards' name once per visit!*

I sat back in my chair and documented his progress in the chart from a heart, lung, and laboratory point of view. I mentioned in my note that he seemed angry and did not want to be fully examined. It was now 8:50 a.m.

"Well, Mr. Harandi, I need to return to the office now. It was nice talking to you," I closed, immediately wishing that I had not said that for a variety of reasons. *Actually, I'm not feeling it has been all that nice to talk to you. You have made it clear that you don't think that it was nice for you, either. You wish I wasn't here. I know you'd rather see Mark.*

I cleared the threshold of his room and was heading down the hall when he called out, "Will you be coming back later today?" I reluctantly returned to the doorway.

"Usually, we make rounds every morning, so the next time I'll be here is tomorrow morning. I can come by earlier so we can spend more time together, if you'd like."

Maybe he thinks I'm too rushed. But I've spent twice as much time with him as any other patient today.

"I don't like this inhaler," he began again.

"What don't you like about it?"

"I don't like it, I said."

Another furtive glance at my watch: *8:51. This is going nowhere.*

"Are you having trouble using it? Trouble getting the medication into your lungs with this inhaler?" I asked, starting through the list of possible reasons he might not like the inhaler given his unwillingness to volunteer the information.

A fifteen-second pause. "No."

"Do you dislike the taste of the inhaler?" Could it be this simple? All inhalers have a bit of a bitter taste, though.

Another fifteen-second pause. Now he was just shaking his head from side to side in a dramatic fashion.

Why am I doing this?

"Are you concerned this new inhaler may not be as effective as the mist treatments you've been getting in the hospital for the past several weeks?" I hoped this was the explanation, because I was out of any other possible ideas. I wasn't going to ask him about the color of the plastic case.

This time there was a thirty-second pause, then more side-to-side head shaking. *Great. We've lost all verbal communication. 8:53 a.m. You will definitely be late for your first patient, David.*

"Well, Mr. Harandi, I will be happy to talk to you more about this tomorrow. I'll also let Dr. Westerman, your lung doctor, know you're not happy with the inhaler he suggested." And then I was gone, racing down the hallway, then to the parking lot, and then speeding in my car to our office one mile away.

"How did your first day of hospital rounds go?" Mark asked with concern and sincerity as I raced into our shared office to put down my things.

"I'll tell you later," I huffed, out of breath from the run, moving immediately back into the hall and opening the door to the exam room where my first patient of the morning waited.

Over our lunch break, I confessed my total exasperation with Mr. Harandi and his mono- and even non-syllabic answers to my questions.

"He's a tough one," Mark responded, but I could tell he was surprised. "How about the other patients?"

"They were all delighted to meet me. Some of them have been worried about you. I think Mrs. Brubaker thinks you are her son, by the way."

Mark smiled. "It's interesting how different each patient can be. Think about the difference between Harandi and Brubaker," he reflected. Mark was a philosopher at heart, and I enjoyed his ability to paint a gigantic wall mural of medicine when I was trapped inside the borders of my one-dollar photo booth snapshot.

"Were *you* able to talk to him?" I asked, still wondering about his apparent surprise at my experience.

"He seemed angry with everyone, including me," Mark confessed. "I hadn't seen him before in the office. In fact, he hasn't seen a doctor in the United States in the three years he's been here. There was nothing in our interactions over the past week that might predict he'd want to see *me* again."

"I called Chuck, and he said he'd stop by again about the inhaler problem. Do you think I should go back to the hospital tonight and talk to Mr. Harandi again?" I wondered aloud.

"No," Mark offered. "I'm not sure there is anything either of us can do to make him happy at this point."

That night, frequent phone calls made up for the silence of the previous night. There were nine calls, including three new admissions from the emergency room. As is often the case, the calls seemed perfectly spaced to guarantee that my brain would experience no REM sleep. I awoke extra early and arrived at the hospital at 5 a.m., determined to see Mr. Harandi first this time.

There hung a note for me, taped to the closed door:

"Dr. Roberts: PLEASE do not
go into this room without
speaking to me first!
Sara Ryan, R.N."

CHAPTER 3

"While we are free to choose our actions,
we are not free to choose the consequences of our actions."

Steven Covey (1932 - 2012), American Business Author

Wednesday, July 8, 6:30 a.m.

There was the very same note, now a bit crumpled, laying on the floor next to Mr. Harandi's lifeless body, where I had dropped it when I began his chest compressions. Seeing it brought me back to this present moment. I had been involved in almost two hundred cardiac arrest situations over my three previous years of training, but this morning, the whole process seemed unusually violent to me. Today was not the first time I had felt a rib crack beneath the heel of my hand while performing chest compressions. Through the years, I had given orders to provide at least several hundred electric shocks to restart beatless hearts, and I had seen the arching chest and twitching arms of each patient in response. Mr. Harandi's shock-induced spasms seemed unusually animated with life. In fact, the third and final time I ordered the use of the cardioversion machine, at the maximum voltage, in a last-ditch effort to restart his heart, his right arm flailed out and hit my ankle. Of course, it was a random set of muscle contractions, but I couldn't help but wonder, *Is he telling me to stop all of this? To let him go? Or is he still just angry with me?*

His skin color was equally bothersome. While many patients turn blue in color, due to an excess of carbon dioxide in their blood resulting from their lack of respiration, Mr. Harandi's face, chest, and arms showed the same mottled and purplish hue. He looked as though he had been bruised, deeply bruised, for years and years, and now the color of his suffering was clearly visible to the medical team in the harsh hospital fluorescent light, in deep contrast to the shining, opalescent tile of the hospital hallway. I can still remember the smell of the recently waxed floor.

"O.K. Let's stop now," I whispered to the resident who was leading the cardiac arrest team. He seemed relieved; it had been an hour of grueling effort with no hint of a positive outcome. He made the official announcement to the team.

Perhaps it was my own guilt over my personal role in his cardiac arrest, or the preamble of my patient's anger over the past forty-eight hours, or, for that matter, the previous sixty-four years of his life. I could not help but think, *You just killed this man, David. Not exactly keeping your Hippocratic Oath here, are you?*

I was seeing my whole future pass away before my eyes: loss of medical staff privileges, loss of medical license, being let go from my new medical practice, friends and family no longer speaking to me. I was just getting to the ten million dollar malpractice suit verdict, followed by the homicide conviction, when I regained my awareness of those around me. As the group dispersed, I looked over at Sara, who also seemed completely overwhelmed. I surmised she too was probably feeling responsible for Mr. Harandi's death, because she had not prevented me from entering his room. I recalled the way she had emphatically warned me that she had promised him she would not let me see him again.

"Sara, can we talk in the conference room?" I asked, gently taking her left forearm and guiding her in her dazed state to the room twenty feet away. We both sat down, and this time I closed the door.

"Look," I began, "this was completely my fault. You did everything you possibly could have done here, and I just ignored you."

She looked up at me with tears and confusion in her eyes. She tried to speak but just shook her head sadly to indicate she could not.

"Your clinical instincts were exactly right. Mine were wrong. I wish I had listened to you."

At this point, it occurred to me she might be playing the same "this is the end of my career" movie in her head as I, fearing her new vocation in nursing, now officially one week old, was over.

"My progress note for today will clearly indicate you advised me NOT to go in his room."

There was a knock at the door, and Char McCartney, the head nurse on this unit and probably our best nursing manager in the hospital, came into the room, closed the door behind her, and sat down. She put her hand on Sara's shoulder.

"This has been a rough morning for you two," she said. "What happened?"

I recounted with painstaking specificity the morning's events while Sara remained silent. Providing excessive detail is my standard approach to describing situations in which I have clearly failed, serving initially as self-flagellation but more constructively as my own way of sorting out what actually happened, in the hopes I can learn something from my mistakes. Unfortunately, I have had little success in my life in learning from the mistakes of others. I think my innate, genetically acquired stubbornness requires me to commit each error myself, so I might develop the motivation necessary for me to fully understand and grow.

Char shook her head as if to exorcise all of the demons floating in our minds. "Well, the family is on their way in. They should be here any minute," she informed us. "Sara, why don't you and I go into my office and talk a bit more?"

As they left, I frantically picked up the phone and called Mark. Talking with pressured speech, I explained all of the morning's events as quickly as I possibly could. With Mark's first question at the end of my story, it was clear that my tortured narrative lacked a few important details.

"So, are you saying he is dead?" Mark asked.

How could you have missed making that *clear?* I wondered.

"Yes, he is. We just ended our resuscitation efforts five minutes ago. The family is on the way in. Now what do I do?"

Mark was blessed with the clarity of thought to which I had aspired during my entire residency training. Even in the messiest situations, with the sickest possible patients, he maintained a calm and clear approach, which put the medical team at ease and helped us all to function at a higher level. I desperately needed this clarity now.

"This is a gentleman who had an extremely poor prognosis. Frankly, he was a time bomb waiting to explode. It's unfortunate you had to be right there when it happened, but it was going to happen, David, with or without you."

My throat began to constrict, and my vision blurred. I was now crying and could not respond verbally. This all seemed so *opposite* of the reasons why I had chosen a career in medicine.

Finally, I blurted out, "But Mark, I killed this man."

"No you didn't," he said in as reassuring a tone as he possibly could. "Nobody will think you killed him."

With the possible exception of Sara, I thought.

"The family is coming in. Do you want to come over and talk to them?" I asked him, desperately hoping he would say yes but knowing the appropriate answer would be no.

"No, you'll do fine. Just tell them what happened. Remember, he was screaming at the top of his lungs at his son-in-law from his hospital bed just three days ago. His family won't be surprised at all. They knew he wasn't going to make it out of the hospital. His daughter told me she had a dream in which he died in the hospital, and I told her not to worry. In fact, I told her I was sure he'd be just fine."

Most doctors learn early in our careers that our specific answers to the often sought after predictions of "How long do I have to live, Doc?" are invariably wrong and have an intensely humbling cumulative effect. I have heard many stories in my career about a man given the clean bill of health who died in the lobby on the way out of his doctor's office. I care for an eighty-six-year-old woman in my practice today who was told she had six months left to live after it was discovered she had a huge, inoperable aneurysm in her aorta, the main blood vessel in the chest. This pronouncement was made six years ago. I'm secretly hoping she outlives the doctor who told her she had just six months to live.

In those early days of practice, Mark and I had regular opportunities to learn such humility. As my mentor, Dr. Reichert used to say, "Good judgment comes from experience. Experience comes from bad judgment." Through our medical training, Mark and I had both been blessed with the abundance of experiences we needed to become better physicians.

There was another knock at the conference room door.

"This must be the family," I said to Mark, and we both hung up.

As I rose from my chair, the ward clerk opened the door and a Middle Eastern couple in their late thirties came into the room. They seemed hastily dressed; his shirt was misbuttoned and untucked. Both looked exhausted, as though they had been awake all night, and now they were burdened with the news of their father's death. After introductions, I ploughed ahead at a level of honesty and concern of which any physician might be capable, once he had resigned himself to the inevitable and total loss of his career. I had nothing to lose.

"I saw your father for the first time yesterday and spent about forty minutes with him. He was concerned about his inhaler." They both nodded as though they were exceedingly familiar with the story. "Your father probably told you about this." More nods.

"I guess he decided he didn't want to see me as a doctor. Something I did must have insulted him. The nurse suggested this morning I not even talk to him, but I felt I had to go in the room to make arrangements with him to transfer to a new doctor." They again nodded knowingly, although this was a part of the story they could not possibly have known. "So, when I did go into the room, he started yelling at me, ran into the hall, and, well, he just fell over and died."

It was not possible to tell his family the story without deep emotion, and I had to stop and collect myself several times, starting again when I thought I was capable of getting at least three or four words out.

"We tried to resuscitate him, but we were unsuccessful. He had such a massive heart attack the first time. If this was another one, then it was probably the last straw."

"We'll never know," pronounced the daughter.

I knew I would need to address her incorrect assumption shortly, but I felt a greater, more urgent need for my own absolution. "Look, I have absolutely no idea what I did to insult your father, but I am deeply sorry for whatever I did." I truly was.

"He called us at home at least six times last night to yell at us about his inhaler," the daughter explained in hushed tones. "We were up all night."

"What did I do or say that insulted him? Or *didn't* do or say?" I needed to know this. I never wanted to make the same mistake again.

"Dr. Roberts," his daughter continued, "my father has spent his whole life being insulted by almost everyone and everything. We never know what will set him off. We don't know what he was upset about yesterday. *You* will never know, either. He kept us up all night with his phone calls two other times since he's been here, equally angry at others for insulting him." She made quotation marks in the air around the word "angry" with her fingers in an exaggerated way, as though this were the one-millionth time she had been forced to deal with her father's anger. "He has been living with us for three years, and we never know when he will explode. It's been like living with a time bomb in your house, always ticking."

"I'm sorry," I said and remained quiet. I noticed she was still talking about her father in the present tense. I knew from experience it would take some time for him to take his place in her past.

She and her husband looked at each other for some time, and I clearly felt some sense within me that they were both deeply sad and were also both relieved.

"I knew he was going to die here. I had a dream about it. I told Dr. Edwards," the daughter explained slowly, without recrimination.

I slowly became aware of the common bond we had: each of us in the room was seeking absolution, I for my feelings of culpability for their father's death, and the two of them for their feelings of relief.

"This must have been an incredibly long and difficult road for the two of you," I suggested, knowing by their physical response to my comment their marriage had been under great duress over the past three years. "I'm sorry that it ended in this way, with you having to rush into the hospital so early in the morning."

They both nodded as a way of accepting my apology without having to speak.

"Well, it's over now," the son-in-law spoke up. "Is there anything else we need to do here?" He began to reach for his coat.

"Well, there is one more thing. According to state law, your father must undergo an autopsy, given the unexpected nature of his death."

Unexpected, I thought. *Why would you use this particular word? His daughter just told you she knew this would happen.*

"From a strictly medical point of view, I mean," I quickly appended.

"Is it really necessary?" the daughter began. Her husband took her hand and shrugged his shoulders.

"I guess the law is the law," he suggested to her.

"You will need to sign a few forms," I explained. "After the autopsy is complete, I'll give you a call, and you can come into my office and we'll review it together if you like." It was clear from their non-verbal response they would have no interest in doing this. They signed the necessary forms and left immediately, each appearing torn by their ambivalence at the loss of her father, and yet clinging more tightly to each other as they left the conference room than upon their arrival.

I wandered through the halls of the hospital and completed the remainder of my rounds. I relaxed only a bit when I realized it might take several days for me to lose my staff privileges and medical license. I could probably at least finish out my week of call, giving Mark a well-deserved seven days off. I had never felt worse in my life, and I hung on tightly to my own guilt over what I had done to Mr. Harandi. The rest of the day was a blur, and I spent the night in a continuous rerun of the morning's events on the movie screen in my mind. It didn't matter whether I was awake or asleep; it was the same movie in my dream.

Jack Kornfield, an eminent Buddhist writer and scholar, comments on how interesting it is to watch our own mind in action if we can learn to step back and objectively do so. "It's like a bad cable TV channel, showing old commercials over and over. Ninety-five percent of it is reruns, it is mostly drama, and it *all* stars you-know-who!" There could no better description of my state of mind as I lay there in bed, tossing and turning, that Wednesday night.

CHAPTER 4

"Bound only by the paper-thin wrapper of mortality,
a soul here lies, struggling to be free."

Eric Ingerson, Bret Mogilefsky, Tim Schafer, Peter Tsacle,
from the movie Grim Fandango, (1998)

The next morning, Thursday, July 9, exhausted but pressing on through hospital rounds, I was paged to call the pathology department at about 8:30 a.m. I responded immediately. It was Sheldon Monthan, a pathologist I knew well from my years of training at St. Joseph's Hospital.

"David, I'm doing the autopsy on Mr. Harandi. Do you want to come down and see this?"

During my residency, I had made it a point to try to attend at least a portion of the two-hour post-mortem examination of any patient of mine who had died. Very often, the actual examination of the patient's internal organs would provide new clues to diagnosis, particularly back in those days when we somehow muddled through without high-resolution CT scans and MRI studies on every patient, as is our practice these days.

I just could not bring myself to go down there, though.

"Shel, I'm swamped on rounds and probably won't make it. I'm sorry. I really appreciate you taking the time to call."

"Well, there's one thing you ought to know: the cause of death." The subsequent pause seemed interminable, and I knew it would only be broken by me. Shel loved suspense.

"Yes? What was it? Another myocardial infarction (a heart attack)?"

"No. He ruptured his left ventricle. He had the massive MI two weeks ago, which took out the entire anterior (front) wall of his heart. You all knew about that, according to your notes. What you didn't know was that there was only a paper-thin sheet of fibrous tissue remaining over the entire anterior portion of his left ventricle. There was no heart muscle left. It tore open, and he bled into his pericardium (the sac around his heart). There was no way he could have been resuscitated."

Pathologists are not generally known for their interpersonal skills and are rarely touchy-feely types. They have chosen a specialty with virtually no interaction with patients. Well, living patients, that is. However, I had the distinct impression Shel was attempting, in his own way, to help me to feel better. I guessed he had heard the whole story about the code yesterday, and he probably knew this was killing me.

"Thanks, Shel. How long until the autopsy report comes out?"

"Ha! Well, you know, we have the gross path to complete today, but the microscopic path will be another month. Maybe six to eight weeks before you have the full report."

I had always been amused how a surgeon in the operating room can obtain pathology results back within twenty minutes from the microscopic examination of a biopsy of a patient's tumor, but it took as long as two months for me to receive an autopsy report. About four thousand times longer, I calculated. *At least they have their priorities right, though. The living before the dead.*

"Thanks, Shel. I'll talk to you later."

"Paper thin," he reminded me as he hung up the phone.

I immediately called Mr. Harandi's daughter and informed her of the autopsy findings. Of course, she did not sound surprised.

"So," she asked, "his heart just exploded?" I confirmed it had. "Just like a time bomb," she replied, offering these words as her apt and succinct summary of her father's death – and perhaps also of his life.

I spent the remainder of my week on call making hospital rounds, seeing patients in the office, taking patient phone calls at night, and pondering whether my career in medicine was over. As the days slowly passed, it began to dawn on me I was still quite welcome in my medical practice and on the hospital's medical staff, my medical license was safe, and there would be no court convictions. My friends and family, as I told them my tortured story, were incredibly supportive.

When I spoke to my good friend and mentor, John, I wondered aloud, "Why did this happen to me? What are the odds this could occur at that exact moment and that I would be the one who was there to cause it? Why am I the one who has to bear this awful weight of guilt? How can I continue in medicine and face this sort of possibility every single day?"

While it now sounds overly dramatic as I look back on it, these were the questions I struggled to understand at the time.

Wise and patient, John waited until I had completely talked myself out.

"Well, perhaps you are the only one in the world who could have been in this position and still move forward in your life. Perhaps if the young nurse had been the one in your shoes, she would have left nursing. Or, if the daughter had taken him home and started to help him up the stairs, and he died right there, which of course he would have, maybe she could have never forgiven herself. Perhaps you can find a way to take what has happened, learn from it, and use it to become a better physician. Maybe you are the only one who could respond in this way. Or maybe you can't."

I opened my mouth to speak; no, frankly, I wanted to argue, to make a point about my own particular version of fairness and how it differed from John's theory. I closed my mouth and decided to let his words sink in. Maybe this *was* my path after all. I had been absolutely certain eight years ago about my sense of calling to be a physician. It would not make any sense to have come all this way, to the official first week of my actual career, only to have it end.

"It's completely up to you, I guess," he concluded.

While I did not want this to be up to me, and while I actually preferred, as Shakespeare once suggested, to "look upon myself and curse my fate,"

I intuitively understood that with such responsibility came opportunity as well.

Medical research has more than adequately documented the effects of chronic anger on the human organism. The first articles appeared during my internship during the late 1970s, reporting the increased incidence of heart attacks in "Type A" individuals. Of course, we physicians, generally Type A individuals, viewed these reports with grave skepticism. Nonetheless, additional studies through the years have only served to strengthen the correlation between poorly controlled anger and health issues. In women, the correlation is strongest between anger and depression, and in men, with a myriad of physical illnesses.

Chronic uncontrolled anger has been shown to directly correlate with abdominal pains, increased anxiety, depression, headaches, higher risk of heart disease, heart attack and fatal heart attack, insomnia, high blood pressure, stroke, higher blood cortisol (stress hormone) levels, poor pulmonary function, slower wound healing, and even a higher incidence of colds due to suppression of the immune system. Interestingly, prayer, meditation, social interactions, Tai Chi, and yoga have been shown in well designed research studies to reduce some of these effects of chronic anger.

Mr. Harandi's anger had effectively killed him. *Are you angry, David?* I asked myself that Wednesday morning. Well, yes, sometimes I am. *Are you an angry person?* No. Or, to be honest, I'm not certain. Maybe I am. There certainly were aspects of the rigors of my medical training that left me chronically frustrated and upset. *Do you want to let your anger kill you, like it did your patient?* No. Of course I didn't. *What does Mr. Harandi still have to teach you?* This question bothered me the most. At that point in my life, I did not realize that those who caused me the most distress had the potential to be my greatest teachers, should I just allow them to be.

The pathology report appeared on my desk on September eighth, the Tuesday after Labor Day, exactly two months to the day after Mr. Harandi's death. I attempted to reach his daughter several times and finally left an answering machine message reiterating my offer to have them come in to go over the final autopsy report.

Somehow, though, I knew they would not call me back; Mr. Harandi had taken his place in their past. When I didn't hear from them, I began to wonder what my process of moving on would look like and how long it would take me to *completely* resolve the events of that day in both my mind and my soul.

At this writing, I'm now at thirty-one years, five months, seven days, and still counting.

CHAPTER 5

An idealist is one who, on noticing that roses smell better than a cabbage, concludes that they will also make better soup.

H. L. Mencken (1880-1956), American journalist and editor

Mark had taken the unusual risk of adding me to his solo practice after only a year out of his residency training and being on his own. Back in those days, a new primary care general internist in solo practice might take four to seven years before being able to financially afford a new partner. Primary care is not a lucrative field of medicine, and specialists, on average, earn about twice the income of their pediatric, family practice, and internal medicine colleagues. However, Mark had been remarkably successful due to his brilliant mind, patient-oriented focus, and thoroughness of approach to medical problems. After about eight months, he simply had far more demand for his services than he could himself supply, and he welcomed me graciously and gave me all of those extra patients I would have otherwise had to find myself.

In our current millennium, the role of primary care physicians has shifted to an almost exclusive focus on seeing patients in the office. Hospitalists, a growing specialty within Internal Medicine, now see our patients when they are admitted to the hospital and provide expert care for their complex problems. After discharge, the patient returns to the primary care physician for follow up care. In 1981 though, the time this story takes place, we cared for our patients in both settings, office and hospital, and our practice was organized along these lines.

Mark and I were scheduled to meet at the office every Monday morning at 7:30 to go over the patients, one by one. We knew each other very well and had worked together on many occasions during our residency training. Mark was one year ahead of me, and he was my chief resident during my second, and his third, year of training. Being named chief resident was an honor accorded to the best resident in each class, and Mark was clearly deserving of this recognition. He was everything a patient could want in a doctor: smart, caring, thorough, and serious. I considered myself privileged when he invited me to join him in his new private practice one year later.

About six feet tall, muscular, blond, and blue-eyed, Mark cut an imposing Teutonic figure. His frameless glasses added an additional aura of seriousness to his face, and I occasionally had the sense I was in the presence of a friendly German mathematics professor. Those who did not know Mark assumed him to be serious to the point of humorlessness; this could not have been further from the truth. Mark's sense of humor was central to his identity, and it was this paradoxical ability to fully grasp both the mirth and gravity in each situation that made him an excellent clinician and the ideal practice partner.

He would often look directly at me when uttering more serious pronouncements about a given patient, his piercing gaze emphasized by his full blond eyebrows and the heavy correction his spectacles provided for his nearsightedness, which made his dark blue eyes appear smaller and more intense. Then, without warning, he would raise his eyebrows to an impossible height, tilt his head downward, push his lenses toward the end of his nose just a bit, and look at me over the top of them. Usually, this new visage would be accompanied by an ironic remark and a broad rolling of his eyes, now appearing twice their size when out from behind the corrective lenses. It was simply impossible for me not to laugh, and as one who, in those days, would have been easily convicted if taking one's self too seriously was a crime, I found his sense of humor an indispensable part of our often long and difficult early days in our medical practice.

Each Monday morning hand-off consisted of passing over a set of three-by-five inch unlined index cards, one per patient, filled with a detailed set of data including basic patient identification information, such as name, gender, age, and birthday. Next, each contained a numbered list of the patient's medical problems and key medications that one of us, as the admitting physician, would record, as well as key lab information and other test results. All of this was in very tiny print, but it was always legible. The hand-off of the cards symbolized the transfer of the practical, legal, and emotional responsibility for each patient, so I asked more questions than necessary the first six months in practice to make sure I clearly and completely understood each patient's situation.

One of the most important aspects of these check-out sessions was the open and non-judgmental way in which we could provide each other with feedback about our care for patients. If I had missed an abnormal lab result, Mark would let me know when he found it. If he had overlooked an important piece of data in a patient's history, I'd fill him in. There was always a strong sense of collaboration and learning, to continuously improve the care of our patients, and never a sense of competition between us. We were both fortunate to have forged such a partnership, uncommon as it was in the medical profession at that time.

Because of our in-depth hospital experience, our close relationships with many of the surgical specialists from our interactions during residency, and our willingness to stay late and come in early to help them with their patients, we quickly built up a large inpatient consultation service. Typically, a surgical specialist would schedule an admission of a seemingly healthy patient for an elective operation, but weeks later, upon arrival to the hospital, the operative candidate might be short of breath or have uncontrolled high blood pressure or an abnormal lab value that was guaranteed to make the anesthesiologist uncomfortable enough to cancel the surgery scheduled for the following morning. This always made for a very unhappy surgeon. Because of Mark's diligence in treating these patients quickly and efficiently, and my adoption of his approach when I joined the practice, we found ourselves consulted on two or three surgical patients every weekday afternoon who needed what we affectionately called a "tune up" in order to keep their operating room appointment the next morning.

Sometimes, these complex cases required staying in the hospital after 8:00 p.m. to observe the first effect of an intervention, such as an intravenous diuretic for a case of mild heart failure. Once we were home, there would often be two or three additional calls necessary to the nurse to further adjust the patient's fluid balance. Then there would be the 5:00 a.m. visit to ensure the congestive heart failure or high blood pressure problem discovered and treated the prior evening was now completely resolved. If so, we would write a progress note indicating the patient was ready, and would be safe, for the operating room. Each week, one of us took call and rounded on the inpatients on our own service, and on the consults, in addition to an almost full day in the office. The weeks on call became quite exhausting and sometimes required incredible physical stamina and emotional fortitude.

One Thursday evening, I stayed late to manage a consult patient, scheduled for thyroid surgery the next morning, who was short of breath that night. At about 9:30 p.m. on a hot and muggy August evening, I pulled into my driveway and watched the neighbor's cat streak into my garage before I could maneuver my noisy diesel Suburban into its spot. I located the cat, shooed her out of the garage, pulled some of my things out of the back of my truck, and went straight to bed. My wife and three children, now nearly one, two, and five years old, were already fast asleep. There were four phone calls that night, two concerning my consult patient in congestive heart failure.

When the alarm went off at 4:15 a.m., I dragged myself out of bed, showered, dressed, and hopped into my truck to drive back to the hospital. I immediately discovered a runny pile of animal feces on the front seat of my car, and, cursing the mildest of oaths under my breath, I cleaned it up, located the neighbor's cat in the back of the truck, and placed her outdoors.

In the quiet hush of my neighborhood at 5:00 a.m., the diesel Suburban engine sounded unusually loud, "Like a spoon in a garbage disposal," my neighbor had once quipped. I cringed as I drove past his house, until I recalled that this same neighbor was the owner of the cat who had just made a night deposit on the seat next to me. Gunning the engine once, I pulled onto the main road and made the three mile journey to the hospital with the windows open, in the futile hope the muggy air might help further deodorize my car. The only good news about the whole mess was that it was ragweed season, and my nose was nicely plugged by my annual allergic reaction.

Grabbing my white coat from the back seat, I trotted through the damp morning air into the air-conditioned hospital, knowing that I had a larger than usual patient census and would need to move more quickly than my normal very fast pace to see twenty-four people that day. The routine was always the same. First, see any unstable patients. Then see new admissions that had come in overnight. Next, see patients in intensive care units. Then consult patients scheduled for surgery that day, followed by our own patients that were going home to complete their discharges as early as possible. Finally, we would see the remainder of our inpatients and consults in geographic order, working from the top floor of the hospital downwards. By creating a predictable routine, this saved us time and allowed the nurses on various floors to give families who wanted to talk to us a rough time estimate of when we would be likely to make our daily rounds.

There had been two new admissions during the night. I knew a good deal about each because the on-call intern had already done a complete admission work-up and called me with her findings. As I walked into the room of my first patient, I glanced up at the television set, which was set to a news channel, but the volume was so low I couldn't actually hear the audio portion of the newscast. My patient was asleep, and I found the remote control beneath her bed sheet and raised the volume to a barely audible level. Two very famous people were getting married, and it was the first I had heard of it.

I laughed at my own complete isolation from the news media and current events, which had subtly occurred over the previous seven years. The eighty to one-hundred hour weeks of both medical school and residency training had very effectively isolated me from the life of the world in which I lived. Here were Prince Charles and Lady Diana Spencer saying their wedding vows in St. Paul's Cathedral, and, according to the announcer, the wedding had been viewed by seven hundred million people worldwide. I mused briefly on the fact that I clearly recognized both the prince and his bride, but I had no recollection of where I might have seen them before.

Then it occurred to me, in an instant, that all of my awareness of world events over the past seven years had come as the cumulative summary of my ten-second television exposures as I walked into patient rooms on rounds. The scene was always the same.

"Good morning, Mrs. Whitney!" I'd crow cheerily, as I rushed into the room. "Do you mind if I turn off the television so we can talk?" Unlike most men, I've been either blessed or cursed with the gift of multitasking, and so it was possible for me to leave the television on, talk to Mrs. Whitney, and almost completely capture everything happening on the tube and in our doctor-patient visit. I learned in medical school that my problem was the *almost* part. If there was something particularly newsworthy and captivating on the patient's television screen, and, to be honest, something less than captivating happening with Mrs. Whitney's hospital stay, I would find after leaving the room that I couldn't remember some of the details of her history or examination. At some point, I decided to just make the turning off the tube an integral part of my ritual. Nobody wants his or her doctor distracted by television, I reasoned.

The frequency of glaring and blaring televisions in hospital rooms has always intrigued me, though. I had already made over ten thousand entrances into hospital rooms at this early point in my career, and it seemed as though the television set had been on about nine-thousand-nine-hundred-ninety-nine of those times. I would walk into the room of an incredibly sick patient, let's say someone who had suffered a heart attack the night before, and there would be the patient, his wife, and one of the children, transfixed by the evening's episode of *Dallas* or *Three's Company*, or even *The Dukes of Hazzard*. Somehow, for reasons that escaped me, television appeared to be a universally effective balm to the fear of death.

Over the years of my training, I had refined my approach to silencing the cathode ray tube in each room. I spent a few months just politely asking people to turn off the television set as I entered the room. Patients were almost always eager to do so. But I found it could take them twenty seconds or longer to locate the hard-wired remote control in their bed, and given my busy schedule each morning, it seemed like an eternity. But that was a relative millisecond compared to what would happen next. The hospital room televisions of the early 1980s lacked our contemporary electronic sophistication, and one could only select a channel by pressing the "advance" button repeatedly until finding it. In addition, there was generally a one-second delay between pressing the button and the advance of the channel, and, to make matters even worse, "off" was only one of the twenty-one channels currently available at the time. As a result of what

34

now seems a prehistoric set of electronics, and the generally weakened state of most hospitalized patients, no patient in these months ever successfully turned off the television on the first try. Patients routinely passed the "off" channel, and the silent black screen was but a fleeting moment in the parade of channels.

Time being as precious as it was to me, I quickly learned to seize the control box as my first physical act on entry to the patient room, and I then began the march through the channels quickly while simultaneously asking the patient's permission to turn off the television. Timing my key-presses perfectly, the entertainment box suspended from the wall at the foot of the patient's bed would be dark and silent by the time they voiced their approval.

Once Lady Di, Prince Charles, their 3,500 guests, and the church full of beautiful flowers had faded from the screen, my attention was drawn to my first patient of the morning, who had been admitted from a nearby nursing home. I noticed she had a bladder catheter and an IV in place, and, in sharp contrast to what must have been a wonderful scent at St. Paul's Cathedral, the room smelled very strongly like urine. She was demented and almost completely unresponsive, and obtaining a verbal history from her was futile. She was so unresponsive, in fact, that she wasn't even watching the wedding coverage!

A bad prognostic sign, I concluded.

Characteristically, there was a wide gulf between the patient's nursing home medical records and what was available in her hospital chart. I made a written note on my daily to-do list to call the facility to obtain more information later that morning. As I moved to examine her with my stethoscope, the foul smell of urine was so pungent it cleared my nostrils, perhaps in concert with my allergy medication. The intern had not mentioned any smell, which I attributed to the lost art of the use of the physician's nose to make a diagnosis. I wrote an order to have her urine sent to the lab for culture so that we could appropriately treat what clearly smelled like an infection.

The next patient on rounds was one who was followed in our office by Mark, had kidney failure, was on chronic dialysis, and had also been admitted in the early hours of the morning with a high fever and respiratory symptoms of cough and bloody sputum. The chest x-ray in the emergency room had confirmed pneumonia, and his blood work confirmed he was due for dialysis this morning. The diagnosis of renal failure could also be made by the smell of stale urine this patient exuded in his sweat and on his breath. Because the non-working kidneys are unable to extract the normal build-up of ammonia in the bloodstream, the skin and lungs do the best they can to remove it until the next dialysis treatment. With the patient's rapid respirations from his pneumonia and sweating from the fever, the room carried an even stronger smell of ammonia than my previous nursing home patient's quarters had.

David, remember to take your allergy medication tomorrow after *hospital rounds, not before. A stuffy nose would be handy right now,* I thought.

While this patient could talk, he was a bit confused, but not so confused to miss the ongoing replays of the Royal Wedding. As I turned off the television, I noted he was clearly very ill and only beginning to respond to the intravenous antibiotics that the intern had started just hours earlier. My eyes watering now from the pungent aroma of urine in the room, I completed my own history and examination, wrote a detailed admitting note, and went downstairs to see if my new consult patient's lungs were now clear and he was ready for his thyroid operation.

He was a friendly and outgoing forty-six-year-old man who had a thyroid tumor producing excess levels of thyroid hormone. Possibly from the strain that this placed on his heart, he had accumulated fluid in his lungs between the time the surgery was scheduled and the day of his admission. According to the new data in the chart this morning from the nurses and the lab, the intravenous diuretics and the beta blockers he had received the previous night had worked their magic.

"This wedding was really something," he commented as I entered the room. "She did not promise to 'obey' him, though."

"Good for her," I replied just as the screen turned black.

On reviewing his chart before I entered his room, I thought he was indeed ready for surgery. Except there was one very big and very new problem. He smelled as if he was now in renal failure. That same uremic smell that had overwhelmed me with my previous patients was again assailing me.

Just your luck, I thought, *three patients in a row who smell badly of urine.*

I knew it was possible that an overdose of the diuretics he received during the night could have shut down his kidneys. I also thought about the fact that severe cardiac failure can cause the kidneys to cease working. However, the patient's kidney function was normal the previous day, his heart failure was mild at best, and there was no unusual odor in the room last night.

And besides, I reasoned, *even if his kidneys had completely shut down, it would take days before the ammonia levels would build up enough to create this level of stench.*

As I leaned over him and finished my examination of his heart, the patient looked at me expectantly, with distress and tears in his eyes.

"Doctor," he choked, "something smells *terrible* in here!" He was staring intently at the left breast of my white coat. *Probably trying to read my name,* I assumed, knowing it was embroidered there and that I had been one of many doctors he had seen yesterday. But he kept staring. And staring. Much longer that it might take to commit the name simple name of David Roberts, M.D., to memory.

"I'm Dr. David Roberts. We met last night," I offered, hoping to jog his memory.

"Yes, I know who you are, Doctor," he replied in the most nasal voice possible. I looked from his chest up to his face; he was now pinching his nostrils closed.

Finally, it began to dawn on me that the odds of seeing three consecutive patients who smelled this badly of urine were improbably low and that there must be some more common denominator than chance alone. Yielding to my patient's gaze, I followed his eyes to my embroidered name on my white coat, which was encircled by an eight-inch radius of a wet and yellowish stain.

"Cat urine!" I exclaimed, and I raced from the room. Attempts to remove the stain and the smell in the sink of the surgical floor's utility room were unsuccessful (as were subsequent efforts at washing and dry cleaning). I returned sheepishly to my preoperative patient's room without the white coat, but with a large wet spot on the left breast of my shirt where I had washed out the traces of the feline excretion that had soaked through. Mercifully, my tie was spared. I explained to him he was ready for surgery and would likely do quite well; his heart and lungs were in perfect shape. I also added that his kidney function was good this morning as well, although this comment was mainly for my own benefit, since up until the arrival of my white lab coat in his room this morning, his kidneys had not been an issue.

He was pleased and grateful to hear the news, but he was quite obviously waiting for what Paul Harvey would call "the rest of the story." While it would still take me several hours to make the transition from seeing the morning's events as humiliating to experiencing them as hilarious, I recounted the events of the previous two hours. He started to chuckle as I described my need to clean up the front seat of my car, and he laughed as I described my two previous patients. By the time I shared with him my thought that *he* might be in renal failure, he was laughing and shaking so hard that an alarmed surgical floor nurse came in to determine the source of the erratic disruption of his cardiac tracing she had observed on the monitor at the nursing station.

Not yet ready to start recounting the story for my peers in the hospital, I told the nurse he was ready for the O.R. and bolted out of the room. Walking down the hall, somewhere in my subconscious mind I began to realize there was some profound truth in what I had just experienced, and if I could really examine it or listen to it, it could change my life over the course of the ensuing years.

And it did. Every time I have told this story, or just recalled it to myself, I have ended with the thought that we all have times in our lives when things aren't going well, and time after time, we think somebody or something else must be to blame. The problem is "out there," rather than "in here." As Steven Covey, an American business author, has wisely noted, "If you start to think the problem is 'out there,' stop yourself. That thought is the problem."

When that happens, it's probably a good idea to pause and take a nice deep breath. Go ahead; take a whiff of yourself, just to be absolutely certain it isn't you.

At least in my case, it almost always is.

CHAPTER 6

I sensed something was not quite right about Brenda Fountain from the moment I entered the examination room. My problem was that nothing seemed particularly out of the ordinary. She was reasonably well dressed and groomed. She had filled out the medical forms in advance of her visit, in a very thorough manner, and the information provided seemed straightforward. Her handshake was perhaps a bit too firm, or was it too stiff? Maybe she seemed just a bit "official" to me, although even then I was aware of my tendency to bristle in the presence of authority figures. Our nurse had recorded her vital signs: height, weight, blood pressure, heart rate, respiratory rate, temperature. All were within the acceptable range, except for her blood pressure of 160/98, with our understanding of "normal" at that time being below 140/90. Hers was too high, but often normal patients who don't really have hypertension post a high reading as a result of the natural anxiety they feel about their first visit to a new physician. This "white coat syndrome" phenomenon is well known by every physician.

As I introduced myself, I noticed she was staring at me with a rather queer expression, a mixture of curiosity and mirth. Having had dozens of similar experiences in my first two months in practice, I knew exactly what was coming.

"You know, I don't mean to seem rude," she began apologetically, "but I must say that you appear much too young to actually be a doctor."

There was no denying my youthful appearance. I had always looked younger than my actual age. When I was seven years old, I was "double-promoted" from first to third grade, skipping second. So, starting in third grade, I was at least one year younger than each of my classmates, and the problem seemed to only worsen as I became older, or, perhaps more accurately, as everyone else aged. More than half of my new patients in the practice, meeting me for the first time, would verbally express some "you look too young to be a doctor" sentiment. The remainder just smiled in a somewhat surprised or bemused fashion when I entered the room, and kept their thoughts to themselves.

I was five feet six inches tall, weighed about 135 pounds, with sandy brown, wavy hair. My high school graduation picture had featured me in a pair of those dark, horned rim glasses so popular in the late 1960s, but since then, I had graduated to contact lenses. This change in visual aids had unfortunately served only to make me look younger. The brutal long and often sleepless hours of my seven years of medical school, internship, and residency had failed to provide me with the wrinkles, gray hair, or other accouterments of aging my colleagues had acquired. Very sensitive to making a good impression with each new patient, I was invariably deflated when the subject was raised, as it was at least half a dozen times each day in the office.

The only blessing in all of this, looking back on it now, was that it would be ten years until the first television airing of the popular television show *Doogie Howser*, the story of a brilliant fourteen-year-old boy who became a doctor. Even then, in my late thirties, I was still hearing the same routine patient comments on my youthful appearance, but now always in reference to this TV show. "What are you," the patient would ask playfully, "another Doogie Howser?"

Back in my first year of practice, many would guess my age, saying, "Well, you look like you're sixteen years old!" and laughing heartily. Eager to put an end to this avenue of exam room discussion, I tried multiple remedies. The first was to grow a mustache, which failed miserably. Patients no longer claimed I looked like I was sixteen years old or in high school. With my exceedingly sparse facial hair, they now were guessing I was fourteen and in junior high.

Next, I went through a phase where I tried using cryptic responses. None of them were effective, but I did have my favorites. "Well, I'm either much, much older than I look, or I'm a child prodigy," I would quip, further confusing the patient.

Finally, I resorted to the truth. There wasn't much I could do about my youthful appearance. When my patients continued to volunteer I looked too young to be a doctor, I would smile, and say, "Well, thank you for the compliment. I'm twenty-nine years old, and I have always looked younger than my actual age. Hopefully, I'll be able to help you to improve your health, nonetheless." Then I would quickly change the subject, as I did now with Ms. Fountain.

"How did you hear about our practice? What brought you in for this visit?" The double question was usually effective in changing the subject.

"Well, I'm really just here for a check-up. Everything is fine. *Really.*"

The manner in which she said "really" made me wonder whether the truth was nearer to, "Not really." So I started into the interview to see if I could find a clue to my vague uneasiness.

She didn't have much in the way of past medical history, had never been married, didn't smoke or drink, and did exercise regularly. She used to be an elementary school teacher but seemed pleased to report she had recently quit this work to devote herself to her "songwriting career." Being a big music fan myself, I immediately perked up and asked her about the writing she was doing. She completely froze to the point of being rigid and was silent for about fifteen seconds, which is a very long time in a typical doctor's office, and almost an eternity when I am in the room.

She seemed completely unnerved, and after taking some time to compose herself, said, "You know, Dr. Roberts, I did want to ask you about multivitamins. Do you recommend them?"

Now it was my turn to be unnerved. Nevertheless, I did politely answer her, sensing that despite her volunteering the information about her own new career in songwriting, she wasn't actually willing to disclose additional details. Being unnaturally curious by nature, I made a mental note to return to the topic in a few minutes, and I continued with the medical interview.

"Is there any family history of high blood pressure?" I asked.

"You know," she responded immediately, "I currently have a Top Ten song on the Billboard charts."

"How wonderful! Did you write the lyrics *and* the music?" I asked, glad to hear more about her work. *Were you just confused in thinking her vitamin question was evasive, David?*

"I just write lyrics. Not the music," she replied, obviously proud of what was an incredible achievement on her part.

"I'm a huge music fan," I offered, hoping to learn more. "I probably have heard the song. Which one is it?"

She instantly returned to her rigid, frozen persona. She became very quiet, seemed intensely uncomfortable, and appeared to shrink before me.

What did you say to her, David? I asked myself. I was perplexed. She seemed to be opening the door to this subject, and then every time I would respond to her, she would slam it closed. *There is a pattern here, though. What is it?*

"Any family history of diabetes, heart disease, stroke, cancer, or lung disease?" I continued.

"No. Everyone is pretty healthy in my family. Actually, I've written the lyrics to *more than one* Top Ten song." She paused and looked at me as if to say, "Your turn."

Don't take your turn, David. Don't ask. That's the pattern. She will tell you, but only if you don't ask.

So, I just went on to complete the medical history interview. The only other problem she mentioned was sleeping fitfully over the past month, waking three or four times each night or not sleeping at all. Occasional insomnia is normal, but it is rare to find a patient who repeatedly stays up all night and is not a college student.

My final question was, "How much stress would you say you've been under lately in your life, compared to normal?"

This is a helpful question to ask most people, and through many years of practice, I have learned that those who come to see me because they are sick feel a much higher level of stress than those who come in for a routine physical. In fact, there is reliable medical evidence showing that more than sixty percent of patients presenting to a primary care physician's office have a significant underlying stress or behavioral health issue.

Her eyes began to well up with tears. "I'm under an enormous amount of stress, the most in my entire life."

I reached for the box of facial tissue I always keep within my reach and handed her a few. We entered another silent period.

The enormous responsibility I feel when there is silence in the exam room fascinates me. I just feel as though I *must* say *something*. Years later, I would come to be a somewhat better listener. This day, I was instinctively learning through our conversation that Ms. Fountain would tell me what she wanted me to know, when she wanted me to know it. Instead of talking, I just counted the seconds in my head: ...*eight, nine ... fifteen, sixteen...*" She was blowing her nose now and composing herself to speak.

"Dr. Roberts," she began slowly, looking at me intently to determine whether I could be trusted with the next piece of information. "It's about my songwriting. It is very stressful."

Although sorely tempted to speak, I just counted my way through the next silent interval: ...*thirteen, fourteen...* I could imagine quitting one's teaching job, with its steady paycheck, to write songs could be quite stressful from an economic point of view, but here was a woman who seemed quite successful with several major hits on the charts. ... *Twenty, twenty-one...* That is, if what she was telling me added up, but it didn't. Something felt highly irregular.

She remained silent, and so I suggested we go on to the in-depth physical examination. I found her to be quite healthy, and there was nothing out of the ordinary, other than a fine tremor in her hands. Such tremors can be hereditary, but they can also be due to other causes, and I went back and checked her thyroid gland one more time just to make sure it was not enlarged. It was normal.

A repeat blood pressure test was still high, and an electrocardiogram, an electrical tracing of heart activity done there in the examination room, showed a slightly increased heart rate but no evidence of the effect of longstanding high blood pressure on the heart. I returned to the exam room after she had dressed and was expecting to summarize our encounter.

As I closed the door, she was clutching a typewritten document. I am naturally skilled at reading upside down, and I saw she held a table of currently popular songs, numbered one to twenty-four on the first page. Most of the song titles were colored with a yellow highlighter, and there was a second page I could not yet see. The number one song, "Endless Love" by Diana Ross and Lionel Ritchie, was highlighted and circled with a red pen. When she noticed my intense interest in the list, she immediately retracted it.

"Well, everything looks fine in terms of your physical examination," I began. "I am concerned about your difficulty sleeping and also your current level of stress, though. We ought to do a few blood tests to make sure everything is fine with your thyroid and adrenal glands."

She held up the list, turning it to face towards me so I could clearly see it. Every one of the twenty-four songs on the first page was highlighted, except for "Start Me Up," by the Rolling Stones. Pausing to be sure I had a chance to take in the first page, she turned to the second, with songs numbered twenty-five to forty. This was the rest of the Billboard Top 40 for the current week. She had highlighted fourteen of the song titles on the second page in yellow.

"I've written the lyrics to thirty-seven of the Billboard Top 40 songs," she insisted. "But someone has stolen them from me, and I'm not getting credit for any of them."

She's mentally ill. That's what is wrong here. My internal use of the very general term "mentally ill" belied my relatively weak training in psychiatry.

"My family thinks I am crazy," she continued, as though she could read my thoughts. "The people at the school where I used to teach all thought I was crazy too. No one will believe me."

There are many ways to carry on a conversation with someone whom society considers "crazy." Usually, the definition of this word stems from the patient's view of reality, which goes so far beyond the probability of what the rest of us "know" to be true that it receives this label. The subject of "who is really crazy here?" has been addressed by many excellent films and novels. I often think that none of us is innocent when it comes to valuing our own view of the world above the perspective of others.

The reflexive human response to "craziness," or what is called "psychotic ideation" in medicine, is to attempt to verbally reorient the patient to the reality held by society in general. In this case, the typical response to Ms. Fountain would be to tell her directly there is no way she could have written all of those songs. A slightly more sophisticated approach might be to obtain the official Billboard Top 40 listing and point out the actual names of the lyricists, who would not, of course, be her.

This approach rarely works. In fact, it can reduce the likelihood of helping the patient. Ms. Fountain would have immediately placed me on her list of people who "just don't get it," along with her family and former coworkers.

The next option is the converse of the first and involves complete buy-in. "Oh my, this is terrible!" one might begin. "Have you reported this to the police and the record companies? You deserve justice here, and I can help you." Using this approach, Ms. Fountain might clearly believe me to be her advocate and place her full trust in me, on the condition that I remain committed to her alternate reality forever. However, when I inevitably attempted to lead her back to society's definition of reality, she would see me as her betrayer.

My favorite option, which works especially well in situations where I can divest myself of my self-imposed role as guardian of all truth for all people, is simply to remain intently curious, while suspending judgment until I have heard more. This tends to be difficult for me to do, though. My family upbringing was clear on one's responsibility to advance the cause of truth in the world. While a lofty goal, I am embarrassed to admit this advancement of truth included responsibilities such as correcting strangers on their grammar. In our family, truth was generally whatever we happened to believe about the topic at hand on any particular day. The concept of simply appreciating someone for their diverse belief or letting a lapse in proper grammar pass (such as "I feel I might faint, so I am going to *lay* down on the couch") would be seen as gross negligence of one's societal duty.

However, open curiosity works in almost every situation (and not just with psychotic individuals).

"Really? Tell me more about this," was my simple response to Ms. Fountain. She provided the whole story without interruption or digression. Her narrative was impossible to believe, but it was replete with clues to her diagnosis.

She clearly saw herself in a grandiose manner. She was not hearing voices in her head. She had recently gotten into significant credit card debt installing three different security systems in her house, in the hopes of preventing further theft of her Billboard Top 40 lyrics. She told me she was staying up all night at least three times a week, sometimes days in a row, without feeling tired, writing new lyrics for recording artists like David Bowie and Madonna. Sometimes, she couldn't write down the lyrics fast enough; they flew into her mind at incredible speed. She had to quit teaching just to keep up with the pace of her creativity. Ms. Fountain had completely cut off all contact with her friends. She didn't worry about paying her bills because she knew she would be a millionaire once people understood she was the author of these songs.

It was clear to me she was in the midst of an episode of mania. She was manic-depressive, and she needed help. It was going to be incredibly difficult to help her understand this.

At the time "Endless Love" was a number one song, physicians in practice were not generally aware that the brains of manic patients were nearly drowning in excessive amounts of the neurotransmitter dopamine, a chemical that is secreted in key areas of the brain and stimulates brain activity. In manic depression, now called bipolar disorder, dopamine levels are exceedingly high and overstimulate the brain. We now know the medications most helpful in treating mania do so by reducing production or blocking the effects of dopamine in the brain and raising the levels of other neural chemicals deficient during manic episodes. Lithium was the mainstay of treatment for such patients at the time I saw Ms. Fountain.

"It's no wonder you can't sleep," I offered tentatively. "I don't know how you can handle all of this pressure. This must be *incredibly* stressful for you." I handed her more facial tissue as her eyes began to tear up again. "I'm worried your sleep deprivation may be adversely affecting your health right now," I continued. In her manic state, she was still suspicious of me, as she was of everyone, but I could tell by watching the corners of her eyes and mouth whether I was headed in the right (eye corners open, mouth corners upturned) or wrong (squinting, mouth downturned) direction. *So far, so good.*

"You have a lot of work ahead of you to straighten out this whole mess," I told her. At first she was agreeing with everything I said, but she squinted and frowned at my use of the word "mess."

"This whole situation is very difficult," I said in an attempt to recover lost ground. "You have to be at your best to find your way through this. I'm thinking you may need some medication to help you sleep, to help you to be at your best." I was getting strong frown/squint feedback that medication wasn't on her list of alternatives. *Okay, let's try this another way.*

"What would you think about some medication to help you here?" I just asked directly.

"Well, as I said, I seem to get by just fine with little to no sleep. I have extra energy, even," she countered.

"There is medical evidence proving chronic sleep deprivation can cause confusion and other serious health problems. I'm worried about you." *She doesn't like the word confusion. She's offended. She's heard this word before from someone who thinks she's "crazy."*

"Doctor Roberts, I'm not confused. I'm just very angry about having my work stolen and other people getting the credit. I'm the one who should be rich, not these other people."

I knew I was running out of ideas. She needed to see a psychiatrist, and she needed to be on lithium. She would need her blood levels of the drug monitored on a regular basis. There was simply no way to do this without her being aware and involved with her diagnosis and treatment. On the other hand, telling her all of this at this exact moment would make it impossible for me to become someone she trusted. Fortunately, I still had one more option: the one question I could always ask when completely stumped and feeling excessively responsible for the success of an interaction with a patient.

I paused and took a deep breath in, slowly exhaling without an obvious sigh. Looking as curious and non-judgmental as I possibly imagined I could, I said softly, "Well, Ms. Fountain, how are you hoping I can most help you in this difficult situation?"

She paused and peered at me through squinting eyes. She was not prepared for this question. She was thinking carefully, formulating a response. What did Ms. Fountain really want?

"I want you to help me convince my family I'm not crazy."

It was simple as that. Could I do this for her?

Well, maybe. It all depended on our understanding of the amount of time she would provide me to do so.

"First, we need to do some blood tests. I know you're not worried about your lack of sleep, but I still am. In order to convince your family, I first need to be certain myself that everything else is fine. Would you be willing to have some blood work done and also a brain scan?" I could tell by watching her eyes and mouth, the blood work would be fine with her, but we would need to discuss the CT scan further. "I need to be certain that structurally everything is fine with your brain. There are certain brain conditions in which people develop quite severe insomnia."

After a brief discussion, in which she determined the CT was not just to check to see if she was "crazy," she agreed. It was not necessary for me to use the term "brain tumor," one of the possible causes of her behavior, to convince her.

"Why don't you have these tests done and come back in about two weeks? Would this work for you?" She said it would.

"I really do think I can help you with this," I confessed as she left the room, understanding the meaning she would take might not necessarily be the same as my own thoughts about her problem.

CHAPTER 7

"Education is not a product: mark, diploma, job, money in that order;
it is a process, a never-ending one."

Bella "Bel" Kaufman (1911 -), Russian-American professor and author

One morning, about three months after I joined Mark Edwards in his solo practice, I was busy hanging my diplomas on the wall above my desk in the small office Mark and I shared. The twelve-by-twelve foot space, illumined by the fluorescent ceiling lighting embedded between the suspended white two-by-four-foot ceiling tiles, barely contained our somewhat oversized wooden desks, but there was ample wall space above each of our work areas to display the tokens of our educational achievements. When I had first moved in, I was impressed with Mark's display of his four most important credentials. He had informed me it would be one of my junior partner responsibilities to have my credentials framed, and I finally had accomplished the task.

Above his desk, Mark had the four framed certificates arranged in two rows of two. In clockwise order, starting at the upper left, was his medical school diploma. Next, he had his residency training program completion certificate, followed by his state medical license, and finally his Phi Beta Kappa award from his undergraduate years. Each was displayed in a small, inexpensive frame, without flourish.

When my mother visited our office, she was impressed with Mark's display of his credentials, and generously offered to pay for "some nicer framing," as she put it, for mine. Like most people, I am more expansive in my creative efforts when someone else is paying the bill, and I was very pleased that morning as I brought the four individually wrapped packages, each with a wide wood grain frame, cream colored matting, and non-reflective glass. I thought it only fitting to duplicate precisely the arrangement of Mark's shrine to higher learning above my own desk. When I was finished, I had the same diploma from the same medical school, the same residency program completion certificate, and the same state medical license as Mark had, all in the exact same positions, each in a much nicer frame.

I was also pleased at the way I had solved my minor problem of not having earned my own Phi Beta Kappa award, and I sensed my selection of another auspicious honor from the annals of my educational history would fit the bill nicely. Shortly after I had hung and leveled the frames, Mark entered our office, placed a few charts on his desk, glanced at the diplomas, said, "Wow, those look great," and dashed out to see another patient. Likewise, I returned to my examination room to my own waiting patient.

Later, as I rushed to my desk to drop off a chart, I saw Mark studying my newly hung credentials more carefully, pausing to glance back and forth between mine and his from time to time.

"Say, David," Mark commented as we were finishing our charting at the end of the day, "I really like your diplomas. The framing is beautiful, and I'm honored you've chosen to precisely duplicate the layout I used above my desk." He was choosing his words carefully, I noticed, as he continued. "I couldn't help but notice the particular academic honor you chose as an alternative to my Phi Beta Kappa, though."

"You liked that, did you?" I said as dryly as possible, never looking up from my desk. One can only travel so deep into the valley of irony when eye contact is involved. "You know, I thought long and hard about what I could put up there, given that I apparently didn't study hard enough in college to earn that designation myself. It really is quite an honor for you, you know. But after reviewing my academic history, this one really stood out."

Mark came over to my desk and stood directly behind me, fixed his gaze on the fourth of my framed credentials, and he began to read aloud, "To David S. Roberts, for Perfect Attendance, Seventh Grade, the E.J. Lederle Junior High School."

"Yes, it is quite an honor, isn't it? Not quite the same level as yours, Mark, but a significant academic achievement, nonetheless."

I would be remiss if I failed to recount here one additional diploma-related event: the visitation of Mark's mother to our practice suite that same fall. She entered our joint office and expressed real interest in me and my joining the practice with her son. She did seem a bit distracted, looking alternatively at me, my diplomas, and those of her son, but otherwise she was charming and engaging.

Mark told me later about the conversation that happened after I left the room to see my next patient.

"You know, Mark," Mrs. Edwards began, "David has done such a nice job framing his diplomas, hasn't he? I notice you have identical achievements, and he has arranged his exactly like yours. What do you suppose he did to get a frame like that?"

"I don't know," he replied cautiously, "but they really do look nice." Mark was debating whether to highlight the Phi Beta Kappa – seventh grade perfect attendance disparity.

"You know, you might want to think about some nicer frames for yours at some point," she said, staring disapprovingly at the wall above Mark's desk.

"You're right, Mother, I ought to do that," he conceded. "I understand that David's mother paid to have his diplomas framed."

That day, at lunchtime, we had our first "practice business meeting" since I had started working with Mark. The accountant, Paul Schurz, had been recommended to Mark when he established the practice, one year before I joined him. In these pre-computer days, he had helped Mark start up with the "peg-board" accounting system so common at the time in physician offices. Patient receipts were attached to the board in sequential order, with copies of charges transferred to the sheet below. At the end of the day, when these receipts had been each peeled off and handed to the patient, there was a complete ledger underneath which summarized all transactions. Looking back on it now, this simple accounting system was the equivalent of using an abacus to solve multiple simultaneous equations.

Mark had gone out of his way to avoid preparing me for the first meeting, to the point of evading my questions about our accountant. I think he wanted me to develop my own impressions of Paul, and so he told me almost nothing other than the fact we would meet with him every other month to go over the financial performance of our practice.

When he walked in the room for our Friday lunch meeting, Paul appeared to be some sort of hybrid between the stereotypical accountant and a Saks Fifth Avenue catalogue. He was short, medium build, and only a few years older than Mark and I, with short hair and a meticulously trimmed moustache and goatee. Wearing pressed navy wool pants, a blue pinstriped shirt, a powder blue sport coat, and a necktie to pull each of the blues together, he seemed friendly and full of purpose at our first meeting together. As we sat down, I noticed Mark providing me with a set of eye signals, directing my gaze toward Paul's feet. The powder blue socks were identical in color to the sport coat, but barely noticeable in the gleam of his navy blue leather shoes.

An accountant with blue shoes, I mused, deciding to reserve further judgment until I heard what he had to say. He had a precise method of speaking, choosing his words carefully as though they all had equal importance, and he clearly talked with the air of one who needed to be in control of the conversation. He also had the habit of predicting out loud what we might be thinking, in response to his comments, which perhaps would have been helpful were any of his guesses even close.

"Now," he might interject, "I'll bet you're both wondering why I used the word 'possibly' in that last sentence."

I never thought it was worth correcting him on his assumptions, but I just learned to ignore them. He did not seem dissuaded by our lack of response to his predictions.

During this particular meeting, Paul showed us some of his projections regarding our practice's income and expenses, emphasizing my own need to see as many patients as possible the first several months, and explaining the three-month lag between seeing each patient and actually receiving the revenue from their various insurance companies.

The practice was experiencing the early signs of a cash flow crisis, according to Paul, but this was expected due to my addition to the practice and the initial three-month time lag in collections. Paul advised us not to worry.

He looks worried to me, though, I thought.

"I know," he suggested, "you're probably wondering what you need to do today to improve matters." I wasn't wondering about that at all; I was still stuck on what he might mean by "early cash flow crisis." He continued cautiously, "You might want to think about adding just two more slots per day to see additional patients, David. I'd hate to see you turn any new patients away, now that your schedule is nearly full."

I have always been a big believer in hard work. Dr. Reichert had once told me, "The harder I work, the luckier I get," and the idea of seeing extra patients didn't faze me at all. The only downside to the extra time in the office would be spending even less time with my family, who had been repeatedly promised, "Things will get a lot better when I finish X." First, X had been medical school, and then residency training. Even I had been surprised to find the private practice of a primary care internist as busy as my eighty-hour workweeks as a resident.

"Sure, I can do that," I volunteered. Kathleen, our highly organized receptionist and office manager, nodded and made a note. A nod from Kathleen was the equivalent of "It shall be so" in our practice.

CHAPTER 8

"For if there is a sin against life, it consists perhaps not so much in despairing of life as in hoping for another life and in eluding the implacable grandeur of this life."

Albert Camus (1913 - 1960), French-Algerian author, philosopher, and Nobel laureate

A few days after I saw Ms. Fountain, I was able to speak with a psychiatrist on the phone concerning her delusions about writing thirty-seven of the Top 40 songs. He agreed with my presumptive diagnosis, my proposed work-up, and also with my cautious attempt to remain a neutral advocate, as he put it, in her diagnosis and treatment.

"We walk a very fine line with manic patients," he said. "It is extremely difficult to get them into treatment because they have to abandon their whole reality to do so. And they have built up some pretty high walls to contain their own reality and to keep everyone else's at bay."

I had clearly been able to feel this wall when I walked into the exam room when I first met Ms. Fountain. That was the something that just wasn't right.

"Of course, we don't have to be manic to place an excessive claim on our own reality, now do we?" he said with self-conspiring mirth in his voice.

"Guilty as charged," I replied, a faithful co-conspirator.

Our discussion centered on the ethics of prescribing medication for a psychotic patient without clearly disclosing the exact reason for the treatment. We wondered whether the end could justify the means in this case. The alternative, and most common scenario, was to simply allow the manic patient to proceed with her grandiose thinking, flight of ideas, and self-imposed sleep deprivation until she became a serious danger to herself – and sometimes others. She would eventually lose her ability to eat and care for herself and would then be committed to a psychiatric hospital for treatment. He suggested she could likely continue, in her current state, for another three to six months, and in that time, she could do a lot of damage to herself before getting to the point where the law would allow her to be committed against her will.

"Should I try to have her see you at this point?" I asked him.

"Based on what you told me about the discussion related to the CT scan, I doubt she would come," he stated. "But you know, even though we would not use lithium for insomnia alone, it is absolutely true that small doses of the drug would clearly help her sleep disorder."

"And perhaps if she were able to sleep more," I responded, "she might be more open to the fact she has a serious problem here and adopt a more comprehensive treatment program? Is this what you're suggesting?"

I knew we were traversing the border into a grey area of medicine and ethics, and I wanted to be sure I understood him completely. The medical profession has been often criticized for our reflexive paternalism; I did not want to be this kind of physician.

"Exactly. Make no mistake about it. She will look up lithium in the PDR." (*The Physician's Desk Reference* is a huge 2000+ page volume that consists of all of the package inserts for each available pharmaceutical.) "So you will need to tell her the medication isn't traditionally used for insomnia and it *is* used for other serious medical conditions. It may help to tell her she has an *extremely serious* case of insomnia." I had never seen a case of manic depression in my practice, and his guidance on walking this diagnosis-and-treatment tightrope was invaluable.

Ms. Fountain returned two weeks later. Her blood tests were fine, and her CT scan was normal. As she expressed significant relief there was "no brain tumor," I realized there was some part of her, buried deep beneath her distorted view of the world, which knew something was seriously wrong and was trying to heal her. When I take the time to look for it, I have seen such an inner force of self-care and healing in every patient I have ever treated, no matter how self-destructive their actions may seem on the surface.

We talked about the insomnia, which, by her report, seemed to me to be worse than two weeks ago, but from her vantage point, it was not a problem. She was writing more than ever. She did admit she was "forgetting to do things, like pay the bills," initially excusing these lapses as being of no real consequence. Thinking back now to our conversation, I am reminded of the quip, "If you think nobody cares if you're alive, try missing a couple of car payments." I knew she was well on her way to losing all ability to function in society. She nearly had her car repossessed earlier that week.

"Well, do you feel like you have to pay your bills in the short run in order to do your songwriting in the long run?" I asked, and she did nod in affirmation.

She agreed to try a daily dose of lithium for eight weeks. I had already photocopied the relevant pages from the PDR and handed them to her.

"When you read this, you'll see this isn't your typical sleeping pill. But I do think it will help you sleep much better, and then you will be able to remember to pay your bills. Once we come to that point, I think I can really help you with your family and their view of your illness."

Ms. Fountain responded very quickly to the lithium, and within six weeks, she had abandoned her songwriting delusion. More importantly, she had an increasing insight into her illness, and she was more than willing to see the same psychiatrist who had been so helpful to me with her care. She returned to teaching the next semester, in the same system, but at a different elementary school. Six months later, in the office, she marveled at the depth of her distorted beliefs about the Top 40 songs.

"I mean, I love music. I've always loved music. I love the Rolling Stones. But it was just completely and totally amazing that my mind could end up where it did, thinking, 'I write the songs that make the whole world sing,' wasn't it?"

"Barry Manilow," I said, and we laughingly sang the last line of his song together.

Looking back over a thirty-year career in medicine, I realize how fortunate Ms. Fountain was to have started and stayed on lithium. Manic depression, schizophrenia, and other major disorders of thinking occur in up to two percent of Americans. One in five adults in this country suffers from some form of mental health disorder, including depression, and very few families remain untouched. Many of these patients, and their families, struggle with taking medications on a regular basis, and they may see wide swings in behavior requiring recurrent hospitalizations as a result. Some patients have enough insight to know the importance of taking their antipsychotic pills every day. Others choose not to. Often, this choice makes the difference between effective treatment, with a return to a meaningful role in society, and repeated behavioral decompensation, homelessness, and even incarceration.

I have seen many patients suffering from delusional thinking. While occasionally a patient will identify himself or herself as the reincarnation of Christ or a prominent historical figure, it is more common to see patients who just see themselves as extraordinarily unique or called to a very special role in the world. This sense of self-importance, so consistent in patients with thought disorders, raises an important question: Is this sense of self-importance always delusional? After all, each human being is an incredibly unique individual. No one in the entire history of the human race, I sometimes remind my patients, brings the same set of talents, experiences, perceptions, perspective, and identity to our world that each of them does. If we believe, as many do, that we have a soul inhabited, in some manner, by a divine presence, then the argument for an unprecedented human uniqueness in every individual is strengthened exponentially. Put another way, we are each truly one in six billion in our uniqueness.

Of course, the individual claiming to write almost all of the Top 40 lyrics, or to be the next messiah, or to be the head of an intergalactic intelligence group all have delusional thinking. But is it *all* really a delusion? What if their mental illness has peeled back some of the normally present protective layers to reveal, in these afflicted and perhaps more insightful individuals, a greater universal truth: we are all unique, and each of us is indeed very special and has an important role to play in this world, one that desperately needs our help? The disturbed and psychotic individual may take this kernel of deeper truth and twist it in a manner that causes them to imagine they rule the world, and the world, in response, calls them "crazy."

In contrast, I have seen far more patients over the years who continually struggle to find meaning or purpose in their lives, seeing nothing special about themselves, even to the point of calling themselves worthless. It is tragic to see this disturbing loss of human potential. In my view, the heartache of suicide, chronic depression, or even the comfortably numb but unhappy life carries with it a much more profound sadness.

I often wonder, *Which is the greater disorder of thought: exaggerating the innate importance we each have in this universe or failing to recognize it within ourselves at all?*

Having seen and done both, I believe it to be the latter.

CHAPTER 9

*"The gulf between how one should live and how one does live
is so wide that a man who neglects what is actually done
for what should be done learns the way
to self-destruction rather than self-preservation."*

*Niccolo Machiavelli (1469-1527),
Italian philosopher and political scientist, in* The Prince

Roger Redmond was a gruff, rough, outdoorsman who made it clear on his first visit to my office on a Monday morning, before I could even speak, that he was not a willing participant in his health evaluation.

"This is my wife's idea," he said, by way of introduction.

Uh-oh, this could be trouble, my inner diagnostic voice intoned. Usually, men who are forced into a doctor's office by their partner are being seen because of the combination of their wife's intuition and their own lack thereof.

Appearing about fifty-five years old, five foot eight inches tall and 170 pounds, he was muscular and solidly built and had a deep tan and pronounced crow's feet in the corners of his eyes. His short, closely cropped salt and pepper hair appeared slightly longer than a typical military haircut, and he sported gray-colored three or four day old stubble on his lower face. As I introduced myself, I quickly calculated from his birth date on the chart he was only forty-five.

A lifelong outdoorsman who loved to hunt and fish, he looked as though he would be leaving my office after this visit to head to the wilderness. It was fall, a beautiful time in the northern Midwest, and he was wearing a flannel shirt, camouflage pants, brown leather above-the-ankle hiking boots, and a hunting cap. Because light waves travel faster through air than the molecules we smell, there was a delay of a few seconds before I smelled additional diagnostic information.

He smells like an ashtray in a bar. Smoking and drinking, no doubt. In fact, both within the last hour. And it's only eleven in the morning.

"How old are you, anyway?" he asked abruptly, perhaps sensing danger in my brief sniffing. "You look too young to be a doctor. Of course, I suppose you already know that, huh?"

For the purposes of brevity, I will spare the reader further descriptions of the conversations concerning my appearance that often occurred upon meeting each new patient. This topic of discussion began the majority of new patient interviews during the first ten years of my practice. However, in their stead, I will confess one personal sin of vanity: the frustration of dealing with this question many hundreds of times in my first twelve years of practice was just slightly less painful than the shock of having the queries end for all time just after my fortieth birthday.

Knowing Mr. Redmond really didn't want to be there, I eventually came to understand that some sort of ultimatum had been delivered to him by his wife: he could not go on his planned hunting trip with his buddies to Montana unless he had a note from a doctor saying that it was okay. I was never privy to any other consequences Mr. Redmond might face if he failed to meet this requirement; it was, nonetheless, clear to me that Mr. Redmond valued compliance with his wife's demand over whatever he perceived the alternative to be.

We spent an hour together, and I learned a great deal about his health history. He rarely saw doctors. Part of his reasoning was, "I know what they're going to tell me to do, and I'm not going to do it." (For purposes of family reading I have omitted here all unnecessary expletive adjectives and other parts of speech that may be considered offensive, at a rate of about one per each of his sentences.) His rare visits to physicians had uniformly resulted in instructions to quit smoking and to cut back on his drinking. He had a startling level of commitment to his bad habits: he smoked two packs of cigarettes daily ("But, hey, I've cut back from four a day.") and drank four shots of whiskey per day ("But, listen, there were *years* when it was a fifth a day.").

Apparently, his chain smoking did not interfere with his job at the lumber yard, and when asked whether his drinking, which started at ten in the morning, was a problem at work, he shrugged and said, "A lot of the guys drink all day. I mean it's a lumber yard. We're not building rockets down there."

When asked about what his wife's specific concerns were, he stared me down and said, "She wants me to quit drinking and smoking. That's what this is all about. And I'm not going to do it."

"Have you had any recent symptoms that concerned her?"

"No. No symptoms at all," he said, staring at my shoes.

"Why do you think she is so intent on having you quit smoking and drinking then?" I wondered audibly.

He just shrugged his shoulders and shook his head. Sometimes, we each experience the love and care of a family member as criticism.

We went through the hundred-question review of symptoms. He had perfected his technique for this with other doctors, and we quickly fell into a rhythm:

"Any visual problems?"

"No."

"Blurred vision?"

"No."

"Wear glasses?"

"No."

"Any problems with your nose?

"No."

And so on. When we came to the respiratory system, I was expecting some change in the cadence.

"Any shortness of breath?" I asked.

"No." He coughed deeply.

"Any cough?"

"No." He coughed again.

"Any coughing up blood?"

"No." He coughed one more time.

The same pattern persisted through every question about the heart as well. No chest pain or discomfort. No arm or jaw pain. No history of heart disease. He never participated in any formal sort of exercise, so it was hard to gauge his physical stamina.

"I get plenty of exercise at work," he reasoned. He had been to Montana the previous fall and said he had a harder time climbing the hills, "now that I'm older." He believed the fact they were hiking at eight thousand feet above sea level explained his occasional fatigue.

But that was it. His father had died suddenly on his forty-sixth birthday. He didn't know the cause of his father's death, but he did note that his own forty-sixth birthday was coming soon. In fact, it fell on a day near the end of the planned hunting trip.

His examination showed about what one might expect: he was more wrinkled than a typical forty-five-year-old man, appearing ten years older than his actual age (a common finding in heavy smokers); I heard coarse breath sounds in his lungs through my stethoscope, suggestive of early emphysema; and there was the fruity smell of alcohol on his breath, likely from heavy drinking the night prior and on the job this morning.

An electrocardiogram showed only a mild abnormality and nothing that would suggest coronary disease or narrowing of the arteries to his heart. Nonetheless, this man was a walking risk for a heart attack, and given what sounded like a high level of concern on the part of his wife, I suggested that he have a stress test.

"We'll put you on a treadmill, have you exercise, and we will monitor your heart for ten or fifteen minutes or so, just to make sure that you can tolerate the high altitude and walking that you'll have to do in Montana," I explained. "We also need to do some blood tests. We should check your blood count and your cholesterol."

"Is this really necessary?" he retorted. "I feel just fine."

"Well, your wife is concerned," I began, seeing immediately in his eyes I had chosen a poor strategy for persuasion. "But I'm worried too. With your smoking and drinking," I continued, as he folded his arms and assumed fortress-like body language, "and your father's early death, we really do need to make sure everything is fine before we send you up to eight thousand feet above sea level to hunt." I hoped that my ending optimistic note might warm him up.

At the end of our time together, I asked him, "Do I have permission to call your wife so that I might have a better understanding of her concerns? I'd like to hear firsthand from her."

"No, you do not," he replied emphatically.

His refusal to allow me to talk to his wife was atypical. In fact, even his wife's absence at this visit was highly unusual. In similar situations, the usually more intuitive woman not only presses the need for her partner to see the doctor but is sitting in the exam room to "supervise." As I have often been told, "I want to make sure that he doesn't forget to tell you *everything*," with a tone of voice that clearly implies that her spouse's memory may not actually be the primary concern. Often in these situations, I also feel supervised myself, expected to tell the unwilling male exactly what their female partner wants them to hear. Despite the complex dynamics of a visit to a physician's office, male patients commonly under-report their symptoms, and I have generally found it to be of great benefit when a well-meaning spouse can be there to help paint a more detailed and accurate picture of the issues at hand.

"Well, it sure would help me to understand why she is so concerned…"

"I'll tell her everything she needs to know," he interrupted, as he abruptly rose from his chair and left the room to arrange for the tests.

End of interview, I guess.

As I talked to Mark later that afternoon, I told him about the bad feeling I had about Mr. Redmond.

"I wasn't sure I could believe anything he said. I mean, he was coughing while he told me he didn't have a cough. And his refusal to let me talk to his wife… Have you ever seen that?"

"Yes, a few times. There's nothing that you can do. The law's the law," he reminded me.

Patient confidentiality is one of the most sacred aspects of the doctor-patient relationship. No matter what is said, no matter how high the concern, physicians are simply not allowed to disclose any information beyond what and to whom the patient authorizes. However, less than ten years earlier, as a result of a famous lawsuit, *Tarasoff versus The Regents of the University of California*, many states passed laws imposing upon physicians and other health care professionals a "duty to warn" the potential victim of a credible threat to their safety. In this particular case, a student had told his psychiatrist of his intent to kill a woman with whom he was infatuated, and then he later murdered her. The court determined the psychiatrist did have the responsibility to warn the woman of the threat, despite the laws protecting the patient's confidentiality. While still controversial to this day, this ruling would not have been any help to Mr. Redmond, or me, since he was posing no obvious threat to anyone.

What was clear was that Mr. Redmond didn't want me talking to anyone about his health, including himself. The ultimate form of confidentiality, I suppose.

CHAPTER 10

"The difference between genius and stupidity is that genius has its limits."

Albert Einstein (1879 - 1955), German-born, Swiss-American theoretical physicist, philosopher, and author

There are times when I am certain my pre-medical and medical school studies caused me to miss the wildness of adolescence. Never was this feeling stronger than during my times working in the emergency department of a small, one hundred-twenty-bed, rural hospital sixty miles from my home. In the early years of my practice, with a stay-at-home wife and three children to support, the twenty-nine thousand dollar starting salary in the practice did not cover our family's expenses, and I found moonlighting in the emergency room to be both an interesting and exciting way to help to pay the bills.

But back to the wildness of youth. I suppose the necessary excellent grades required for the admission to medical school also require, as a prerequisite, an above-average level of good behavior, at least for the typical student accepted for a medical education. While my youth was certainly not mischief-free, in retrospect, I suspect I exercised a modicum of restraint beyond my peers. Perhaps I missed out on some enthralling experiences; at the same time, I never was required to avail myself of the services of an emergency room as the result of my own poor decisions. Over the course of my life, I certainly have exercised my fair share of bad judgment. I have lots of "experience." However, most came after my formal education was completed. Some of the adolescent patients I cared for in this small emergency room had clearly cornered the market on bad judgment on the days they staggered through our doors.

Richard and John, two high school friends, had procured and consumed sufficient alcohol to disable completely whatever good judgment they may have been able to piece together when sober. At the age of sixteen, this probably meant drinking four to six beers each, although some would deem a single bottle sufficient to do the job at this age and in this gender. From their history, which was anything but coherent, there had been some sort of contest between them, and they had consumed their two six-packs within about ninety minutes while sitting in a car at a railroad crossing near the outskirts of town.

"You see, all this was in preparation for our high school's homecoming football game later tonight," John confided, giggling, but in a manner conveying that any person with half a brain would understand the obvious connection. Not I.

Somewhere between beers three and five, good judgment reached its nadir, their creativity began to well up to overflowing, and they logically decided handguns could enhance their experience further. These were procured quite easily from their homes, and they drove to a nearby field to amuse themselves further. Richard was the one who had suggested throwing the empty beer bottles skyward and then shooting them before landing. Initially, one played the role of bottle launcher and the other marksman. They were unable to hit any of the bottles in mid-flight, and they blamed each other for poor bottle-throwing technique. Neither cited bad marksmanship as a possible reason for failure. Over the ensuing half hour, they had thrown each empty beer bottle enough times to ensure all twelve were now lost or shattered on impact with the earth.

"Fortunately," to quote his ironic word choice, John then remembered the bottles of Pepsi-Cola in the trunk of his car. Being full of the soft drink, these glass bottles were much heavier and could be thrown higher, providing the boys with more time to fire multiple rounds as the soft drinks hurtled back to earth.

"To intensify the challenge," despite the fact not one bottle had yet been hit, "we decided we would each toss the bottle upwards and then shoot it ourselves. In that way," John prophesied, "we'd have no one to blame but ourselves."

No one, indeed, I mused.

I must sympathize with the reader at this point, understanding the tension created by the use of the following words and phrases in a single story: beer, railroad crossing, handguns, and teenage boys. I did not experience a similar tension. Both were alive, both sat before me in the emergency room, both could speak, and neither possessed an obvious bullet hole anywhere on their person. Seeing them there, I knew they were comparatively indestructible.

Finally, the boys had some "success," as they called it. John hurled a full sixteen-ounce bottle of Pepsi skyward, directly overhead. Looking up, he could see it superimposed over the almost-full moon above him. "Blam," the gun went off, "ker-crack," the bottle exploded, (I'm now quoting Richard's onomatopoetic word choices, each of which he bellowed lustily), and then "clunk," the majority of the bottle crashed into John's own forehead, resulting in the four-inch laceration I had just inspected under the mass of toilet paper he was using to compress it when he came in to the emergency room.

"Thank God we had the toilet paper in the car," Richard intoned, with all of the reverence this drunken sixteen-year-old could muster.

Since childhood, I had always been appalled at the long list of occurrences for which people held God responsible, from wars and famine to the most minor form of personal inconvenience. This was the first time, hearing Richard's gratitude, I had the conscious awareness of the human tendency to thank the Almighty for equally unrelated favors.

"It was really cool," John boasted, obviously unaware of how the scar across his forehead would be likely to appear in the mirror twenty years from now, especially when sober. To his benefit, cuts from broken glass can sometimes be quite clean and straight, and, with the aid of fine suture material and twenty-four stitches, we were able to leave him with a scar that might someday be difficult to spot on first glance – from a reasonable distance, in dim light.

The cleaning of the wound had taken some time, followed by the even lengthier process of suturing it, and after some time, their alcohol-induced euphoria gradually gave way to the more sobering prospects of the imminent arrival of one or more of their parents. This transitional period contained a repetitive motif in which one of the boys would say something like, "Man, my dad is going to kill me when he finds out I borrowed his gun." Both boys would then nod, solemnly, as if actual death was the most likely possibility.

Then, they would trade conspiratorial glances, and the other would say, "Yeah, but it was *so cool!*" A form of mutual giggling would commence and continue until the next sobering image of a parent would step through the ethanol fog to the center of their mind's stage. After about one minute, they would then repeat the same conversation.

Meanwhile, each of the emergency staff and I considered it an act of divine providence that the combination of alcohol, cars, a railroad crossing, and shooting guns had resulted in nothing more than a facial laceration. In the hospital setting, usually a mixture of any two of these items produced either emergency trauma surgery or death.

Both sets of parents arrived within minutes of each other, and the boys left the emergency room with far more troubled faces than several others who had been escorted earlier by the local police from our premises to the city jail.

As Richard and John left, the head nurse muttered to me, "Those boys should have known better than to be shooting Pepsi bottles with guns while drunk!"

I nodded solemnly.

"Besides, as everybody knows," she continued, now borrowing from a popular ad campaign of the era, "things go better with Coke!"

CHAPTER 11

"Faced with the choice between changing one's mind and proving that there is no need to do so, almost everybody gets busy on the proof."

John Kenneth Galbraith (1908 - 2006), Canadian-American Economist

The day before Mr. Redmond's follow-up appointment, I received a phone message. "Mrs. Redmond called. Wants to talk to you about her husband."

Well, the law says that you can't disclose anything without the patient's permission, but it doesn't say you can't listen, I reasoned.

I called back immediately. "Hello, Redmond residence," the female voice whispered, barely audible.

"This is Dr. Roberts calling. I had a message that a Mrs. Redmond called."

"Um, yes. Just a second." In the background, I heard footsteps and then a door closing. "My husband said he came to see you several weeks ago, and he is coming in to see you tomorrow. Is that true?" she whispered, even more softly now.

"Mrs. Redmond, I'm sorry, but I can't provide you with any information about your husband without his written permission to do so."

"That's ridiculous! You can't even tell me if he was there?"

"No, I cannot. However, if you have particular concerns, there is no law that says that I can't listen to what you have to tell me."

There was a long pause, as she seemed to weigh the pros and cons of providing information as opposed to receiving it. "Well," she began, extremely tentatively, "I'm worried with all of his smoking and drinking he is headed for…"

"Hello? Hello? HELLO?" There was now a harsh male voice on the line, as loud and demanding as the other voice was soft and tentative. It was Mr. Redmond. "Hello. Is somebody on the line?"

His wife did not respond. I heard a soft click, then a loud expletive and a more definitive click. Wife, then husband, hanging up the phone, I surmised.

Mr. Redmond missed his appointment the following day. The day after that, I received a phone message, attached to his chart. "2:10 pm. Roger Redmond called. Needs written note saying it is okay to go to Montana."

I thumbed through his lab results in the chart. High cholesterol, slightly elevated hemoglobin, the oxygen-carrying molecule in red blood cells, often increased in heavy smokers because of the chronic carbon monoxide poisoning provided by cigarettes. Liver enzymes slightly elevated, indicating mild liver damage, likely from alcohol. No exercise test.

"Call cardiology lab for results of the exercise test. Tell patient he needs to come in to go over the results," I wrote in response, and sent the chart out to the nurse's desk.

It reappeared shortly. "2:45 p.m. Doesn't think it's necessary to come back in. Just wants note for hunting trip," was the response from Cynthia, our office nurse, summarizing her phone conversation with him. "Cardiology lab has no record of test."

Now I was writing in a spiral fashion along the margin, the small phone message note being otherwise filled with writing. "Call patient. Did he have exercise test? Needs to have test and come in to see me." Now the phone message slip was completely full. Like the game from elementary school where two opponents progressively grab a baseball bat, closer and closer to the handle, I had the last word for that phone message slip.

At the end of the day, Cynthia popped her head through the open office doorway. "He says he had the test on October second. The lab schedule shows he came in that day, but they can't find the result. They're looking for it. Mr. Redmond says he's leaving for his trip this Friday and it isn't going to be his problem if the lab lost his test. Now what?"

I explained to Cynthia my dilemma and the nagging bad feeling I had about Mr. Redmond.

"Have him come in tomorrow or Thursday. I'll call the cardiologists." I picked up the phone and called the physician who headed up the lab, explaining my dilemma. "He's coming in tomorrow. Can you find the tracings by then?" He said he was sure that they could. While I had him on the phone, I explained my dilemma. I never passed up the opportunity for a free consultation.

The cardiologist was quite helpful. "Well, if his dad actually dropped dead of a heart attack, with his smoking and high cholesterol, he's clearly at risk. If he died of something else, he's also at risk for coronary disease, but not as much. Either way, if the exercise test is negative, I'd let him go. I'd also document his risks in the chart. Don't worry – we'll find that tracing. We know it's here somewhere. The cardiologist who supervised the test seems to recall it was normal."

Wednesday night, before I went home, I checked with our secretary, Jean Marie. "Did we receive Mr. Redmond's GXT (graded exercise test) yet?"

"Nope. I just called them. They're still looking for it. They know he is coming in tomorrow morning." She smiled and gave me the "don't worry, we'll take care of it" look I so often relied upon, and I left for the day.

The next morning Mr. Redmond called again, asking if he could just pick up the note and not have an appointment. Without my involvement, the staff knew what to tell him, and there he was, scowling at me, when I entered the exam room at 10:00 a.m.

"I really don't think this is necessary," he said by way of greeting.

"Good morning, Mr. Redmond," I responded. "I'd like to review all of your test results and…"

"Are you going to write me that note?" he quickly interrupted.

"…and then talk about your planned hunting trip. I do have some concerns." We walked through the lab results. I talked about his cholesterol, his diet, his smoking, his drinking, his risk for heart disease, his need to exercise. I could tell he was experiencing the entire conversation, as he had with other doctors in the past, as though he was in his own personalized *Dante's Inferno* section of purgatory.

"Did they ever find my treadmill test?" he challenged.

I had seen the phone message clipped to the front of the chart as I walked in the room. "Cardiology lab called. GXT normal. 8 METs. Stopped due to fatigue." Eight METs referred to the level of energy he was able to reach before he was too tired to continue. It was low for a man his age.

"We don't have the final written report here in the office, but the cardiologist says it was normal. That doesn't mean there aren't some things you can do to improve your health, though. For example..."

"So I can go on the hunting trip, right?" he pressed. "You'll write me the note. Right?"

I took out my prescription pad and carefully printed the following message: "Exercise test normal at low level of exertion. OK to go on hunting trip. Should avoid heavy exercise, start low cholesterol diet. Should avoid heavy smoking, drinking. Needs to follow up with me after return from Montana. David Roberts, MD"

I handed the note to him and watched him frown as he read it. "Does it have to say all of this?" he asked, somewhat threateningly. "Can you just say 'OK to go on hunting trip' and leave it at that?" His face reddened.

At this point, I had almost completely lost my patience. "This is a note for your wife, for God's sake!" I wanted to shout. "I've written notes for work, notes for insurance companies, notes for airlines, but I've NEVER written a permission slip for somebody's spouse! Get a grip, man!"

Fortunately, though, somewhere from the ragged end of my last remaining shred of patience, I managed to say instead, "Mr. Redmond, this note provides a summary of the tests we've done and my opinion of your condition. I'm sorry if this doesn't meet your needs. It's the best I can do."

With that, he simply rose from his chair, left the examination room, and strode down the hall, ignoring our secretary calling after him. He marched out through the waiting room and disappeared from the building.

I never saw him again. Unfortunately, though, this was only the second chapter of my very long story of Roger Redmond.

CHAPTER 12

"That is not dead which can eternal lie,
yet with stranger aeons, even Death may die."

H.P. Lovecraft (1890 - 1937), American writer of weird fiction

I generally worked one or two twenty-four hour shifts per month in the small-town hospital emergency room setting, alternating these weekend shifts with being on call for my practice. In some ways I found the work stimulating, and in other ways it was exhausting. After a full and challenging week in the office seeing patients, I would drive sixty miles to the small hospital early Saturday morning to begin a twenty-four hour shift at 7:00 a.m.. Not only was I the only doctor present in the ER, I was generally the only M.D. in the whole hospital for most of the day, as the patients' own physicians would make Saturday morning rounds by 9:00 a.m. and then be gone until Sunday morning. It was, therefore, also my duty to handle inpatient hospital emergencies, such as cardiac arrests and other critical patient situations. In addition, the late evening and early morning hours often found me tending to more mundane matters involving routine hospitalized patients, which might take me only a few minutes to handle, thereby sparing the community physician a drive to the hospital in the middle of the night.

One such call came at 10:30 one evening, during an atypical lull in the normally circus-like atmosphere of the ER on a Saturday night.

"Dr. Roberts," the nurse intoned respectfully, "this is Cheryl calling, from Unit 400. I hate to bother you, but we have a patient of Dr. Bhatia's up here who has expired, and, well, you know the drill. We need a physician to officially pronounce her dead."

"Ambulance with a motorcycle accident victim coming in, five minutes out," the ER nurse called to me.

Speaking into the phone, I said, "I'll be right up," hung up, and made my way to the stairs. I took the steps two at a time and arrived on the fourth floor in about thirty seconds.

"That was fast," the nurse beamed. "A new record, I'm sure."

"Probably by about twenty minutes," the unit secretary added dryly.

"There is an ambulance en route," I gasped, out of breath from the run up the stairs. "It will be here in about four minutes. Where's the patient?"

"Right down here. Follow me, doctor." The nurse was in her early twenties, within a few years of graduation, I guessed. She wore baggy blue scrubs, the night shift uniform in this hospital. She seemed unusually grateful for my quick response, and she carried the air of hierarchical respect for physicians that seemed, to me at least, to emanate from some bygone age of medicine. I was never a fan of the artificial "physician – nurse" authority system, and it was much more firmly ensconced in this rural hospital. Usually, I would take a moment to establish a more egalitarian relationship. "You can call me David," I would most often say, reaching out my hand. Being in a hurry, with three and one-half minutes until the arrival of the ambulance, I passed on this approach and just followed the nurse as she scurried down the hall and into the room.

It was a semi-private, two-patient room. The first bed was empty, and in the far bed, by the window, laid a woman in her nineties, perfectly motionless, with white hair.

"Okay, thanks," I said. "I'll be right down there to fill out the paperwork."

Three minutes until the ambulance arrives, I calculated, and I quickly placed my stethoscope over her heart.

"Lub-dub, lub-dub, lub-dub," said my stethoscope. *Not exactly what I was expecting to hear.*

"Shooooooosh," it said next, as the patient took an exceedingly long breath. I jumped backwards. Why a single breath from a woman presumed dead should be more startling to me than hearing her heartbeat, I cannot say.

I gently pulled up one of her eyelids and briefly shone my penlight on her pupil. It contracted immediately, the normal reflex in the living human eye.

Two minutes. I was always timing things. I regretted now not having introduced myself, not remembering this nurse's name. *There's always the nametag,* I reasoned.

I found her at the nursing station. Only the C of her first name on her nametag peeked out at me from beneath the diaphragm of her stethoscope. *Cathy? Candy? Charlene?*

Ninety seconds.

"Listen, I hate to tell you this, but the patient is not dead. Not yet. She still has heart tones, is taking slow respirations, and her pupils react to light."

The nurse, *(Connie?)* looked appalled and began to speak. As she did so, the stethoscope moved slightly to the right, revealing the letter "h" after the capital "C." *Must be Charlene.*

"I'm so sorry to have called you up here..."

"Listen, Charlene," I interrupted, "I'm really sorry, but I have to go. There's an ambulance arriving in less than a minute, and I have to be there. Call me when you're sure she's dead!"

What a stupid thing to say, I thought as I bounded down the stairs to meet the motorcycle driver now arriving at the doors of our emergency room. The ninety-year-old woman on the fourth floor was obviously only minutes away from death, but as a physician, I couldn't certify the event until it actually happened. *Still, David, you could have been much more kind to the nurse.*

It was a very busy Saturday night, without the slightest lull until about three in the morning. As usual, a few deeply inebriated souls darkened our doors at about 2:15 a.m., shortly after the official bar-closing time in the town, but their problems were relatively simple, and I found myself crawling onto my own gurney in the doctor's five-by-nine-foot sleeping quarters at about 4:00 a.m. As usual, it took me all of twenty seconds to fall into a deep sleep.

There was a faint knocking on the door, which became progressively louder until I realized the sound was not the audio portion of my current dream.

"Dr. Roberts," the nurse called through the door.

"Yes, come in," I responded, groggy but now awake. "Come in" was clearly a euphemism, as the desk and the gurney filled the entire square footage of my sleeping closet. It was 6:55 a.m. according to my glow-in-the-dark watch. My twenty-four hour shift ended in five minutes.

She cracked the door open a few inches. "Unit 400 called. They have a patient up there they want you to pronounce dead."

"Okay, I'm awake." *As awake as I am going to be after three hours of sleep, anyway.* "I'll head up there in a minute."

"The nurse told me to tell you they are certain she's dead this time." I could tell, by the tinge of laughter in her voice, the story had made the rounds throughout the entire hospital last night.

"What was the nurse's name?" I asked, realizing "Charlene" had been a bad guess. "I wasn't very nice to her."

"Oh, Doctor Roberts, give yourself a break. Everybody thought you did the best you could, what with the motorcycle wreck coming in and all." While I did not consider myself deserving of forgiveness, her reassuring voice in the dark did provide some absolution to my confession. I sat up in the gurney and searched in the dark for my white coat.

"It was Suzie who called this morning," she continued. "You talked to Cheryl last night."

"Cheryl?" I repeated, hoping to memorize the correct name this time. *Where did I come up with Charlene?* I wondered.

"Yes, but she won't be there now. I think she went home a few minutes early, to avoid death by embarrassment."

I stumbled out of the physician's closet, as I affectionately called my combined sleeping room and office, and made my way to the stairs, this time ascending only one step at a time. Suzie was waiting there for me with the chart, smiling. I walked down to the patient's room to re-examine her.

The patient was no longer breathing. There were no heart sounds. Her pupils did not react to light. Her body was room temperature.

In all likelihood, she had died just a few minutes after I left her the night before. I wandered back to the nursing station and filled out the necessary forms, with Suzie standing by in case I needed help. When I came to the box to fill in the time the patient had expired, I said "Time of death" aloud and looked at Suzie.

She just smiled and said, "We knew you were really busy, and then we heard you were asleep. We didn't want to bother you."

I felt ashamed to be treated with such kindness and respect in return for my abrupt and unkind manner the night before. Something in the Bible about having hot coals heaped upon one's head came to mind.

"Look, can you tell Cheryl I'm sorry about last night? I was rude. I wasn't angry with her at all. I was just preoccupied."

"We all knew that," she responded. "I'll tell her when I see her tomorrow. And thanks for responding so quickly. We all really appreciate it."

As I drove the sixty miles home that morning, I thought about the differences between the high levels of intuition and expressed caring I routinely experienced from my nursing colleagues and about the conversely low levels I experienced among physicians, myself not only included, but perhaps the a primary example.

What is it about the selection and training of nurses and physicians that produces such a noticeable, if not even stereotypical difference? More importantly, what do I need to start doing as a physician to express more regularly such a caring attitude to my colleagues? How do I acquire the insight into myself needed to have a better understanding of the needs of others?

I was exhausted. I had no idea. But I sensed these were the right questions, and they were a good start.

CHAPTER 13

"A wise man has doubts even in his best moments.
Real truth is always accompanied by hesitations.
If I could not hesitate, I could not believe."

Henry David Thoreau (1817 - 1862), American author and naturalist

It was early November, ten days since Roger Redmond left for his hunting trip in Montana. On a Thursday afternoon, I received a phone message: "Mrs. Redmond called. Wants to talk to you about her husband."

That's odd, I thought. *You've already talked to her about confidentiality. What's up?* I called her back and immediately felt as though I was on the witness stand.

"What, *exactly*, did you tell my husband about the hunting trip?" she began.

"Mrs. Redmond, I understand your concern about your husband. I really do. But as we discussed several weeks ago, I can't release any information to you without his written permission. I'm sorry."

"You mean you can't tell me anything as long as he's still alive, right?" she countered.

What an odd response. No one has ever said anything like that to me before. "I'm not sure I understand what you mean, Mrs. Redmond," I responded, thinking out loud while feeling a "caution" sign pop up in the back of my head.

"I said, 'You mean you can't tell me anything as long as he's still alive,' but, you know, he's not still alive. He's dead." Her tone of voice was ninety percent anger and ten percent sad.

It is quite common for family members of patients who have died to experience an initial reaction of anger. In fact, it is the second of the official five stages of grief: denial, anger, bargaining, depression, and acceptance. She was obviously well past her initial denial.

"Mrs. Redmond, I am so sorry. What happened?"

"He died of a heart attack on his hunting trip. I told him not to go!"

I had no idea what to say next. Completely speechless, stuck in denial, I was not quickly progressing through my own stages of grief.

"What did you tell him, Dr. Roberts?" she queried. "He said you told him he'd be fine, and you gave him a note that said so. Is that right?"

"I did give him a note the last time he was here, Mrs. Redmond."

"What did it say?"

Fumbling through the chart, my hands shaking, I slowly uttered, "Well, let's see ... I have the note right here somewhere... I mean, a copy of the note..."

What are the rules about confidentiality after a patient dies? I wondered. I had no idea, actually. Also, I wasn't finding a copy of the note I had given to Mr. Redmond. *Now what should you do, David?*

"Uh, Mrs. Redmond, can you tell me more about how he died?"

"I really don't want to talk about this over the phone. Believe me, I have all the details of what happened, and I think you need to hear them. Can you go over his records with me, now that he is gone?" she asked and demanded.

"I need to check, and I will let you know. We can still meet, though. I'm anxious to hear exactly what happened." After checking my schedule, I determined I could talk to her that same afternoon. She said would come right in.

I was able to reach our hospital's attorney for some general advice. After a patient died, I was told, it was usually considered reasonable to share relevant information with the family. After I hung up, it occurred to me that virtually everything would be relevant here.

Mark came back from the hospital, and he winced when I told him what had happened. He clearly recalled the case, and asked, "Did you ever get the official report of the exercise test?"

He was as worried as I was about the possibility of being sued for malpractice. Ours was a young and still struggling practice, and while we had medical liability insurance, neither of us had any idea of how a lawsuit might affect our financial viability. For all we knew, it could put us out of business.

"No," I told him, "we never received a copy of that missing report."

"What about the note you gave him? You copied it, right?" Mark remembered my ambivalence about this man and his stormy exit from our office.

We routinely copied everything that we gave to patients. Since Mrs. Redmond had called, though, I had slowly pieced together the details of my last encounter with her husband. I had penned the equivocal note, handed it to him, he became upset, and then he immediately stormed out of the office.

"No, I didn't have a chance. He ran out with it before I could copy it."

Mark already possessed rather prominent masseter muscles from holding his jaw clenched in times of stress. I could see them growing before my eyes at this moment, bulging out much wider than his temples.

"Well, I guess we just need to do the right thing and tell her what happened," he concluded. Honest to a fault, Mark always applied the Golden Rule to his interactions with others.

I spent the few remaining minutes of the noon hour reviewing my office notes from the two visits with Mr. Redmond. Mostly, I was angry with myself. I had a clear inner sense of concern about the whole case; something was wrong, and I had known it. Medical school training tends to be much longer on facts and shorter on feelings. The lessons about listening to one's inner voice come from experience and not from medical texts, another version of the good judgment – experience – bad judgment equation.

At the appointed time, Mrs. Redmond arrived with her brother. As I sat down with them in the examination room, I could tell this was going to be a difficult session. After I had introduced myself to them and expressed my genuine sorrow for their loss, she pulled out an electronic device from her purse and asked, "Do you mind if I tape record this conversation?"

In my advance mental rehearsal of this meeting, I had not considered the possibility of a tape recorder. I had no idea whether this was a good idea or not. *If you say "no," it will sound like you have something to hide*, I reasoned, *and if you say "yes," she'll use this against you.*

Seeing my hesitation, she quickly added, "You know, we're a big family, and everyone wants to hear more about what happened. I knew we couldn't fit everyone into one of your exam rooms. I thought it would be easier to tape record the conversation and play it for my family."

Her brother looked down at the floor and shifted uncomfortably.

"Sure," I responded, not wanting to seem withholding. "So, can you please tell me what happened in Montana?" I asked her.

"We don't really know the details. We just know that Roger died of a heart attack. Of course, it's all his own fault, with all that smoking and drinking. No one is to blame but him for what happened. But Dr. Roberts, what we're wondering about is what happened in the office here over the past month."

Wait a minute! The whole point of her coming in was for her to tell me how he died. Is this some sort of a trick? My inner voice tried to warn me I was walking into an ambush. Nonetheless, she did have a legitimate right to know what happened.

Using the chart, I walked through my detailed notes. Pretty much everything was documented: his heavy smoking and drinking (to which she pointed out that he had underestimated both), his lack of any chest pain ("he had some every day"), his negative exercise test ("that's funny, because he could hardly make it up the basement stairs without stopping to rest"), and his anger about my wording of his note ("interesting that he refused to show it to me").

Between my explanations and her responses, it was now clear Mr. Redmond had actively worked to misrepresent the truth to me. While I was frustrated about this, I also began to assume Mrs. Redmond must clearly understand that no physician could possibly have penetrated the thick fog of false medical history her husband had generated.

"Dr. Roberts, can you tell me one more thing?" she asked somewhat innocently. "Would you say my husband was misdiagnosed?"

In the nearly thirty years since being asked this question, I have generated dozens of clear and forthright answers, each of which would have both represented the truth and protected me from future litigation. Such responses include:

"No, based on the information given to me and the test results, I'd say the conclusions we reached fit perfectly with his history and the test results."

"No, his history and test results would have predicted that he had only a twenty percent chance of eventually developing heart disease. There was no way to know what was going on, especially given his complete misrepresentation of the facts."

"No. It is impossible to diagnose every case of heart disease in advance."

Et cetera, et cetera. Instead, I opted for the more direct, "Well, yes. Given his tests were normal, and, if what you say is correct about him dying of a heart attack, then he was clearly misdiagnosed. I am so sorry that this happened, Mrs. Redmond."

"So," her brother interrupted, in what was to be his sole utterance of their visit, "you're admitting he was misdiagnosed?" The tape recorder in Mrs. Redmond's hand perceptibly rose toward my mouth.

"Yes. I'm sorry," I said, crafting my response from one hundred percent guilt and zero percent self-protection.

Years later, in the subsequent millennium, a research study would show conclusively that the risk of malpractice lawsuits decreases when treating physicians clearly explain their medical mistakes and then apologize. Being twenty-five years earlier, though, the Redmonds can be excused for not being aware of, or influenced by, this data.

"I guess that's all we need to know," Mr. Redmond's wife replied, clicking off the tape recorder. They both rose to leave. Exasperated, I realized immediately I had somehow been tricked into incriminating myself in a way that did not represent the facts of Mr. Redmond's case and that the probability of my comments being used against me was quite high. On the way out, I again expressed my sympathy for them and my sorrow for their loss. I knew I was Mrs. Redmond's necessary villain for her husband's death: someone was to blame, and it wasn't going to be Mr. Redmond himself, after all. I recall feeling very angry with the Redmond family at that moment, not realizing in those days that most of my anger came from that part of me that coped with stress by blaming others for my own misfortune. The black and white concepts of right and wrong would not serve me well in managing my emotions around

Mr. Redmond's case, especially at a time in my life where I could see very little gray in anything.

$\mathscr{L}$

In those early years of our practice, I often wondered whether Mark felt that bringing me on was a mistake. That afternoon, my doubts were particularly acute. While we thoroughly enjoyed practicing together and trusted each other implicitly in the care of our patients, it seemed I had some predilection for unusually large errors in judgment, which, at least in my view, were generally unrelated to the quality of my medical decision-making. As I recounted for him the tape-recorded interview earlier that afternoon, I could see those bulging jaw muscles in his chiseled Teutonic face getting an even more robust workout than they had earlier. As the junior partner, I felt acutely I had put our practice at risk.

"You know, I think she tricked me. When she said, 'No one is to blame but him,' I just got sucked in." It was part of my nature to believe everyone wanted to hear the truth and that telling it could only help a situation. As a result, I was often quite forthright in my "truth telling." "Brash" would probably be a better word for my approach on many occasions.

Characteristically, Mark said little, just listening and then offering a bit of optimism at the end. "They're probably still in the 'anger' phase of their grieving," he said and left it at that. But the tense stare of his tiny spectacled steel-blue eyes belied the optimism as it cut right through me.

$\mathscr{L}$

I spent the next several months sleeping and waking, reviewing every possible alternative scenario to the two visits that Mr. Redmond had made to my office. Of course, each of these two-act plays ended with my prohibiting him from taking his hunting trip to Montana. In these repetitive instant replays, he had thousands of heart scans, hundreds of heart catheterizations (never done back then for patients without reported symptoms), and countless referrals to smoking cessation classes and Alcoholics Anonymous. His survival rate in my fantasies was one hundred percent! If I had a dollar for each time I had asked myself, in reference to his case alone, "Well, what if I had..." then I could have retired by the end of that year at the age of thirty.

My medical training had been devoid of any discussion of the personal effects of "making mistakes." On my surgery rotation in medical school, I had attended a monthly "Morbidity and Mortality" conference, where the chair of the department of surgery would go through each case in which a death occurred and ask questions concerning the patient's care. The focus was always on the clear understanding of the patient's death, which is, of course, commendable, and never on the personal impact on the physician and family.

Now facing my own patient's death, I was without compass as I wandered lost through this wilderness of guilt and self-recrimination, hoping to understand how I might someday cope with being in a profession whose mistakes can cost people their lives. It never occurred to me that I might talk with my colleagues about this episode. Those discussions just weren't a part of the fabric of medicine at that point in our profession's history.

Of course, I had an unbelievably high index of suspicion for coronary artery disease in any heavy-smoking, heavy-drinking middle-aged male I saw for the next several years. I recall another patient, nine months later, who didn't smoke or drink and did jog regularly, but who came in to be checked out because he was headed out west for a "strenuous hunting trip." Ordinarily one of the pleasures of practice, seeing this healthy man who was clearly taking optimal care of himself put me into a cold sweat for the entire visit, and it kept me up most of the night after I had seen him.

This patient was in great shape, and I told him so. He looked somewhat confused as I recounted to him, in inordinate detail, the symptoms of early coronary artery disease and described what he should do in the event he began to have chest pain.

"Of course, you probably won't have these symptoms," I countered at that point, primarily for my own reassurance, and completely confusing him.

In addition, during this decade, I myself was making an annual pilgrimage of sorts to the Rocky Mountains with good friends, hiking and climbing the highest peaks in the American West. Being the only physician of a group of anywhere between six and sixteen other men my age, I had carried a fairly simple six-ounce first aid kit in my pre-Redmond days: various types of adhesive bandages, antiseptics, aspirin, acetaminophen, and some medication for heartburn. Post-Redmond, my upgraded mobile doctor's office weighed about five pounds and was loaded with surgical materials, syringes with attached needles, and even adrenaline. I suppose this was all part of my subconscious plan to be fully prepared in the event one of my perfectly healthy and physically fit friends should experience a coronary event high on some mountain pass in Colorado or Wyoming.

Fortunately, the practice of medicine is full of positive, affirming moments, and gradually, over time, I was able to grow in my confidence as a physician and know I was helping others on a daily basis. It also dawned on me one day that no matter how excellent of a diagnostician I could eventually become, I would never develop the power to read the minds of others. At some point, I came to better understand the shared responsibility necessary for an effective patient-physician relationship. Just as research has proven patients must desire to quit smoking and actually be ready to do so to be successful, I learned that the Roger Redmonds of the world had their own necessary responsibilities in the complex relationship they each have with their physicians.

Of course, there was always more that I could do to improve my skills in medical interviewing, making people comfortable to be open with me about their symptoms, concerns, and fears. There is probably no career better than medicine to provide one with a life of challenge and continuous improvement. In time, I was able to move past the daily dose of self-recrimination and return to a more balanced sense of my role as a doctor. It was as though I had graduated from "Medical Errors 401," a senior year college course in living with one's failures.

Somewhat predictably, having reached this false summit, I soon would be given the opportunity to enroll in the graduate level course in "Making Mistakes" – on the day the subpoena arrived.

CHAPTER 14

*"Your work is to discover your world
and then with all your heart give yourself to it."*

*Hindu Prince Gautama Siddhartha (563 - 483 B.C.E.),
the founder of Buddhism*

About nine months after I joined the practice, we called an emergency practice business meeting to address a cash shortfall. We did not have enough money in our account to pay ourselves, and barely enough to pay our staff. The situation with Mr. Redmond had left Mark and I both quite concerned for the viability of our practice, and our meeting that day would do nothing but deepen those fears. We had no business experience whatsoever. Medical school and residency training provides a level of education in biochemistry and other topics far beyond what is needed to be a physician. In contrast, there had been no instruction for either of us in any aspect of managing a small business, so even the most primitive concepts of revenue and expenses seemed substantially more complex and mysterious to us than phenylketonuria, a rare metabolic disease of infants.

As such, we were completely dependent on Paul, our accountant, to manage the practice those first several years. Too small a business to have our own professional office manager, we tried our best to understand the economics of our medical practice and lead it wisely.

As usual, Paul arrived fifteen minutes early for the meeting, and he was dressed in splendor, sporting white loafers – before Easter and somewhat out of season.

Our accountant approved our initial plan of temporarily withholding our own paychecks that week, and then he went further to explain to us that our payroll problem was not a one-time event, but rather something we could expect to see continuously, because there seemed to be an imbalance between our revenues and expenses.

"What do we do to fix this?" we asked, panicked.

"Well, it is much simpler than you might think," he said reassuringly. He pulled out a yellow legal pad and put together a summary table of our expenses and revenue. He walked us through our sources of revenue and our various expenses. I noticed at this meeting, and through the years, that Paul never actually called any attention to the fact his consulting services were also an expense of the practice, but at this particular point in time, we were all ears. Using some very round numbers, he carefully attempted to guide us through the maze of dollar figures and toward his conclusion. Despite the fact that neither Mark nor I actually understood much of what he said, we both intuitively sensed Paul was now getting to the point, and our attention was heightened.

"So," he concluded, after a short and apparently intentional dramatic pause, "I suspect you are both thinking there is no way out of this predicament." He smiled like a magician just before the close of an impressive trick.

We're paying you to come up with a solution here, Paul, I thought, but neither Mark nor I spoke.

"Well, if David was to see only two additional patients each day in the office, you would fix your problem."

Mark and I glanced at each other across the table and both nodded.

"I can do this pretty easily," I offered.

In the back of my mind, I was already feeling a bit overwhelmed by the time commitment of the practice. While certainly less than the eighty or more hours per week of residency training, we were each averaging twelve hour days during the week, and on the weekends we were spending a total of ten additional hours in the hospital. And then there were the sometimes quite frequent on-call pages from outpatients.

But two extra patients was only thirty minutes of appointment time, plus maybe another fifteen minutes of associated paperwork, and over five days, this meant a total of about four more hours per week. We wanted the practice to be successful, we needed to pay our employees, and since my family saw very little of me anyway, another four hours didn't seem too onerous in the bigger scheme of things. Thomas Jefferson once said, "I'm a great believer in luck, and I find the harder I work the more I have of it."

Maybe the extra work will bring the practice better financial performance, I figured. I added the scheduling slots that afternoon and began seeing extra patients the next day.

Up to this point in life, I hadn't really given deliberate thought to how I spent my time. Since my high school paper route, work had been a central point of my life. I had worked all the way through medical school to pay my tuition, and "doing whatever needed to be done" was reflexive for me. Once I became a physician, I was impressed with the degree my patients' work was most often central to their identity as well.

Like any conversation between people meeting for the first time, I am always looking for something unique and interesting about each person who comes to see me. Through the years, this search has produced some of the most satisfying moments in my clinical practice. I have had the privilege to provide care for a United States president's campaign manager, the same president's personal aide, one of the men who helped to develop sonar, an internationally known author, famous musicians, undercover drug officers, CEOs, and people from every walk of life, even Madonna's dance teacher. (The rock star, that is, not the mother of Jesus.) Each patient has an interesting story to tell and is usually flattered at my interest when asked to educate me about their life and work.

There are also people who work in positions that, up until meeting them, I never knew existed. I didn't know there were people who actually watched every minute of recorded television coverage of NASCAR racing, in slow motion, timing and totaling the number of seconds each company logo appears on the screen. These statistics are compiled into reports for the sponsors, which demonstrate the return they are getting in terms of brand name exposure on the investment of their advertising dollars. Of course, it made sense someone would do this work once I had heard of it, but it also isn't the sort of thing I would ever imagine on my own.

One of my patients worked in child care at a bowling alley. Prior to hearing about her work, it had never occurred to me that bowling could require a level of intense concentration necessitating child care. I had, on at least one occasion, rolled a ball down the alley with my right arm, while holding one of my children with my left. Of course, I don't make my living bowling. (It was a gutter ball.)

I have also seen all the variations in approaches patients may take toward their work. I have seen people die from heart attacks, related, in large part to work-related stress. There are the people who work over eighty hours per week and those who don't work at all. Some hate their jobs and live miserable lives; some love their jobs and feel quite fulfilled in them. I have cared for those who were injured or killed on, or because of, their jobs. I have written countless notes to excuse people from their work and equal numbers permitting patients to return to their employment.

Work can be the source of an individual's identity; it certainly has been for me for a significant period of my life. Work is so important to most people that it is included in their introduction to another. "What sort of work do you do?" may be the most common conversation starter, particularly between men.

One's occupation can also create a specific medical hazard. Asbestos workers (a now almost extinct occupation) have a significant risk of mesothelioma, a rare form of cancer of the lining of the chest. Health care workers have a higher risk of hepatitis and HIV infections through accidental needle sticks. Rare occupations can provide important clues to even rarer diseases. Were it not for my medical training, I would be unaware there were people who filled silos for a living, nor would I know "silo filler's disease" was a serious lung condition occurring in people with this occupation due to their exposure to nitrogen dioxide. Considering a career as a shepherd on the island of Malta? Sounds romantic, but be careful you don't contract brucellosis, a rare bacterial infection acquired from sheep and other animals.

Despite its various occupational risks, I can't imagine a career more fulfilling than medicine. It seems every human being has an innate desire to make a difference, either in the world or just for one other person, and medicine has offered me the opportunity to do both, every hour in practice. While there are a number of infectious risks to being a physician, the biggest occupational hazard I have incurred is the damage that comes from working an excessive number of hours caring for those who are ill and in need of care. While it may be true that practice makes perfect, perfectionism is a double-edged sword for the physician, which also carries risks of burn-out, alienation from family and friends, and more serious physical and mental health challenges.

Up to this point in our practice, every interaction I had with a patient presented me with an opportunity to learn more about the world. Absent any internal sense of the negative effects of my growing overcommitment to the practice, the idea of two extra patients per day sounded like a great plan.

CHAPTER 15

"All things share the same breath - the beast, the tree, the man...
the air shares its spirit with all the life it supports."

Chief Seattle (1780 - 1866), leader of the
Suquamish and Duwamish Native American tribes

I had first met Alma Clark in my Resident Practice. In those days, interns and residents called it "clinic," our shorthand term for the ten percent portion of our internal medicine training in the outpatient (non-hospital) setting, the venue that would eventually occupy ninety percent of our time in private practice. At this time, Internal Medicine residents worked between seventy to ninety-five hours per week, and over the course of three years, we spent most of our time caring for hospitalized patients (called inpatients). We spent the remainder of our time, averaging eight to twelve hours per week, in seeing patients in a variety of outpatient settings, including our resident clinic, the emergency room, and rotations where we spent time in the offices of private physicians. The inpatients were generally much sicker, and their diseases and problems were much harder to treat, and the dictum was that inpatient work was the hard stuff and the outpatient cases were easy.

"If you can take care of a patient in a diabetic coma in an intensive care unit," our program director would promise, "then you'll have no problem at all treating diabetics in the outpatient setting." In other words, if you can care for the most difficult version of any condition or disease, then, by extension, it should be easy to handle all of the simple details.

On June thirtieth of every year, when the class of third-year internal medicine residents would graduate, those who were not doing additional training in a subspecialty went from spending only four hours per week in the office setting to a practice on July first that was at least fifty hours of time in the relatively unfamiliar outpatient arena. Of course, this left each of us feeling totally unprepared for the "real world" and sometimes angry at our training program.

As Mark put it somewhat facetiously, "My first patient in my practice came in with left shoulder pain. After about ten minutes, I said to myself, 'Well, it's not an acute myocardial infarction (heart attack), it's not septic shock (low blood pressure due to bacteria in the blood stream), it's not lung cancer. I think there is something actually wrong with his shoulder! What do I do now?"

Over the subsequent decades, the organizations responsible for ensuring that residency training did indeed prepare its students for the real world recognized this growing disparity and expanded requirements for outpatient training, creating a balance more appropriate for the private practice of internal medicine. There was a silver lining to the dark cloud of our first several years of self-taught outpatient medical practice.

Back in our resident clinic, our patients viewed us as their primary care doctor, although law and standards required residents to review our work on each case with a faculty physician, who actually carried the ultimate legal responsibility.

When I first met Alma Clark, she was only forty years old, five feet tall, and weighed eighty pounds. She was a hard-looking woman, expressionless, all bone and muscle, with a copper tinge to her skin. *You could paste her picture in the dictionary next to the word "wiry,"* I thought when I first laid eyes on her.

Her case was fascinating. Since age twenty, she had difficulty exercising, becoming winded almost immediately.

"Even when I carry groceries into the house," she explained, pausing to breathe, "I can only carry one bag at a time," pausing again to breathe, "and sometimes I just have to stop and rest."

Reflexively, I began to breathe with her, immediately needing to double my respiratory rate. *Twenty-four breaths per minute*, I estimated silently. *Too fast.*

"Now, I feel short of breath all the time, even now," she added, although this was evident to me by her frequent mid-sentence pauses to breathe.

I'd been with her for less than a minute and was already rattling off possible diagnoses in my mind: heart valve problem or "hole in the heart," emphysema, restrictive lung disease, old tuberculosis infection, asbestos-related pleural cancer, chronic and perhaps hereditary anemia, old blood clots clogging the arteries to the lungs. Most of the possibilities were lung diseases. I was feeling lightheaded from pacing her respirations, and I resumed my usual breathing rate.

We went through the usual list of questions about her past medical history, family history, and her habits. She never exercised, and, to my surprise, she had never smoked a cigarette in her whole life. No alcohol intake. No other problems apart from her now constant breathlessness. She did occasionally wake up at night with air hunger, a horrible sensation akin to drowning. She hadn't been on an airplane in several years; she had become extremely short of breath the last time she had flown, and she decided never to repeat the experience.

"Open your mouth and take long, deep breaths," I said as I placed the stethoscope on her back. I didn't hear anything in her lungs. This was a problem. Normally, human beings have what are called "breath sounds" in medicine. With inspiration, the in breath, air first fills the lungs, sounding through the stethoscope like wind traversing a crack in a masonry wall of a house, just a slow "whoosh," without the whistling. Then, in expiration, the out-breath, the physician hears a slower and longer swoosh as the air leaves the lungs. Hearing nothing in the lungs isn't the worst possible finding on the physical examination; the absence of heartbeat reigns supreme in this regard.

Step 1: Check your stethoscope, I thought, having made the mistake of thinking a patient's lungs were inaudible in medical school, later finding an obstruction in my instrument's tubing. The stethoscope was clear; I could hear the sound of my finger tapping on its diaphragm.

Step 2: "Mrs. Clark, could you open your mouth this time and try breathing more deeply for me?" Breath sounds are louder with the mouth open.

"I have my mouth open," she insisted.

Step 3: I used a trick taught to me by Dr. Westerman, and took the right stethoscope ear piece out of my ear. I could listen to the breath coming in and out of her mouth with the right ear and also hear it in the lungs through the stethoscope with the left.

"Let's try again. Deep breath!" I said enthusiastically, in an attempt to cheer her on.

Right ear: "Shooooosh. Swoooooooooooooooosh."

Left ear: Complete silence.

Step 4: There is no Step 4, I reflected. Distracted, I finished her physical exam, still worried about her lungs. She had multiple findings of chronic oxygen starvation, with pale blue lips and nail beds, and clubbing, a change in the fingernails resulting from low blood levels of oxygen. The only other finding worth noting was that her liver was easily palpable in her abdomen and clearly enlarged.

"Mrs. Clark, we're going to need to obtain a chest x-ray today in order to figure out what is going on here," I said, calculating that I had just bought myself forty-five minutes to pull out a textbook or talk to my supervising physician in clinic. I had probably listened to about five thousand human lungs up to this point in my career, in pairs. Each pair produced audible breath sounds. I had heard all the possibilities: bronchial (coarse) and vesicular (quiet and wispy) breath sounds, egophony (increased resonance of voice sounds, with a high-pitched bleating quality, heard especially over compressed lung tissue in pneumonia and other illnesses), pleural friction rubs (scraping of the two lung surfaces together like sandpaper), rales (clicking, bubbling, or rattling sounds), rhonchi (sounds that resemble snoring), stridor (a high-pitched crowing sound), wheezing (hoarse whistling sounds), whispered pectoriloquy (whispered voice sounds with increased resonance), crackles and pops, and even severely decreased breath sounds, but never just plain nothing in a living patient.

The textbook provided no help. My clinic supervisor was in an exam room with another resident. On the phone, Dr. Charles Westerman, the pulmonary medicine specialist who was the director of our medical intensive care unit, explained that in advanced cases of emphysema, patients may have barely audible or even inaudible breath sounds, but the latter would be very rare. I had learned some of my obsession with complete differential diagnosis listing, or coming up with every possible explanation for a symptom or finding, from him.

"Of course, you can also hear the absence of breath sounds with bilateral pneumothorax (collapse of both lungs), complete tracheal (windpipe) obstruction, and death. I suppose she wouldn't have been able to walk into your office with any of these, though," he added with his usual wry humor. "Particularly death."

Mrs. Clark returned a bit later with her x-ray films in hand.

"Let's look at them together," I offered, walking quickly over toward the view box to put the films up, leaving her panting behind me in an effort to keep up. I switched on the fluorescent tubes that provided backlighting to the films. I began in my usual style, with the appropriate gestures, "You see here, this is your spine running from the top to the bottom of the x-ray. Here's your heart in the middle, this bright white part. You can see your ribs as well, sort of half-white," I continued, sweeping my fingers in a curvilinear manner to direct her gaze. "Now, the lungs, since they're full of air, don't really block the x-ray beam, so they're always black."

This lay translation was not actually true. The lungs are never completely black, just relatively so. There are still many wispy whitish-gray lines that traverse these dark areas in the chest radiographs of all patients: the shadows of blood vessels and walls of bronchial tubes that course through the human organs of respiration. To the average patient, though, the heart looks white and the lungs look black, and most people either find my quick radiology orientation helpful or just politely feign comprehension. I have learned patients seem completely fascinated with any guided tour of their own anatomy as pictured in x-ray, ultrasound, CT, and MRI images. While a bit of an inconvenience to ensure the images are available at a visit, most *homo sapiens* are visual learners, and providing patients a picture of their problem often saves me a thousand additional words of explanation.

Mrs. Clark gazed upon the blackness of her lungs with me. While she appeared interested, I had no idea how much of this she actually understood.

"Wow," she chimed in, as though answering my question, "they really are black!"

"Yes, as I said, the x-ray beam doesn't really..." and then I cut myself off. Her lungs were completely black. The usual pale white shadows were missing in most parts of her lungs. This is the worst emphysema I've ever seen. *What has happened to this woman's lungs? Have they collapsed?* Checking along the lung margins on the x-ray, I quickly confirmed her lungs to be fully expanded.

"Well, actually, Mrs. Clark, you are quite observant. There should be a few more markings in here, your lungs shouldn't be this black."

"Do I have black lung?" she asked, still expressionless, innocently misled by my "black and white" terminology. I explained that "black lung" was a disease we see in coal miners where the actual lungs, and not the x-ray image, turn black. Upon being asked, she reported she had never worked in a coal mine. Despite her expressionless face, I did sense a look of incredulity in her eyes when I asked her the question, as if she wanted to respond, "Do I look like a coal miner to you, doctor?"

Based on her chest x-ray, her problem seemed to be with the loss of much of the oxygen transfer capacity of her lungs.

"Are you certain that you've never smoked?" I asked again. These lungs looked worse than those of the heaviest smoker I had ever encountered.

Aware that I had asked her this question before, she responded in her expressionless manner, "Well, I think that's the sort of thing I'd remember."

David, make a mental note: don't ask her this question ever again.

After we reviewed my findings back in the examination room, I explained that we would need to do some blood and lung function tests to make an accurate diagnosis. Then, we could start treatments to help her with her breathlessness. This encounter took place many years ago; today in my practice, we can instantly and painlessly determine the oxygen level in a patient's blood stream by attaching an oximeter, an oxygen level machine, to their finger. Back then, we needed to obtain an arterial blood sample, much more painful to obtain than a regular venous blood test. Today, I would know immediately that her blood oxygen saturation while resting was eighty-four percent, well below the normal level of ninety percent, and I would have arranged to have oxygen equipment delivered to her home later that day. Instead, she had to wait another two weeks until the final results of her tests arrived. Fourteen more days of breathlessness.

Pneuma is the Greek word for breath. (Actually, πνεῦμα is the Greek word.) Through the past several millennia, it has carried a meaning broader than the simple in and out breathing we each are doing at this very moment. Pneuma is also the Greek word for spirit, and the same word is used for the Holy Spirit in the New Testament. Buddhists, known for their focus on breath as a doorway to deeper states of meditation, experience the quieting of the mind, opening of the body, and deeper concentration as a result. In Chinese philosophy, Ch'i, as in Tai Chi, is the word for the vital energy of life, the breath. Many familiar medical terms are derived from the root word "pneuma," pneumonia, or infection of the lung, being the most common. Pneumothorax, or collapse of the lung due to air (pneumo) in the chest (thorax), would prove to be another critical word, derived from its Greek root, for Alma Clark one day.

Chief Seattle says: "All things share the same breath - the beast, the tree, the man...

the air shares its spirit with all the life it supports." You can sit in a grove of ancient redwoods, or in a desert landscape, or anyplace where you can find something green and alive and observe this connection. As you breathe in, you inspire oxygen, which is transferred to your red blood cells, courses through your heart, and then travels via your arteries to every cell in your body. Oxygen is necessary for human metabolism and life. As you breathe out, you expire carbon dioxide, the byproduct of the same human metabolism, which has been collected by these same red blood cells, coursing back through your veins, and heart, to your lungs. However, as you exhale, everything green you see is "inhaling" that same carbon dioxide, the necessary compound for plant metabolism, called photosynthesis. As the great redwood or piñon tree "exhales" the by-product of its metabolism, oxygen, you are inhaling it and sustaining your life.

Alma returned for her appointed visit with her husband Chuck, and all of her tests results were in my hands. Bothered by the combination of severe emphysema and liver enlargement, I had ordered a single diagnostic test for the one disease that might explain both findings at the same time.

So, in addition to finding the very low level of oxygen in her blood and destruction of three-fourths of her lung tissue, her tests also confirmed the presence of a severe form of alpha-1 antitrypsin deficiency, a very rare hereditary disorder causing protein deposition in the liver and emphysema in the lungs. The changes in her lungs were profound, with large cavities in each.

"Before we go through your results, Mrs. Clark, I'd like you to try something for me," I began. I fitted the plastic tubing from the oxygen tank I had ordered for her around her ears, and I placed the two small cannulae, or prongs, into her nostrils. "Now, let's see how this feels." I turned on the oxygen at a flow rate of two liters per minute.

The effect was almost immediate. Her lips turned from pale blue to a light shade of pink. Her eyes brightened. She took a long, deep breath and then let out a slow sigh. I was watching a miracle take place.

After about one minute, she spoke her first uninterrupted sentence in the office. "Doctor, for the first time in twenty years, I don't feel like I'm fighting for air." Her husband Chuck was beaming.

"She looked like this when she was sixteen," he crowed, and he gave her a big hug and a kiss on the cheek. In the radiance of her husband's exuberance, I almost missed the slightest upturn of the corners of Alma's ordinarily expressionless mouth: her version of happy.

We talked through the details of her disease, based on my own review of the limited information available in textbooks and journal articles. She had a severe and advanced form of alpha-1-antitryosin deficiency, and a very poor prognosis, but with careful attention to daily care for her lungs, she could live a good while. I have found "a good while" to be a helpful expression. It has no specificity in terms of time and allows the patient, hearing a grave diagnosis for the first time, some breathing room to think things through before asking their caregiver the question of ultimate courage: "How long do I have to live?"

She'll ask when she is ready. No need to push it today.

I wanted the best for Mrs. Clark, despite her fatal disease. We arranged for home oxygen and scheduled her to see a pulmonary specialist to provide her expert care in addition to her regular visits with me. I knew I would not likely see another case of this rare disorder in the next twenty years, and I wanted her to also see someone who had greater experience. Dr. Westerman had seen a total of sixteen cases, by his own rough estimate.

Alma fared surprisingly well. "I have to. I have two teenage kids, and my husband wouldn't know where to start," she said one year later, summarizing her family system in a single sentence.

We treated her increasingly frequent episodes of bronchitis aggressively, and two years later, she was still using an oxygen flow rate of two liters per minute. These were the pioneer days of portable oxygen, and in order for her to go grocery shopping, she had to drag a rather heavy tank around the supermarket on two wheels.

"Lugging this oxygen tank around uses up more oxygen than I get through the tubes," she quipped one day. Absent a twinkle in her eye or a sly smile, I learned to identify her humor solely by the slight inflection of her voice.

Nonetheless, with her new mobility her portable oxygen provided, Alma had a plan for her life and, as it would turn out, for her death as well.

CHAPTER 16

"For death begins with life's first breath,
And life begins at touch of death."

John Oxenham (William Arthur Dunkerley) (1852 - 1941),
English journalist, novelist, and poet

When I graduated from my residency program, many of my patients from the resident clinic decided they wanted to follow me into my new private practice. Chuck and Alma Clark were two of them. The night before her first visit to my private practice office, I had a memorable dream. Alma and her husband had arrived at the desk in my office; she was completely expressionless, he had his bright, engaging smile, as usual. Dr. Frank, one of my esteemed but slightly eccentric neurology teachers, was walking quickly through our office, an event that would never actually happen in real life, as his office was miles away.

In the dream, I could audibly hear his thoughts. *"That woman has the worst Parkinson's disease I have ever seen,"* he thought. I looked back at Alma.

"Of course she does!" I exclaimed, waking myself up in a cold sweat. Patients with Parkinson's disease have what we call "masked facies," according to our medical compulsion to describe much of what we see and do in Latin, a dead language, rather than using terms patients can readily understand. In this case, it would be "no facial expressions." I have heard medical conspiracy theories that suggest our use of Latin is indeed a subterfuge foisted upon the unsuspecting public to "keep them in the dark" about their health, but I do not believe this to be true. Instead, I suspect that medicine, like many fields, values tradition highly and is too busy to do the work of completely overhauling our method of communication, much like the United States' failed effort to convert to the metric system many years ago.

For the next four hours of the morning, I was distracted by the thought I had missed this important diagnosis. Dr. Frank was rarely wrong when it came to neurologic matters during waking hours, although I had no idea how accurate he was in dreams. I couldn't wait for Mrs. Clark to arrive. When she did, I immediately escorted her and her husband into the exam room myself, rather than waiting for the nurse, and performed several physical examination tests to see if she did indeed have Parkinson's disease. These tests suggested that she did not. Tests of her seventh cranial nerve, which stimulates facial muscle contraction, showed that she had the ability to move her face when so directed in all three branches of each of the two nerves. Apparently, my dream induced uncertainty was strong enough to keep me in pursuit.

"Mrs. Clark, I've noticed that you rarely move the muscles of your face. How long has this been going on?" I realized immediately as the words left my lips that they were devoid of all tact and politeness.

She turned and looked at her husband with a blank stare, as if to say, "Do you want to take this one, dear?"

Taking her cue, he replied cautiously, "Well, Doctor, facial expressions don't exactly run in Alma's family." Chuck provided me with a big smile, sufficient to overcompensate for her absent expression, even when averaging the two together. Seeing my persistent questioning look, he added, "She's always been this way." She nodded, providing me with a modicum of relief that I was not the first to identify this finding.

At her next visit, about four weeks later, her husband brought in a wedding picture from sixteen years prior. There was Alma, expressionless, looking like most of my own driver's license pictures through the years, no matter how hard I try to smile. She appeared to be about ten pounds heavier back then. Mr. Clark told me she looked "pretty happy" in that picture. I nodded, feigning understanding.

We all knew Alma would begin to deteriorate rapidly at some point in the future. For the next two years, she had a slow deterioration in her pulmonary function tests and required correspondingly higher oxygen flow rates. One January, about four years after her diagnosis was established, she had to temporarily turn her oxygen up to five liters per minute, the highest sustainable rate with home oxygen equipment. When she came to see me at the office, she had a short bout of bronchitis, which responded nicely to treatment. After feeling better for two or three days, she developed a fever of 102 degrees Fahrenheit, muscle aches, and gastrointestinal symptoms. She had influenza.

Twenty-four hours after the first muscle ache, she was in our hospital's medical intensive care unit on a breathing machine. Once her influenza had run its course, she remained attached to the ventilator, with little hope of getting off it. Her lungs simply weren't strong enough anymore to keep her alive without the machine, which Dr. Westerman and I explained to her two children, ages thirteen and sixteen. The kids, speechless, were doubly terrified. Five days earlier, their father had suffered a heart attack while visiting their mother. He was in the surgical intensive care unit, recovering from four-vessel bypass surgery. I simply could not imagine how difficult it had to be for them at this moment, with their mother and dad barely clinging to their lives.

As often happens when doctors provide the family with a dark and gloomy prognosis, Mrs. Clark immediately improved. In fact, the next morning, her blood tests and respiratory parameters suggested she was ready to be taken off the ventilator. She did well off the machine, was walking in the hallway the next morning, and asked to go home the following day. Her husband had made a similar rapid recovery, and Chuck and Alma were both discharged the same day, back to their trailer, in what amounted to a home health care tour de force of hospital beds, oxygen, and other medical equipment.

About twelve months later, her condition had worsened to the point of being short of breath on the five liters per minute flow rate continuously. She had stopped all of her housework and only left her home for her visits with me. At a family conference, Alma, Chuck, their two children, Maija and Adrian, and I openly discussed her wishes for her end-of-life care. Given her level of lung damage, we all understood that if she ever went back on a ventilator, or breathing machine, she would not get off again.

"I could never... live that way," she insisted, breathing rapidly even on the oxygen and pausing to inhale in mid-sentence. "I hated that... machine! Just let me... go if it comes... to that."

The children, missing school to be part of this meeting and at the time only fourteen and seventeen years old, looked on in complete disbelief from their adolescent perspective. Chuck also struggled to grasp the idea that his wife might die soon. Having a sixth-grade education, he worked in a minimum-wage job at local auto factory. However, Alma was quite clear about what she wanted, and the family followed her lead. She signed the documents clarifying her wishes, and despite her blank stare, I had come to know her well enough that I knew she was sad.

I only had one final opportunity to talk with her, about one month later. For the only time since her very first visit to my private office, I found her in the exam room alone, without a family member.

"Rather than worrying... about my health... today," she informed me, again breaking her speech into two-second intervals in order to breathe, "we need to talk... about my husband. I'm very concerned... about him."

Interesting, I mused silently. *She is so close to dying. Chuck is doing better than ever.*

"He won't have the... slightest idea how... to manage the children... when I'm gone," she continued. "Since he was thirteen... years old, Adrian has been... at war with... his dad. He won't listen... to a word... Chuck says. Maija and her... father rarely speak... to each other. I tell them... their Dad... loves them... but they just... don't understand... that all of his... hard work... all the double shifts... all the weekend time... at the plant... earning a living... for our family... is just his way... of loving them. I've told them... if it wasn't for... my illness... we could live... on what... he would make... working forty hours... a week."

Both of our eyes were tearing as she took some extra breaths to steady herself. "The children talk to me... tell me everything. What will they do... when I'm gone?" Now sobbing quietly, her shoulders began to heave. I held her hand.

How strange and wonderful, I thought, as I handed her a facial tissue with my other hand. Alma, the "expressionless one," has the deep bond with her children, and Chuck, with his emotions on his sleeve, seems so far from them. I understood the natural advantage she had as their mother, but there was a more profound truth here.

"I'm sorry... Doctor Roberts. I didn't mean... to be just... sobbing here."

"I just feel privileged that you feel comfortable being so very honest with me, Mrs. Clark," I replied truthfully. "There's no need to apologize. You can say anything you like."

"Chuck will listen... to you... Dr. Roberts. He'll need your help. Please do... what... you can... for him."

It was obvious she was saying goodbye to me. I suspected she was going through a similar process with everyone else in her life, sitting down with each one, planting key words in their memory banks, giving them final instructions on how to live without her. I wanted to reassure her, to tell her that I was certain her time to die had not yet arrived. I held my tongue; I would not have been truthful. She had convinced me the end of her life was quite near.

"Thank you for... all that you've done... for me. I've... been lucky... to have you... for my doctor."

"And thank you, Mrs. Clark, for being such a wonderful patient."

To this day I can't be quite sure, but I do believe she may have smiled ever so slightly, then took a few moments to compose herself and rose to leave. I took her oxygen tank and wheeled it behind her to the front desk.

Only four days later, her husband called, frantic, saying Alma was gasping for breath.

"She's the worst she's ever been," Chuck cried, which was saying a lot, since she had been desperately ill on more than one occasion.

"What should I do?" he gasped into the phone. "It looks like she's dying. She can't talk, she's breathing so hard."

Despite our discussion in the office, he was not prepared to have her die at home. I called 911 for them, and the ambulance rushed Alma to the emergency room. I met her there and saw this gaunt, sixty-seven-pound, five-foot tall, forty-five-year-old woman, whose skin was a pale shade of blue from head to toes, with dark blue lips and fingertips, despite the mask that had been delivering 100 percent oxygen to her during the ten-minute race from her home. Every ounce of her energy was now focused on the impossibly deep contractions of her diaphragm and rib muscles, needed to bring air into her lungs, or so I thought.

As I had been taught in medical school, I breathed along with her respirations, which were occurring at about one per second now. My hands quickly became numb. I slowed my breathing and took out my stethoscope. As usual, I could hear no breath sounds in her left lung. Listening now to her heart, I could hear it beating about 180 times per minute, about twice her normal rate. Last, checking the right lung, I also heard no breath sounds, her usual finding. Something was horribly wrong here, and I could think of only one explanation.

I stepped out of the room as the portable x-ray machine arrived. Mrs. Clark's blood pressure was dropping. Following the x-ray technician back down the hall to her lab, I stood by the developing machine as the film came out. At first glance, it looked no different. Looking more closely at the view box, though, I could see the problem.

Patients with alpha-1 antitrypsin deficiency are at much higher risk for pneumothorax, the spontaneous collapse of a lung from the extensive destruction of pulmonary tissue by the disease. Pneumothorax literally translates to "air in the chest," the place where the average lay person would think air should go when we inhale. However, when the air passes through the lung and fills the chest cavity instead, it may accelerate the collapse of the lung itself, and very little oxygen will enter the bloodstream through respiration on that side. Both of Alma's lungs now appeared to be collapsed. I ran back to Mrs. Clark's room.

"Probable bilateral pneumothorax!" I shouted, indicating that I believed that both of her lungs had collapsed.

The emergency room physician had already inserted the endotracheal tube down her throat, through her vocal cords, and into her trachea, inflating the small cuff to hold it in place. Hearing my pronouncement, the ER doctor quickly inserted tubes through the walls of both sides of her chest in the hope of expanding her lungs, the only possible way to save her life.

Unfortunately, the holes in both lungs that had caused their collapse were too big; her lungs did not re-expand. When this failed, efforts commenced to connect Alma to a breathing machine, now her one remaining hope for life. Compelled by her expressed wishes, I had to stop the effort. I explained she was a "no code" and that she had specifically requested, in writing, that she not be intubated. The team quickly disassembled, and the nurse turned off the cardiac monitor. There was a brief but reverent stillness in the room, which had been so chaotic only a minute before, as Mrs. Clark breathed her last, only a few seconds later. Her face, in death as in life, was expressionless.

Walking slowly out to the family waiting area, I could only imagine the impact Alma's death would have on the family. Chuck also had told me on more than one occasion he had no parenting instincts. "I don't know how I'd manage the kids without Alma," he had confessed only weeks ago at his own office visit. The concept of taking over his wife's role at the climax of his children's turbulent teenage years completely terrified him. He was a simple, honest man. I really liked him, and I considered it an honor that the whole family seemed to trust me so deeply.

I walked Chuck and his two children into a small conference room opening directly off of the emergency department waiting room, intended primarily for the purpose I was about to use it. As they sat down, I quietly closed the door and sat across from them.

"Both of her lungs collapsed," I began. "We tried to re-expand them, but as you know, her lungs were too damaged and too weak. I'm so sorry. She's gone." They each stared at me, full of the same disbelief that had characterized our conversation in the office five weeks earlier. We all just sat there together, tears in our eyes, for quite some time, in complete silence.

Finally, Chuck spoke up, in his simple and ever-practical way. "Well, what do we need to do now?"

I explained to him about funeral arrangements and asked them all to come back to see me in the office sometime in the next week. As I was about to leave, Chuck grabbed me in a tight bear hug that stopped my own breathing for a moment. His children followed his lead.

"Thank you for all you've done for Alma. She wouldn't have lived this long if it wasn't for you, Dr. Roberts," he choked.

Personally, one of the most difficult aspects of being a physician is reconciling the deep expressions of gratitude families so often provide at the moment of their loved one's death, the same moment where I always feel a deep sense of failure. The family is thankful, but I am thinking, *Could I have done something different? Is there some way this could have been anticipated? Prevented? Should I have seen her back in the office sooner?*

At the time of a patient's sudden or unexpected death, a physician can generate twenty such questions in less than a minute, and they can drown out the quiet and tender appreciation the family needs to express. Through the years, I have found the best approach is to simply quiet my internal critic, with all of his questions, and open myself fully to the sincere thankfulness families so generously give to me when I most need it.

Yet it remains a struggle for me to do so. I believe we humans are generally provided what we need, at the time when we truly need it, if we can just recognize the gift right there in front of us. For me, the only effective approach is to recognize this gift of kindness, hold out my hands, and take what is freely given to me.

CHAPTER 17

*"In forming a judgment, lay your hearts void of foretoken opinions;
else, whatsoever is done or said will be measured by a wrong rule;
like them who have the jaundice, to whom everything appears yellow."*

Sir Phillip Sidney (1554-1586), English statesman

Entering our practice office after making rounds at the hospital, with about forty-five seconds to spare before seeing my first patient, I said hello to Jean Marie, a new employee on her very first day at work. She was a young and enthusiastic recent high school graduate with bright green eyes, wavy shoulder-length brown hair, and an eager and cheerful disposition. She joined Cynthia, our registered nurse, and Kathleen, our receptionist, in ensuring our rapidly growing practice of patients were receiving the excellent care and service they deserved. Out in the hallway, I saw Mark handing Jean Marie a plastic eight-ounce cup half-filled with a yellow liquid. Mark had an unusually serious expression on his face as he "oriented" Jean Marie to the office process of analyzing a patient's urine.

"Write Mr. Carson's name on this paper towel and then put it on top of Cynthia's desk, and then set this on top of it," he said, handing her the glass. "Cynthia will then perform a dipstick analysis and set up the microscope if we need to look at it further." She looked quite tentative and squeamish while first touching the cup, and she had the "they didn't tell me about this in the job interview" expression on her face so common among new health care employees on their first day of work. Nonetheless, she dutifully followed Mark's instructions, and as she was finishing, Cynthia emerged from one of the patient examination rooms and handed me the chart for my first patient.

"He's yellow," she quickly told me, clearly distracted. Smiling at Mark, she went over to her desk, sat down, and just before our new employee walked away, picked up the plastic cup and drank half of the contents before Jean Marie could scream, "No! No! That's urine!"

I could hear the uproarious laughter as I closed the examination room door behind me and greeted my new patient, Professor Yarrow. He was a small and very thin thirty-four-year-old man whose most obvious characteristic was the yellow tinge to his skin.

Jaundice. Possible biliary obstruction. Gallstones. Cholangitis. Cirrhosis. Acute hepatitis. Hemolytic anemia. Now in private practice for over a year, with my Internal Medicine Board examinations behind me, my mind automatically began to rattle off the "differential diagnosis" list of possibilities, often before I even said my first words to the patient.

"Well, I'm in my mid-thirties now, and I thought it would be best to become established with a physician. I want to be sure I'm doing everything I can to be healthy and stay in nutritional balance."

This is interesting, I thought. *He's not raising the issue of his yellow skin.* After several additional questions, it became clear he had no symptoms such as pain, fever, or history of travel to a foreign country, which might help me "rule in" some of the possibilities in my differential diagnosis list. In fact, he seemed annoyed at any implication whatsoever he might be "sick."

This isn't working. You need to try a different approach, David. I decided to stick to the usual routine of performing a complete medical history and physical, figuring I would have the opportunity to ask him everything I needed to at some point in time without any further suggestion he might be ill. He was an associate professor of history at a local university, and he answered every question quite succinctly. However, I knew something was wrong here. I could just feel it in my bones. The patient maintained a somewhat cool and distant demeanor for the remainder of the visit, which made my attempts at diagnosing the etiology of his yellow skin exceedingly difficult.

He had a completely unremarkable medical history and had almost no contact with the medical profession. We breezed through all of my queries about past surgeries and illnesses. His "review of systems," which consists of about one hundred questions regarding symptoms that might indicate a more serious illness, was completely negative. For example, the gastrointestinal review of symptoms disclosed he had no nausea, vomiting, diarrhea, constipation, swallowing difficulty, history of stomach problems, heartburn, ulcers, liver or pancreas disorders, vomiting blood, passing blood per rectum, or jaundice. Sitting before a bright yellow man who purported to have had "no history of jaundice" piqued my curiosity even further. "Jaundice, you know, is an accumulation of bilirubin in the skin. It turns the skin yellow." As I said this, I looked at him straight in the eye.

"Yes, I know that," he said as he flashed an annoyed smile. It then dawned on me that every square inch of him looked yellow except for where I was now looking: the sclera, the whites of his eyes, were indeed white. *Normal.* However, when bilirubin, produced by the liver, accumulates in the skin, as it can in all of the diseases on my differential diagnosis list, it always turns the sclera yellow.

Because of the encyclopedic level of knowledge required to be a physician, most of us can categorize our information database as follows: things I know, things I used to know but have forgotten, things I have never known, and then a final category where I know something sounds familiar but I don't have the details handy in my conscious level of memory. When my need for additional knowledge was immediate, my usual recourse was to leave the exam room, find Mark, and ask him. If Mark or, as our practice grew, all of my other colleagues were busy, I would pull out an appropriate medical textbook and begin hunting. This was my practice in the pre-Internet days, and it could take a very long time to find an answer to an obscure question in an 1,800 page textbook.

So, having finished taking the professor's complete medical history, I excused myself to allow him to undress for the physical examination. In the hallway, I saw Jean Marie, who glared at me as though I were a co-conspirator in some very recent crime. Mark and Cynthia were in rooms with other patients. I pulled out my huge internal medicine textbook at my desk.

I did know there were various medical diseases that did turn the sclera different colors, including red, yellow, green, and blue. I also recalled there was some nutritional factor that could turn every inch of a patient's skin bright yellow but leave their sclera and the mucous membranes inside of the mouth unstained. I remembered hearing about it on my pediatric rotation as a third year medical student, which was now six years in the past. *Good luck finding this one, David,* I moaned to myself. My first discovery was that there was no entry in this huge tome's index for "yellow."

However, it was a good day, and I was able to find the reference to "carotenemia" in my textbook in less than a minute. As often happens when our door to a particular memory cracks open just a little bit, it all started coming back to me, and I recalled excess consumption of carrots by children could cause their skin to turn yellow. This could be mistaken for jaundice and a serious liver problem, or other medical disorder, and cause the patient to undergo a very expensive, sometimes dangerous but unnecessary medical workup. In fact, the yellow skin is just due to excess deposits of carotene, a chemical precursor to vitamin A, in the diet. The textbook reminded me that many vegetables contained high amounts of carotene, and this was not always just a problem due to carrots.

I re-entered the room and began the physical examination on the professor. Close and careful scrutiny revealed his skin was perfectly yellow, but his sclera and the inside of his mouth were not. The rest of the examination was normal, except he was five feet, five inches tall and weighed 108 pounds, seriously underweight. There was nothing in his physical examination implicating serious liver disease.

Usually, at the end of a complete history and physical, I go over all of my findings with the patient and make plans for any further needed testing.

"Well, Professor Yarrow," I began, "almost everything looks good on your exam. I really have only two concerns. The first is your yellow skin, and the second is you seem to be quite underweight." He stiffened and folded his arms. It was obvious I had offended him halfway through my last sentence, but I pressed on. "I'd like to talk to you about your diet for a few minutes," I said. I glanced at my watch to confirm my next patient appointment was in just less than five minutes. "How would you describe your diet?"

"Well," he began slowly, as though he was weighing every word carefully, "I like… to focus on…foods with a high… fiber to calorie ratio." He then glared back at me as if to say, "Well, see if you can figure *that* out!"

"Foods with a high fiber to calorie ratio?" I echoed. I had never heard of this particular mathematical relationship, but I could begin to imagine substances high in fiber and low in calories. Cardboard came to mind. "What type of foods meeting this criteria do you prefer?"

"Foods with a high… fiber to calorie ratio," he replied, taking even longer this time to articulate the phrase.

At this point, I was aware we were becoming locked into some sort of duel. As much as I love to stay on schedule, I made an internal decision: the professor was not leaving my office until I determined what, exactly, he was eating. Part of me was simply curious; the larger part of me was stubborn.

"Well," I countered, "there are many foods with a high fiber to calorie ratio." I wondered if my attempts to sound authoritative about a concept completely unknown to me were convincing. "Of course, whole grains, fruits, vegetables, nuts and beans are all high in fiber," I suggested. He rolled his eyes.

"I'm more concerned about… the *ratio*… than the fiber content alone," he responded, derisively. He was clearly being condescending now. While there may be some readers who don't mind a condescending or deprecating remark, in those days of my life, I always felt the need to retaliate. *David, you definitely are going to get to the bottom of this.*

The conversation took another thirty minutes. As mentioned, I have a strong preference for staying on time. To be perfectly honest, I am obsessed with timeliness, so clearly the professor had touched some sort of nerve in me that caused me to press on. Gradually, step by step, I was able to determine after an additional ten minutes that his dietary focus was vegetables, and among this broader category, he felt lettuce had the best "fiber to calorie ratio."

That's true, I thought. As his "mystery diet" was slowly being revealed, Cynthia, per our office protocol, recognized I was running fifteen minutes behind schedule, and she had first knocked and then later came in to the exam room to remind me my next patient was waiting. I thanked her for the update and, ignoring her message, continued to ask yes or no questions, which seemed to be the only ones the Professor would answer. After another ten minutes, we had made further progress. I now understood that my yellow professor's diet consisted primarily, if not exclusively, of iceberg lettuce. *Now we're getting somewhere!*

While nutritionists never talk about "fiber to calorie ratios," iceberg lettuce is somewhat a joke in dietary circles and considered one of the most nutritionally devoid foods on our planet. I recalled one of my quickly and poorly selected on-call dinners in the hospital cafeteria as a resident, when a dietician friend and co-worker had looked at my plate, rolled her eyes, and said, "Well, that tray contains all the nutritional value of a head of iceberg lettuce!"

"So, how many heads of iceberg lettuce would you say you eat in your average day?" I gently asked the professor.

"How many heads of iceberg lettuce... do you *think* I could eat in a day?" he countered.

This is ridiculous. I'm now twenty-five minutes behind schedule and playing Twenty Questions with a history professor about his diet. He was clearly in control here, but I was stubborn, and I was not leaving the room until I knew the answer.

As calmly as possible, I replied, "Oh, I don't know. I suppose if you really liked iceberg lettuce you could maybe eat one or two heads per day."

"More than that."

More than two heads of lettuce per day!??! Are you kidding me? This is unbelievable, I was thinking, while on the outside I remained calm and acted nonplussed. I couldn't coax him to just come out and tell me directly how much lettuce he actually did eat.

After another five minutes, I had finally pieced together his story. The yellow professor bought his iceberg lettuce by the crate, twenty-four heads per crate, two crates per week. He picked it up at the loading dock of a nearby grocery store every Monday afternoon, right after it was delivered to them. He ate almost nothing during the day, and then at 11:00 p.m. each evening, he would sit down and, over a period of about two and one half hours, eat seven heads of iceberg lettuce while reading history texts. Being particular about mathematics, I pointed out on the last night of each week he would have only six heads of lettuce left, and he smiled and replied this was true. On Sunday evenings he would only eat six heads, and then, for dessert that night, he would have a "bunch or two" of carrots.

I told him I was quite concerned about the lack of nutritional content in his diet, and he responded he was not. We did reach a compromise where he agreed to obtain some blood work and return to see me in another two weeks. In additional to obtaining the beta carotene levels, which I knew would be quite high, I checked other more common nutritional parameters on the lab order sheet, handed it to him, and we said goodbye.

As he was checking out of the office at the front desk, I noticed Jean Marie was in much better humor and was now chuckling with Mark and Cynthia. In fact, they were all laughing deeply and holding their sides.

"Mountain Dew," Cynthia explained to Jean Marie, "is one of Mark's favorite beverages. We wanted to make you feel welcome on your first day and thought it would be funny to fill a cup with the soft drink and tell you it was urine. Once you set it down, the plan was for me to drink it before you could stop me."

By now, Jean Marie, who turned out to have an excellent sense of humor over the ensuing years, was laughing as hard as I was, along with the others.

"I'm just not sure it's the best joke to play on someone on their very first day of work in a medical office," she said in a completely unsuccessful attempt to make at least one of us feel guilty.

There is a certain gravity in the physician role that can oppress even the most optimistic soul over time. Dealing with life and death, literally, providing emotional support for others when one's own internal resources are depleted, working long hours, and enduring consecutive nights with little sleep can all take their toll. There was something about the way Mark and I were able to combine the pathos of our day-to-day practice with a daily dose of humor that sustained us through the most trying of times. While sometimes cynical in nature, or perhaps "ironic" might better capture the tone of our banter, we intuitively knew our survival depended on creating a workable balance between the grave and the humorous aspects of medicine.

We had learned within a month of our first meeting that we shared a common hero in this regard: Eddie Haskell, the sixteen-year-old character on the now ancient "Leave It to Beaver" television show. His trademark scene was his ceremonious entry into the Cleaver household, where he would effusively greet Ward and June, the sit-com parents, with politeness so extreme it was nauseating. "Good afternoon, Mr. Cleaver. Hello, Mrs. Cleaver. My, what a beautiful dress you're wearing today! I was hoping to pay a visit to Wallace and Theodore, if they are available and if this is a convenient time." Then, he would bound up the stairs and burst into the boys bedroom, without knocking, saying, "Hey, Wally, how's it going?" Then to Theodore ("The Beaver"), he would say, "Beat it, chump, I need to talk to your brother. Alone! Now! Scram!"

I'm not exactly sure how we made the connection between life, death, and Eddie Haskell, but there was a form of "on-stage" seriousness we always tried our best to adopt for our patients and an "off-stage" mischievousness we appropriated for ourselves, which kept us sane during the arduous early years of private practice.

Laughing about the practical joke in the hallway, I realized I was now thirty minutes behind, which meant every subsequent patient would find me about a half an hour late that day. I apologized to each of them for the delay and simply stated that I had encountered an unusual problem that took longer than I had anticipated to resolve. I knew I had been stubborn; I also felt quite strongly I knew what was best for the professor and his diet. Discovering the reason for his yellow skin was worth being late. He may not have known it then, but eventually he would understand.

CHAPTER 18

*"The people who live in a golden age usually go around
complaining how yellow everything looks."*

Randall Jarrell (1914-1965), American poet

The yellow Professor Yarrow returned to the office for an appointment
two weeks later, as scheduled. His beta carotene levels were the highest
the lab had ever seen, so high, in fact, the pathologist called me to find out
more about this patient. In addition, the professor had a low vitamin B12
level, which could eventually cause neurologic problems, and low protein
levels in his blood, which over time could result in suppression of his
immune system and make him susceptible to serious infections. Yet he was
completely resistant to any modification in his diet, and despite repeated
attempts on my part over the next several months to convince him of the
need to make at least some minor changes in his diet, I made no progress
other than to persuade him to begin taking a multiple vitamin tablet daily.

I tried everything. I found the data on the nutritional value of iceberg
lettuce. One cup contains: 8 calories, 0.5 gram protein, 0.7 gram fiber, 10
mg calcium, 78 mg potassium, 1.5 mg vitamin C, 16 mcg folate, 13.3 mcg
of vitamin K, and 164 mcg of beta carotene. Given there are about five
cups of lettuce in one head, he was consuming 240 servings every seven
days, and 39,360 micrograms of beta carotene per week. Clearly, this was
far more than was needed and was the cause of his yellow skin.

He argued that my data proved his point. He was getting protein. He was getting vitamin C. He challenged me to find a food with a higher fiber to calorie ratio. I did. I found a food with a fiber to calorie ratio that is fifty percent higher. It was romaine lettuce.

"I don't like romaine," he replied dismissively. He would not have been much better off eating forty-eight heads of romaine anyway, nutritionally speaking.

Eventually, he also revealed he really liked the color of his skin and had no interest in doing anything to change it. On each of a half-dozen attempts on my part during the visit, he adamantly refused my suggestion to see a nutritionist.

In retrospect, I believe this struggle basically boiled down to the fact that I thought there was something unhealthy and "sick" about his eating the way he did, and he thought I was overstepping my bounds, even as a physician, in pushing him to change. At this visit, we came to the acute realization of our irreconcilable differences. Sometimes, the best intervention to unlock a stalled negotiation is to bring in a third party. To my surprise, he willingly agreed to see a psychiatrist for another opinion on the matter.

I wrote out the referral slip and internally claimed victory on the spot. Surely, a psychiatrist would see the self-destructiveness of eating forty-eight heads of lettuce per week, *iceberg* lettuce for that matter! At the time, my need to be "right" about this was an all-consuming fire, the smoke from which had undoubtedly clouded my vision.

I knew the date of his appointment with the psychiatrist and I figured it might take five to seven days before I would see the referral letter on my desk. Each day I would skim through the tall stack of incoming lab results, x-ray reports, and consultant letters, looking for the psychiatrist's opinion. About ten days after the appointment, the verdict arrived. While in his note the psychiatrist observed the man "appeared unusually yellow," was somewhat malnourished, and was evasive in answering his questions, his final conclusion was that Dr. Yarrow was, in fact, quite sane and "just happens to like eating lettuce a lot more than anyone else I've ever met."

Not surprisingly, the professor didn't come back to my office to see me again.

Two years later, I received a short but friendly note from my yellow patient, saying he had obtained a full professorship in history at an east coast university and that he was feeling well.

"I am still on the same diet ☺," he wrote. (I found his inclusion of the smiley face to be a particularly annoying form of punctuation. *He's mocking me*, I brooded, with mild paranoia, the old conflict re-emerging after lying dormant for two years.) His letter went on to ask if I would please send his medical records to his new physician at the address he had provided.

I was brooding with some sense of righteous, although likely misplaced, indignation that he continued to do well. Much later, after so many wrong turns, I would come to see more clearly the supreme challenge, in my own life, of simply determining what is best for me. Older, and perhaps more introspective at that point, the absurdity of having even mild opinions about what was best for others became clear, given my own struggle to understand what was best for me. It is easy for physicians to believe we are imbued with "superior knowledge," and it can be tempting to impose upon people our opinions about what might be better for their bodies. There are numerous jokes involving God, physicians, and the lack of role clarity between the two that speak to patient perceptions regarding this issue.

What motivated this man to eat forty-eight heads of lettuce per week? I pondered again. *Why does he like having yellow skin? The whole thing is just too weird!* Just thinking about our past encounters made me just as agitated as I had been at his last visit, two years prior.

Of course, it wasn't the forty-eight heads of iceberg lettuce that was the problem, though; it was just my reaction to it. Anyone who knows me well can testify to the fact that I have my own pronounced eccentricities. Some of them might seem more arresting than my professor's diet. I am thinking of the incredulity I have faced over the years when informing people of my lifelong adult habit of awakening at 4:00 a.m., or earlier, and spending an hour in reflection, prayer, reading, and meditation, followed by my drive to the gym in total darkness to exercise before work. I would guess, by their "Are you crazy?" reactions to my habit, that about half would choose the lettuce diet if forced at gunpoint to make one of these two lifestyle modifications. Each of us chooses our own unique path through this world. Dr. Yarrow's just happened to be paved with iceberg lettuce.

In my practice now, I place more complete precedence on the patient's own preferences, what they desire to change and are able to change, understanding they may sometimes choose to ignore certain pieces of medical evidence. Until a patient herself actually wants to make a change, no force of my will alone can produce even a brief lifestyle alteration.

I scribbled a quick note to the staff to copy and mail the chart and hurried out of our office to go back to see a very sick patient at the hospital. On my way out, I saw Jean Marie "orienting" a new medical assistant who was working her first day in our office. Jean Marie held a plastic cup about half full of a yellow (and probably highly caffeinated) substance, and she was providing deadpan instructions to her new coworker as to how to handle urine specimens. A nearby examination room door was cracked open approximately one inch; Cynthia's left eye was peering through it. She was waiting for her cue.

CHAPTER 19

"Judge others by their questions rather than by their answers."

Voltaire (1694 - 1778), French writer and philosopher

It was seven o'clock at night on a cold and sleeting Midwestern winter Friday evening, and I was wandering the stacks, alone, in our hospital medical library. Before the days of broader access to the Internet, doctors relied on the large volumes of the "Index Medicus" to find journal articles relevant to the medical question at hand. My own quest this evening was a greater understanding of the cardiac complications of influenza.

Nancy Martin, my thirty-nine-year-old patient, mother of four children ages two to twelve, lay dying in our medical intensive care unit (MICU), and amongst the ten physicians struggling to save her, we were devoid of further ideas on how to help this woman. Up to this point, we had not yet even made a definitive diagnosis beyond knowing she had influenza, or "the flu." I had just walked down to this quiet and peaceful library from that noisy intensive care unit, which was now full after the admission of two new critically ill patients. I had never seen the unit so hectic, nor the library so quiet.

I finally located a review article on "The Cardiac Complications of Influenza" from *The New England Journal of Medicine*. The review had been written twenty-five years earlier, after antibiotics were discovered, but, to a young internist like myself, seemingly from the prehistoric ages of medicine. Well, that may be a bit of an overstatement. Let's just say I assigned the article to the just-post-leeches era. It was the only review available, according to the enormous index, and time was running very short.

Mrs. Martin had come to the office only three days ago as a new patient. Her answer to, "Why are you here today?" had been scrawled in almost illegible handwriting on the questionnaire: "horrible case of flu." The medical history form we asked our patients to fill out was four pages long; Mrs. Martin had answered only the one question. It was a cold and grey February in our Midwestern town, and I had seen dozens of patients over the past two weeks who had a horrible case of the flu. This had been a very bad year for influenza, and according to our Department of Health, the worst was yet to come; some of our elderly patients had become so dehydrated they needed hospitalization.

How horrible can a bad case of the flu be in a thirty-nine year old? I pondered as I flipped open the chart and walked into the room.

I cannot recall which of the two terrifying signs I noticed first: her vital signs or her appearance. In any case, they combined instantly to completely reverse my initial judgment on entering the room. Our nurse had written, "BP 80/p, HR 120, RR 24, T=103.6," which meant her blood pressure was so low it could barely be obtained (normal would have been more like 120/80), her heart was racing (normally sixty to ninety beats per minute), she was breathing much too rapidly (normally less than 16 per minute), and she had a high fever. However, it was the look on her pale and graying face, shouting silently, "I am dying," which fully captured my attention.

The ability to immediately discern the difference between a "severely ill" and "just a bit sick" patient is the single most important skill of a successful physician. I could feel my heart begin to race, and my own blood pressure go up, before I even had time to close the door. I didn't bother to do so. Spinning on my heels, I went into the hall to summon Cynthia to bring in the equipment so we could immediately start IV fluids on this desperately ill woman. My nurse was, as usual, one step ahead of me, and I ran into her as I rushed out the door, knocking the IV bag out of her hand.

"Jean Marie," I shouted down the hall, "call 911!" Then I rushed back into the room. "Mrs. Martin, are you allergic to any medications?" I began. She was now lying flat on the exam table, and Cynthia was preparing her skin and vein to accept the large-bore IV needle. She pursed her lips, attempting to make what looked like a "p" sound, answer my question, but she could not form words, so she shook her head up and down to signify "Yes."

"Penicillin?" I quickly asked.

She nodded again, this time more feebly. "Yes."

I remembered being taught the "one question rule" by Dr. Santini on an emergency medicine rotation during my internship. Our emergency room attending asked us, "If you knew you could ask your critically ill patient only one question before he or she lost consciousness, what would it be?" Clueless, we looked at each other, provided sufficient body language cues to indicate we had no idea, and strenuously avoided eye contact with our teacher.

A patient man, and an excellent teacher, he allowed the silence to weigh on us, and then said, "Okay, let's just go around in a circle, and everyone can share what your question would be." Now it was just a matter of which intern or student he picked to answer first. I was sitting to his immediate right.

"Sally, you start," he said, choosing the student to his left.

Great. This will give you a bit more time to think, I calculated. *I don't know the answer, so I'm going to guess "blood type."*

"Well, if the patient was bleeding, I'd certainly want to know their blood type," Sally offered.

"Nope," he responded. "The lab won't provide blood unless they run the blood type and crossmatch themselves, so even if the patient knew their blood type, it wouldn't help. Bill, what are you thinking?"

Bill was in the middle of an extended pause, buying time. *Maybe it has something to do with medications*, I was guessing to myself.

"What medications are you on?" Bill chimed in. I was beginning to wonder if my peers were reading my mind.

"Well, you're very close. Knowing medications is important, but that's not the 'one question.' Lisa?"

Lisa was ready, and she immediately suggested, "When was your last period?" We all laughed. Not only had she missed the clue about medications, but her proposed question seemed absurd.

Seeing a "teachable moment," Dr. Santini jumped in. "Actually, it's not the right answer for a critically ill patient. However, Lisa is making an important point. It is your responsibility to ask every woman of childbearing years if there is any possibility she might be pregnant. Every single one. But our hypothetical patient is dying right in front of you, and you are allowed only one question. What is it, Jim?"

Jim was stalling too. Based on our teacher's response to Bill, it had to be something related to medications. *Maybe it's, "Do you have any medication allergies?"* I thought to myself. I was next to answer.

"Do you have any medication allergies?" Bill piped in. I was torn between believing they were all reading my mind and knowing that thinking this way is an early symptom of schizophrenia.

"Right! Very good, Bill." Dr. Santini was pleased his patience had paid off. "*Primum non nocere.* Anybody ever heard of this?"

"First, do no harm," I said, anxious to say something out loud.

"Exactly," Dr. Santini acknowledged. "The patient is about to lose consciousness. They may never say another word the rest of their life. There's a lot you can do to help them, no doubt, in a well-equipped emergency room like this one. But the biggest thing you can do to hurt them is to give them a medication they're allergic to. They'll be unconscious, having some massive anaphylactic reaction, and you think it is due to whatever illness they came in with. And then, they'll die." He took a very long pause for effect. It wasn't needed. We were all busy memorizing the "one question rule." Someday, we knew, it would come in handy.

Here it was, proving itself quite useful at this moment with Mrs. Martin. A cardiac arrest in a medical office may seem to the average reader to be a near-ideal place to have your heart stop beating, especially when contrasted with one's own bathroom at three in the morning or the bowling alley at any time of day. To a physician in private practice, it is the worst nightmare scenario. Mrs. Martin was dangerously close to a cardiac arrest, and this small ten-by-ten-foot exam room, while so perfect a setting for so many different kinds of healing experiences, was wholly inadequate for this one.

We were actually able to accomplish a great deal while waiting for the ambulance. She had received over a half liter of IV fluids, which had caused her blood pressure to rise twenty millimeters of mercury, into a safer range. We had obtained an ECG, electrocardiogram, a reading of the electrical activity of the heart, which was somewhat abnormal, informing us that her heart was under severe stress, but this was not a heart attack. We had even drawn a tube of blood in the hopes of getting a head start on her necessary diagnostic studies. When the emergency medical system crew arrived, she still looked desperately ill, but she was no longer quite as grey. She would make it to the hospital. The tube of blood would be lost somewhere en route.

After three days in the medical intensive care unit, she was no better. In fact, each day her condition had worsened. She was on a ventilator, unable to breathe on her own. Her cardiac function continued to deteriorate, and high doses of medication were required to push her blood pressure up to acceptable levels. I have seen the thirty-nine-year-old human body survive against incredible odds, but the combined failure of both heart and lungs can rarely be transcended.

Speed-reading the review article in the silence of the library, I searched for some clue to what this obviously severe and rare strain of influenza might be doing to Mrs. Martin's body. After four years in private practice, I still had a complete command of the skeleton of the medical knowledge base acquired during my seven years of medical training, as well as enough experience now to add flesh to this structure and to also temper my expectations about the frequency of rare diseases in the routine outpatient world of internal medicine. For example, during my first year in practice, every new patient with hypertension, high blood pressure, was another patient who just might have a rare adrenal tumor, a narrowing of one of the kidney arteries, or an overactive thyroid. Each of these conditions, plus others, make up what we call secondary hypertension, meaning the patient had an elevated blood pressure due to a potentially treatable cause. Of course, ninety-nine out of one-hundred patients presenting to a physician's office will have the more common "essential hypertension," or garden variety high blood pressure.

Unlike the surgeon, the general internist has no opportunity to cure her patients through a dramatic operation. Finding a rare cause of secondary hypertension is a true joy, and this reinforces the compulsive and sometimes exhausting discipline required to practice medicine. The patient may be spared a lifetime of medications to control her blood pressure, and a potentially life threatening disease is cured. Of course, in a good portion of these cases, there is still an operation required to remove an adrenal or thyroid tumor, or to repair a narrowed artery, with the skilled surgeon justly regarded as the hero, but for the primary care internist, the satisfaction of "making the diagnosis" of a rare disease is sufficient.

This singular pride in discovering the one-in-a-hundred or thousand or even million diagnosis is also the source of occasional ridicule. On my surgery rotation in medical school, a proud surgeon once mocked, "When the internist hears hoof beats, he thinks of zebras. When we (implying wise surgeons) hear hoof beats, we know they are horses."

In certain parts of Africa you'd be wrong, I recall thinking on first hearing this clearly prejudicial remark. It seems to be the nature of much of humankind to regard most highly our own particular view of the world and, when necessary to bolster our own sense of personal security, to place others in an inferior position to our own. Healthcare is no more immune to this fatal error than any other walk of life. We all want to feel good about what we do, sometimes not realizing it is unnecessary for others to be worse off in order that we may feel more safe ourselves.

Yet the rare disease still occurs with predictable frequency. (You can't diagnose a disease you don't consider.) With the advent of advanced technologies like sixty-four slice CT and MRI scanners, which provide three-dimensional detail of almost every human anatomic structure, this is no longer strictly true, as these remarkable new technologies find abnormalities never considered by the ordering physician. Scanning technology in the 1980s provided watercolor-like pictures; now, we routinely obtain high resolution, digital photograph-quality images.

My patients rarely come to me fearing the most common possibility. They begin by fearing the worst; this indeed may be the very nature of fear itself. The seventy-four-year-old patient with new high blood pressure, absent any additional abnormalities, has less than a one percent chance of harboring an adrenaline-secreting tumor. A detailed workup is not necessary and would be wasteful. In contrast, the thirty-two-year-old woman or man with episodic, severe anxiety, palpitations, headaches, and periodic, unexplained episodes of rage may well be the victim of such a tumor and should have the simple blood test to confirm or rule out the possibility.

In other words, while I agree with my surgical colleagues that the sound of hoof beats should not trigger an assumption about zebras, all physicians benefit from at least waiting until the remuda, or dazzle, of beasts is close enough to determine the presence or absence of stripes before making even the simplest of diagnoses.

Distracted by my train of thought, I returned to the large, bound tome of *New England Journals of Medicine* before me. Everything in this article about the cardiac complications of influenza seemed exceedingly rare. No horses here; this article contained a virtual zeal of zebras. Influenza can be an extremely virulent disease, as the pandemic of 1918 had proven, killing somewhere between twenty and forty million people. In fact, more people died in a single year from influenza than in the four years of the world's second worst pandemic, the Black Plague, from 1347 to 1351. Tonight, though, influenza was killing this mother of four who had been, according to her husband, "healthy as a horse" only one week ago.

In the quiet of the library, I realized that I had not heard back from the intern caring for her. I had left Mrs. Martin's bedside about forty minutes ago to see if I could find something – anything – to guide our diagnostic efforts. Here before me, in the article, was a possible answer that tied together her abnormal electrocardiogram, dropping blood pressures, and the unusual findings we had seen on the echocardiogram, or heart ultrasound, earlier that day.

There was no answer when I called the MICU main desk. *That's odd. There's always someone there.* I asked the hospital operator to page the intern, and she said, "Oh, he's trying to call you right now. 4126."

I dialed the number, and he answered the phone immediately, on the first quarter-ring.

"She's been coding for thirty minutes. It doesn't look good. No blood pressure, heart rate 160. Dr. Branson is here, and he's getting ready to call the code." In layman's terms, the cardiac arrest team had done everything possible, nothing was working, and one of the ICU medical directors was about to have the team stop their efforts. Mrs. Martin was dead.

How can this be, David? You didn't hear the code announced. You should have been there.

I instantly remembered that the only place in this large hospital where there are no speakers to announce a "code blue" is the medical library.

"No wait!" I responded.

At the same moment, I heard the intern say, "I have to go. Another patient is crashing," followed by the click of the receiver in its cradle.

CHAPTER 20

*"The pieces of my broken heart are so small that
they could be passed through the eye of a needle."*

*Brian Helgeland (1961 -), American screenwriter, director, and producer, from the
screenplay,* A Knight's Tale

Ours was a big hospital. I ran the three-hundred yards down the hall,
hearing the loudspeakers blare, "Code Blue in the MICU." I knew that the
announcement would come only once, as most of the code team was in
the MICU already. I could picture the team of already exhausted doctors,
nurses, and respiratory therapists running from their failed efforts at the
bedside of Mrs. Martin, having done all they could, to the other patient
who had a cardiac arrest, starting over again with someone who still may
have a chance at life.

Taking the flight of stairs two and three steps at a time, I arrived on the
fourth floor landing at the back entrance of the MICU, which was directly
adjacent to Mrs. Martin's room. Entering the room, I saw live footage of
an erupting volcano on the television screen opposite my patient. Below
the image, in ticker-tape style, ran the caption, "Kilauea erupting on the
Big Island of Hawaii."

There was only one other person in her room now, a respiratory
therapist named Bill, whom I knew well, and who had helped me many
times over the past five years. Bill was hurriedly disconnecting Mrs. Martin

133

from the ventilator equipment. The breathing machine was off, yet she still was breathing shallowly on her own.

"Please leave her on the machine for a few more minutes," I protested. "We need to do a pericardiocentesis."

"But David, they called the code just a minute ago. They couldn't bring her blood pressure back up." While he was very respectful, it seemed clear to me he thought I was delusional.

"Look at the monitor," I insisted. "There is a rhythm there." While he looked up to see the miniature version of a normal cardiac rhythm, about twenty percent of its normal height, I began rummaging through the crash cart finding the four things that I needed.

The crash cart, as it is called, contains virtually all of the possible medication and equipment necessary to resuscitate a dying patient. A cube on wheels, about thirty inches on a side, it is full of ampoules, little tiny glass bottles, of cardiac and blood pressure medicines, equipment for intubating the patient (putting a tube down their throat to connect them to a breathing machine), and needles and syringes of every size and caliber, to describe just some of its contents. In the midst of rescuing a dying patient, there is no time to send the medical student out searching for a rarely used piece of equipment, so these carts are fully stocked. I knew that I would have everything that I needed, if I could just find it myself. Normally, I had people hand me what I asked for. I realized that I had participated in over one hundred cardiac arrest situations, most of them as the leader of the team during my residency training, but I never once had to find anything myself in this maze of drawers and compartments. However, with some luck, I now had the items I needed: sterile gloves, antiseptic solution, a fifty-cubic centimeter (approximately two ounce) syringe, and a pericardiocentesis needle. I could tell I had secured the cooperation, however tenuous, of the respiratory therapist when I heard the ventilator switch back on and resume its breathing cycles.

"Can you sterilize her skin quickly, right at her xyphoid process, please?" I pleaded. He applied the Betadine antiseptic in three courses of expanding concentric circles, while I donned the sterile gloves and unwrapped the other equipment. The xyphoid process is the sharp little triangular shaped bone that sits at the bottom of the sternum, or breastbone. The reader may choose to depart from the excitement of the story to locate his or her own xyphoid right now, if so desired.

The pericardiocentesis needle is six inches long and about one-sixteenth of an inch in diameter, and it is used to withdraw fluid from the sac around the heart. I had never seen one outside of the sterile envelope I was now peeling open. I had never held a needle that large before now. I attached it to the large syringe and placed the tip of this sharp probe just below my left index finger, which was now pressing on Mrs. Martin's xyphoid bone. I had seen a classroom slide, an artist's drawing, depicting this procedure in medical school, about ten years prior, and again, three years later, during my internship. I had never seen anyone perform it.

We have a dictum in medical training, "See one, do one, teach one," which quite literally described the fact that most procedures we performed on our patients for the very first time were often preceded by only one observation of the technique.

Well, David, you're one behind here. Maybe Bill is right – you are delusional. On the other hand, this woman has been pronounced dead, so it's not like you can make things worse.

The pericardium is a thin sac that covers the heart. Picture a human heart sealed inside a balloon. Normally, there is no real space between this balloon-like sac and the heart itself. In influenza, but more commonly in other disease processes, the heart's surface may become inflamed, and fluid may slowly fill the pericardial sac around the heart, expanding the balloon to potentially great dimensions. On chest x-ray, the "heart" can become enormous, appearing to extend almost the full width of the chest. In reality, the organ itself may remain its usual size of a human fist and be surrounded by the massive fluid-filled pericardial sac.

On her heart ultrasound that morning, Mrs. Martin's heart did not appear to be enlarged. Because of the extent of the influenza in her lungs, the study was technically quite difficult and the results somewhat equivocal. There seemed to be only a small amount of fluid in her pericardial sac, but nothing to the magnitude described above. In my rushed library reading, I had learned that influenza patients were more susceptible to *constrictive* pericarditis, in which the same inflammatory process can occur, but in this case the pericardial sac is rigid and cannot expand like a balloon. As the viral inflammation increases the fluid volume in the sac, the pressure literally constricts the heart from its normal operation. In typical pericarditis without any constriction, the fluid will gradually disappear over time. When there is constriction, the patient may die unless the pericardial sac is drained. The drainage procedure is called pericardiocentesis, the Latin version of "draining the fluid from the sac around the heart."

I advanced the pericardiocentesis needle about three inches beneath the skin, half the needle's length, my motion parallel to the floor, up and to the right, directly toward her heart. *Wait.* From somewhere in a relatively inaccessible region of my memory bank, I was receiving a message. In one of those classroom photos, there was an electrical lead from an ECG machine attached to the needle. When the needle approached the surface of the heart, the electrode would signal the physician the pericardium had been reached. This was an important signal, because advancing the needle another quarter of an inch could put it into the heart itself, where it could tear a coronary artery or trigger a serious heart rhythm disorder, both potentially fatal complications.

"Her blood pressure is still 40," the respiratory therapist offered, now a full participant in the procedure.

Forget the ECG electrode. You don't have time. Plus, you don't know how to do it, I decided, and I again began to advance the needle, an eighth of an inch at a time, while pulling back on the plunger of the syringe. I was timing my advances to the beeping rhythm of Mrs. Martin's heart monitor, beating 160 times per minute, but moving no blood forward. *Four beats, advance the syringe. Four more beats, advance the syringe. Keep the suction on the plunger.* At this rate, the needle was moving one inch closer to the heart every five seconds. My hands were trembling only slightly when I felt the distinct signal: the slightest tap from the end of the needle, transmitted back to my left index finger. Instantaneously, the syringe began to fill with straw colored fluid. *You're in the pericardial space!* Five cubic centimeters (one teaspoon), ten cc's, fifteen, twenty, the fluid came easily, with only the slightest suction applied to the syringe. It was filling itself with almost no help from me!

Above us, the cardiac monitor tracing began to slow noticeably. The heart rate dropped from 160 to 140, then to 120, eventually to 100, almost to a more normal value of less than 90. This was a positive sign. The height of the electrical heart tracing on the cardiac monitor, which started abnormally small and dampened because of the fluid surrounding the heart, first doubled, and then doubled again, to nearly normal size – another positive sign, suggesting the heart was no longer constricted now that the fluid had been withdrawn. Bill grabbed his stethoscope and repeated the blood pressure reading.

Unbelievable! This is just unbelievable! I thought to myself. *This worked!*

"Blood pressure is 90 over 60!" he exclaimed. This was a blood pressure compatible with life. "This is just unbelievable! I can't believe this worked! I've never seen…" He stopped abruptly and looked at me sheepishly. "I'm sorry," he apologized. "It wasn't that I didn't think you could…"

"Look, I can't believe this worked either," I interrupted. "I am as stunned as you are."

Then it hit me. "Oh, my God, Bill! Do you know if anyone has talked to the family?"

Mrs. Martin's husband and oldest son were probably still in the waiting room, where I had left them two hours ago. I told them I would be back; they were planning to spend the night there. They would have heard the first code blue announced over the loudspeaker. Shortly after, a nurse would have informed them that it was their mother and wife who was in distress, and assured them they would be kept informed.

Bill grimaced. "Dr. Branson left the room to tell them she didn't make it, right after he called the code."

I staggered out toward the MICU family waiting room. My hands were really shaking now. Relatively cool and calm minutes before, I immediately became drenched in sweat.

So sticking a big needle almost into somebody's heart without ever actually seeing it done before wasn't that bad. But you've never had to tell a patient's family that their loved one wasn't dead after all. Not that it isn't good news, but how do you explain this?

In the seventy-five-foot walk out of the MICU's main entrance, around the corner, and into the waiting room, I had tried and rejected at least ten opening lines. Tentatively committing myself to, "I have some good news," I walked into the crowded waiting room, in which about twenty anxious people sat, grouped into five or maybe six different families. It was clear that every person in the room was worried about their own family member. Each pair of eyes was riveted on me, each face was silently questioning me:

"Was Mother the one that coded?"

"Did my husband have a cardiac arrest?"

"Is our sister dead?"

"Is my wife still alive?"

The only audible sound was the sleet pounding against the wall of windows on the south side of the waiting room. I realized that as a physician, I had always heard the "code blue" as my call to action. It now dawned on me: every time the speaker announced, "Code blue in the MICU," and a stampede of medical professionals passed the waiting room door and burst into the unit, each waiting family member feared the worst. That night, this exact sequence had occurred twice within a forty-minute period. Their terror had been exponentially increased.

I knew nothing about the other patients in the MICU that night. Mrs. Martin was the only one under my care. Hers was the only family I could inform.

"I'm sorry," I began, speaking to everyone, "I'm Doctor Roberts, and I'm here to talk to the Martins. I'm sorry, but I can't tell you anything about anyone else. I'll ask the ICU staff to keep you up to date. I'm sure you're all aware they have their hands full at the moment."

I cringed at my choice of words, but stayed focused on the Martin family. The father and his teenage son sat together in the crowded room, holding each other's hands, their gazes riveted on me, searching my face for some clue as to the fate of wife and mother – and their own as well.

"Let's go outside and talk," I said as they came forward. There was a conference room back inside the MICU we could use, which would afford us some privacy. By now, I had abandoned, "I have some good news," and another half-dozen equally awkward sounding conversation-starting attempts. I had no idea what to say. I still couldn't discern what exactly they did or did not know.

Fortunately, Mr. Martin saved me. Just after he and his son sat down, as I was closing the door with my back to them, he spoke up. "Doctor Roberts, please tell us. How is she doing?"

I paused to let the wave of relief pass over me. *Thank you, God.* Dr. Branson hadn't talked to them. He probably ran directly to the other cardiac arrest patient. (The only bigger crisis in a hospital than two consecutive cardiac arrests is two simultaneous ones.) My head slowly inched forward, finally resting against the closed door. I sighed deeply, feeling my rigid muscles all suddenly relax together. Holding the door handle to steady myself, I slowly turned around to face the expectant father and son, both searching my face and my every movement for a sense of the news I was about to deliver. I had my opening line.

"Well, we have figured out what is wrong with her heart."

The following Monday, I transferred the responsibility for our hospital service, including Mrs. Martin, to Mark, who kept me informed over the following week regarding her status. While her "miracle cure" had allowed her to live longer, she had not regained consciousness. In addition to her pericarditis, there appeared to be more extensive involvement of the cardiac muscle itself. According to the journal review article, influenza myocarditis, inflammation of the heart muscle, had a high mortality rate. After another four days of progressive deterioration, her heart had failed completely and her chances for recovery were zero. At her family's direction, she had been disconnected from the ventilator, and she died within the hour.

Restoring the life of someone who has been pronounced dead can feel like an act of biblical proportions. That sort of rescue is rare among primary care internal medicine doctors, and I knew it was something I would remember all my life. I was quite aware I would never again be called upon to perform a pericardiocentesis.

Upon hearing of her death, it was clear I had simply restored her blood pressure that night in the MICU and not her life. The perfectionist in me kept chattering away, *What if you had figured it out earlier? What if the pericardiocentesis had been performed before her blood pressure dropped? What if? What if? What if?* Of course, the influenza virus would have destroyed her heart muscle, and she would have died anyway.

What if: the occupational hazard of a profession where life and death are daily outcomes of one's work.

One of the regular responsibilities of the primary care physician is to assure each patient is adequately immunized against preventable diseases.

Even to this day, in the face of a new, worldwide influenza pandemic, I encounter many patients who say, "I don't believe in flu shots."

Do you mean you don't believe flu shots exist? I always think, but never say. While I certainly respect each patient's decision (the law does not allow us to just hold people down and inject them), I can't help but wonder whether anyone would ever refuse the vaccine had they known Mrs. Martin – age thirty-nine, mother of four – and seen the fatal consequences of what most people think of as a relatively mild virus.

I also have some bias toward the public health aspects of influenza immunization. The more people in a community who are immunized, the less likely the non-immunized individuals are to contract influenza.

"You don't have to have a flu shot for yourself, you know," I tell my patients. "I get my flu shot for you, so I won't spread the disease. You can get yours for the elementary school children in our community. That's where influenza spreads most quickly."

While Nancy Martin's death was certainly a dramatic example of the seriousness of the virus, I have seen many other patients die from what most blithely call "the flu." The vast majority of these fatalities have been unvaccinated individuals.

We've probably all had the muscle aches, the headache, cough, fever, and gastrointestinal symptoms that come with an episode of influenza. We spend a day or two at home, in bed, drink plenty of fluids, take something for the fever and pain, sleep twelve hours per day, and then gradually get better and return to work, school, or our regular activities. We think of "the flu" as though it is just a "bad cold."

But it is one that kills 40,000 Americans each year.

I haven't personally missed a single influenza vaccine since the day Mrs. Martin died. Nor have I seen images of Kilauea, which is still erupting thirty years later, without recalling her "horrible case of the flu."

CHAPTER 21

"He's a pinball wizard
There's got to be a twist
A pinball wizard
He's got such a supple wrist
How do you think he does it?
(I don't know)
What makes him so good?"

Pete Townshend, from the song Pinball Wizard,
first recorded by The Who

Johnny Moon literally swaggered into our office for his appointment one day in early spring, looking all for the world like a rock star of the early eighties. With dancing bright blue eyes, he was as thin as a rail, with shiny shoulder-length black hair, tight jeans, an equally tight-fitting black leather jacket, and a long silver chain hanging from his belt, looping down and back up into his pocket.

At the front desk, Kathleen was speaking to him in unusually soft and welcoming tones; she had abandoned her captain-of-the-ship persona for this new patient as she asked him for the paperwork we mail to each patient a week or so in advance of the visit. Standing in the hallway, I could hear him apologize and say he had left it at home.

"Well, that's no problem at all," Kathleen responded even more sweetly, "you can complete them here in the waiting room until Dr. Roberts is ready to see you."

This is a first, I thought. Normally, Kathleen could be quite unforgiving to patients who had failed to produce the required paperwork on demand. I had another fifteen-minute appointment before I saw this new patient, though, and figured at the age of nineteen years, he could quickly complete the forms in a timely fashion.

When I entered his examination room, I saw this energetic and likeable young man with a warm smile on his face rise to greet me with a handshake.

"What's up, Doc?" he crowed rather rapidly, without any actual attempt to imitate the intonation of Bugs Bunny.

My physical examination of the patient began immediately: *Very cool right hand. Fine tremor. Glistening skin, very moist.* There were a small number of possible diagnoses, and my internal differential diagnosis generating center in my head rattled them off almost as quickly as Johnny's rapid speech: *Severe anxiety, drug use (amphetamines, cocaine), drug withdrawal (alcohol or almost any other drug), pheochromocytoma, mania, hyperthyroidism.* A pheochromocytoma is a tumor of the adrenal gland that secretes epinephrine, commonly known as adrenaline, in quantities hundreds of times larger than the body requires.

"Well, Mr. Moon, we have you scheduled for an hour for a complete physical examination. What brings you in today?" As I spoke, I was shuffling through his paperwork to see if anything stood out. He had left the "occupation" question without an answer. I really was wondering, both from his appearance and demeanor, if he was a rock star.

"Well, I feel pretty good, actually. My girlfriend says I'm getting pretty hard to live with, though. She thinks there is something wrong with me. I'm not exactly sure why. Like I say, I feel just fine." Simply reading these words can't convey the experience of hearing them. Mr. Moon was the fastest talker I had ever heard in my life.

It is possible for humans to hear and understand as many as three hundred spoken words per minute. Most of the time, we speak at a rate of one hundred-twenty to one hundred-sixty words per minute. Consequently, even when someone speaks twice as fast as normal, we can often understand quite clearly. As a physician who ends up asking patients over one hundred fifty questions about their medical background the first time I see them, Johnny Moon was a blessing, as I knew we would complete the interview portion of the visit in short order.

The converse situation is the bane of the internist's existence. I ask my first question, such as, "What brings you into the office today?" and the patient begins by taking a long, deep sigh, followed by a five-second pause, and then launches into their novella.

"Well," he might begin, "when my sister was pregnant, she had this awful skin rash. And there wasn't a *single* doctor who could tell her what it was. She went to *five* different dermatologists!"

Where on earth is this going? I would wonder during the next five-second pause while the patient peered into my eyes to see if I was as upset as they were about this vast failure of the dermatologic community. I never was. Usually sooner than later, I would no longer be able to listen patiently and would interrupt, "How long ago was your sister pregnant?"

"Oh, well, this was all thirty years ago, but as I was saying, no doctor could figure out what it was. It wasn't until after she had her third child. She had the rash with each pregnancy, and it would go away about four weeks after she had the baby. You know what it was?" The patient would here insert the longest pause.

Oh, this is a quiz. Perhaps just a test of your diagnostic abilities, David.

"No, I don't," I would say nicely and smile. *It was thirty years ago. I wasn't there. I didn't see the rash. I wasn't even born yet,* I would think, admittedly not amicably.

"It was the prenatal vitamins." Another pause, another deep piercing gaze to ascertain whether I was now prepared to condemn the vitamin industry. I never was.

"So, my sister ended up…"

There is now some fairly good medical evidence, unavailable at the time of Mr. Moon, which shows that allowing the patient to tell his story in an open-ended fashion usually results in a more satisfied patient and often results in the delivery of a key piece of information that might not be obtained through the rapid-fire question and answer format I preferred.

The poet Muriel Rukeyser writes, "The universe is made of stories, not atoms," and nowhere is this better exemplified than in the physician's exam room. Meaning well, patients gather data and may spend hours, or days, preparing their own stories for their doctor. Many believe each detail has the potential be the important clue to their diagnosis and, not having spent four years in medical school, take the responsibility for serving up any fact or impression, no matter how obscure, for the doctor's careful consideration. Meanwhile, the physician has already formulated a hypothesis as to the patient's diagnosis within about fifteen seconds.

On good days, I could let a patient verbally wander off into seemingly irrelevant territory for over a minute. I have seen doctors remain silent for over four minutes. Much less able to control my impatience at this point in my life, on most days I would invariably interrupt again after another twenty seconds.

"I'm sorry to interrupt," I would lie, "but I want to be sure we adequately address your concerns in the office today in the time we have scheduled. Perhaps you could connect this episode of your sister's prenatal vitamins thirty years ago with what is bothering you today?" Sometimes this strategy worked nicely and the patient would steer his own way back into the present. Other times not. Sometimes there was a logical link between the story and the patient's current ailment, at least one I could understand. Other times not.

It's probably time to return to the story at hand, lest the reader begin to assume I am afflicted with the same tendency toward rambling history as the patients I decry here.

So, Johnny Moon was the physician's "dream historian." Short and to the point, he spoke quickly, and we covered his entire medical, social, personal, family history, and review of systems in about five minutes, a task usually requiring twenty. In this brief period, we determined he had the following new symptoms, all gradually increasing over the past four months or so: outbursts of anger, trouble in his primary relationships, insomnia, excessive warmth (he felt hot all of the time), a tremor of his hands. He was not a student, and he did not have a job. He supported himself playing pinball.

"Pinball?" I asked, surprised. "How does one make money playing pinball?"

At the risk of presenting a story about my own sister's prenatal vitamins, it is worth pointing out that this story takes place in an era before cell phones, high-resolution home video games, and even the regular use of desktop computers in business. Atari had developed the first video game, called "Pong," which was, in comparison to modern technology, more primitive than the first prehistoric wheel. When attempting to describe these early video games to young people, they laugh uproariously and consign me to the same age of human civilization in which the first wheel was invented.

So, pinball machines were the primary source of arcade entertainment, and my young patient had figured out how to make money over the past ten months, since his high school graduation, by wagering against others on these games. He reported that as he had improved his skills, he was able to win as much as two hundred fifty to three hundred dollars on the average weekend, which, as a nineteen-year-old, was enough to live on comfortably. In addition, he had won five hundred dollars in a regional tournament several weeks prior.

"My friends call me the 'Pinball Wizard,'" he said, smiling with pride.

"As made famous by the Who," I replied. He seemed pleased to see his doctor had some background in rock and roll music. When I told him the immensely popular rock band had played at my own high school, including that particular song, he was even more impressed.

As part of our medical history review, completed in record-breaking time, he stated he used only limited amounts of alcohol, smoked marijuana twice in the more distant past, and had never used amphetamines, cocaine, or heroin.

"I don't use any drugs at all—they mess up my pinball game." Did the tremors and "hot flashes," as he called them, come and go, or were they more of a constant phenomenon? "They're there all the time." *With an adrenal tumor, he might be more likely to have episodic symptoms.*

His physical examination held additional clues: elevated blood pressure, heart rate of 110 (normal for a male his age would be between sixty and eighty), an enlarged thyroid gland, the fine tremor in both hands, hyperactive reflexes, and lid lag. Lid lag is a subtle finding on the examination of the eyes, noted when a physician asks the patient to follow her fingers as she moves them. When moving the fingers from a position well above the patient's eyes to well below, the eyes normally track quickly, with no visible white space seen between the upper lid and the iris, the colored part of the eye. In one condition in particular, the white portion of the eye, or sclera, can clearly be seen. This phenomenon was visible in both of Mr. Moon's eyes during the maneuver, but not when simply looking forward.

After he dressed, we went over my findings in detail.

"Mr. Moon, I am fairly certain your symptoms are caused by your thyroid gland, which is making much more thyroid hormone than your body needs. We'll need to do some blood tests to confirm this diagnosis, and we will probably want to do a scan of the thyroid if the blood tests show elevated hormone levels."

"Could this have anything to do with these anger outbursts I've been having?" he wondered aloud, and I could see he was reviewing the last ten months of his life from a completely different perspective. I nodded. "Because my girlfriend basically told me I couldn't live with her anymore because of the way I have been treating her. I'm here today as a sort of compromise."

I explained that in my short career in medicine I had seen a number of individuals on the brink of ending their most important relationship when diagnosed with hyperthyroidism.

"When the blood tests come back positive, I'll be happy to call your girlfriend and explain this to her if you like. Or you can bring her in to the office next time. It's up to you."

"That would really help me," he confessed. "How soon can all of this testing be done?"

It turned out to be very quickly, in keeping with Mr. Moon's rapid pace through life. His blood test results were available the next morning, showing he had an extremely overactive thyroid gland, and due to a cancellation, we were able to obtain the thyroid scan the same day. It showed an extremely high level of uptake, confirming the diagnosis of Graves' disease, the medical term for this form of overactive thyroid gland.

I called him later in the day to tell him the results, and he put his girlfriend on the phone. I explained his mood changes were likely related to the thyroid disorder, and I promised her with treatment he would likely return to his "old self," the way he was ten months ago. She thanked me, sounding incredibly relieved.

I have learned a great deal from my work with patients who have Graves' disease. The first lesson came in medical school, when I simply informed a female patient in the university hospital endocrinology clinic about the diagnosis. The woman, in her mid-forties, turned white and looked as though she was about to pass out.

"What's wrong?" I immediately asked.

"Did you say, 'Graves' disease?'" she gasped, horrified.

"Well, yes. It's a state where your thyroid becomes enlarged and very overactive. It's called Graves' disease." I was trying to be supportive but still did not understand her apprehension.

"Graves' disease? *Graves'* disease? So, I'm going to die then. How soon?"

I was mortified. The world of medicine is chock full of anatomical structures, symptoms, signs, lab tests, or diseases named with what we call eponyms, usually after the doctor who first reported them or the historical character with the malady. For example, there are over four hundred fifty such eponyms beginning with the letter A alone, from Aarskog's syndrome to Azima battery, including the more famous Achilles' tendon and Addison's and Alzheimer's diseases along the way. None of these eponyms have quite as frightening an alternate interpretation for the layperson as Graves' disease does, I learned.

The "Grave" in Graves' disease refers to Robert James Graves, an Irish physician who, in 1835, first described a patient with an enlarged and overactive thyroid gland and bulging eyes (the latter finding called proptosis). There is, in medicine, a certain level of "eponym competition," and in 1840, the German Karl Adolph von Basedow independently reported a similar patient. On the European continent, the disease went under the Basedow moniker for some time. Lest I forget, there were also others laying claim to the eponym, having reported their findings earlier but in less widely circulated medical journals: Parry's disease, Begbie's disease, Flajani's disease, Flajani-Basedow syndrome, and Marsh's disease have all faded, and Graves' disease has become the most commonly used term.

Since that moment in medical school, after I say the words "Graves' disease," I always immediately add the phrase, "named after Robert Graves, an Irish physician who first reported the disease in the early 1800s." No matter how thoroughly and reassuringly I explain the thyroid problem prior to using this eponym, I still see a momentary flash of panic in each patient's eyes. It's unfortunate Dr. Flajani didn't publish in a more widely circulated medical journal.

CHAPTER 22

"Do not consider painful what is good for you."

Euripides (c. 480-406 BC), Greek playwright

Several days later, in the office, I reviewed the options for treatment with Johnny Moon. At that time, there were four treatment options for Graves' disease: medications intended only to control the symptoms, medications to return the thyroid to normal functioning over time, surgery to remove the entire gland, and the nuclear option, which was total ablation of the thyroid gland with radioactive iodine. In the first category, he was already taking propranolol, a medication used to slow his heart rate and perhaps diminish the flushing; I had prescribed the medication over the telephone when his lab results came back. He was feeling noticeably better already.

However, he needed to choose one of the other three treatment options as well. Without treating the thyroid gland directly, he would likely go on to develop other medical complications of his hyperthyroidism. Most readers would assume one of the non-nuclear options would be preferred; generally, they are not. Because of the need to take the medication three times per day for up to several years, some very serious potential side effects of the medication, and the need to follow thyroid blood tests for many years until the gland finally fails, as it often does, or the desire to avoid surgery, many patients opt for the single dose of radioactive iodine during an overnight hospital stay, followed by a lifetime daily replacement dose of oral thyroid medication. "I might just as well get it over with now," most patients say when choosing the nuclear option.

But not Johnny Moon. Still in the great "invulnerable" adolescent psychological stage of life, he understandably wasn't ready for the nuclear thyroid ablation approach.

"I can take the pills, and I don't mind the blood tests," he noted, sounding as philosophical as one can when speaking between two hundred fifty and three hundred words per minute. As I discovered later, he also had other concerns. I wrote a prescription for the second medication, and we agreed to meet again in two weeks.

When he returned to the office for a follow-up appointment, his thyroid hormone blood levels were greatly improved and now only slightly elevated. His heart rate on the two medications was sixty-six beats per minute, normal. He still had a bit of a tremor, and his lid lag was still present. Usually, the eye changes from thyroid disease are irreversible. He did not seem particularly concerned about this, since there was nothing any non-physician observer would notice: he did not have the "bulging eyes" that some Graves' patients did, and also, referring to the lid lag, because, "the only people who have to move their eyes way up and way down like that are the Three Stooges." His girlfriend had already noticed a positive personality change and had given him a one-month extension on her eviction notice because of his good behavior. On paper and on examination, just about everything was going in the right direction.

Everything, that is, except pinball.

"Could these medications mess up my pinball playing?" he wanted to know.

I smiled and excused myself to locate the *Physician's Desk Reference*, a 2000+ page book with the drug monographs, or package inserts, for almost every available prescription drug. I hated the huge tome and the difficulty of finding needed information, but at this point in medical history, it was all we had. Returning to the room, I explained the purpose of the book and noted I was certain there would be no mention of pinball in the lists of side effects. He laughed heartily as I tracked down the side effects of propranolol.

Running my finger down the list of the dozen or so "Precautions" and the fifteen "Adverse Reactions," I quipped, "Nope. No mention of pinball!" He laughed again, just as enthusiastically. "Also, there isn't anything about loss of coordination. Just fatigue and dizziness. Are you having those symptoms?" He was not.

Turning back to the almost impossible to decipher index (there were actually four separate ones), I eventually found methimazole, the medication he was taking to directly control his overactive thyroid. Passing over the precautions, which always make me shudder since one is the drug's ability to stop the production of blood cells in the bone marrow, sometimes resulting in a fatal anemia, we looked at the adverse reactions together, a longer list. Nothing was listed that would affect coordination or mental speed.

"Why don't we just watch and see how your pinball playing goes over the next few weeks?" I offered. "I'll see you again in three weeks, and you can have your blood drawn a few days before the visit." This sounded fine to him, and we agreed to meet as suggested.

He was waiting at the office door at 7:30 the following Monday morning, only four days later.

"Doc, I have a real problem, here. A disaster. We need to talk."

Probably the girlfriend, I surmised quickly. I was thirty minutes early for my first patient, so I led him back to one of the exam rooms. Contrary to my presumptive diagnosis of his "disaster," it was not his girlfriend; it was his pinball game.

"I lost over three hundred dollars this weekend, Doc. Three hundred dollars! Something's wrong here. My reflexes are shot, and my concentration isn't as good. I used to be able to play for six to eight hours straight. Now I am tired after two. It has to be the medication." He said all of this at a slightly slower pace now, about two hundred twenty-five words per minute.

"Let me examine you first, and then we can talk further," I said by way of compromise, and also to give me a little more time to think. His physical exam was fine, just as last time. I rechecked his reflexes, and they were now normal. Whereas three weeks ago his legs kicked out briskly and firmly to ninety degrees the instant I tapped his patellar tendon, now the legs moved three inches forward like every other normal person. The underlying cause for his recent economic downturn was beginning to dawn on me.

"How good were you at playing pinball before you started having your very first symptoms?" I began, thinking along an entirely different line now.

"What, you mean a year ago?"

"Yes, ten months or a year ago. Last May. Before you were feeling hot all of the time. Before the anger episodes."

"Well, I was just graduating from high school, and I didn't have much time to play then. It was over the summer that I really started shooting the lights out. But it was because I was playing eight hours or more a day. That's what really made the difference."

"How much money did you win playing pinball prior to last summer?"

"None. I didn't even start betting until August."

"No tournaments?"

"Nope."

"Did you play pinball with your friends when you were in high school?" He was nodding. "How often?"

"A few times per week, maybe. Why?"

"How often did you win when you played with your friends?" I was becoming conscious of the fact I was turning the interview into an interrogation; this was not my intent. I tried to lighten up a bit. "Did you win most of the time?"

"Well, actually, no. Brad generally won. Then, sometime in July, I started winning, and he couldn't beat me after that. Until this weekend, that is. I couldn't beat him!"

I reviewed the blood tests report from last week one more time just to be certain I was on the right track. The methimazole can actually take a patient from an overactive thyroid state to an underactive one. Careful monitoring is required to be sure the patient's dose is exactly right. The blood tests showed his dose was appropriate. If anything, his thyroid gland was still just barely overactive.

It was now clear what was happening to Johnny Moon. How was I going to explain it to him, though? Pinball was his vocation, his source of income.

"Here's what I think has happened here, Mr. Moon." I went on to explain my theory. He had started off, like most people, an average pinball player. Then, in June, his thyroid gland started making more

152

and more hormone and began to pour the excess amounts into his bloodstream. While we usually think of the effects of excessive thyroid hormone in a negative way, the hormone is necessary for life in all humans, and at proper levels, it provides multiple beneficial effects, including a sense of general well being, enhanced alertness, more active reflexes, and enhanced ability to perform mathematical calculations. For most people, these are good effects, but in excess, the hormone can create additional problems.

His extremely high blood levels of thyroid hormone had made him a superb pinball player – a pinball wizard, in fact. The enhanced reflexes, the shortened reaction times, the sharpened vision, the increased stamina, each effect enhanced his game. Now, with treatment, these superhuman powers were fading.

"Can't we just stop the medicine then, Doc?" he pleaded.

"Well, as we talked about last time, there are lots of serious side effects of untreated hyperthyroidism. Besides, Graves' disease often lasts for a few years and can resolve on its own, only to recur later. As your doctor, I'm more concerned about your heart than I am about your pinball abilities." He shifted in his seat, bristling mildly. "I hope you can understand that. You're paying me to keep you healthy, right?"

He nodded slowly, still thinking, still looking for some loophole. "What would happen if I was on the medication most of the time but went off it from time to time, just for a few days?"

"Well, it takes up to two weeks for the medication to achieve its full effect, and about the same amount of time for it to be eliminated from your system. So I'm not sure this would really be the best idea." He was nodding and frowning in a manner suggesting I had told him what he needed to know, but not exactly what he wanted to hear.

"I know this isn't what you wanted to hear," I said, attempting a partial reconciliation. "It's not like you are planning to play pinball the rest of your life, though, is it?" His somewhat shocked and embarrassed look made it clear I had actually described his plan.

Why not? I reflected. *He's earning a living, he's a folk hero here in town, he's the best he can be at what he loves to do the most.* Having chosen the arduous path of a physician, I realized I was feeling a bit envious of his simple goals and his remarkable success.

"This means I'm going to have to either find a job or go to college," he spoke, almost in slow motion for him, followed by a long deep sigh, as though he was exhaling every molecule he had inhaled over the past ten months. His shoulders slumped for a minute, and then he collected himself and sat back up straight in his chair. He was already working himself past the idea that either school or a job would be a death sentence, but it would still take him time to decide on a new plan.

The next six months came together into a pattern. He became very careful about the timing of his appointments and blood tests, and he now carried a small pocket calendar he would open and consult, holding it close, in an apparent effort to ensure I did not see what was written inside. He started to call frequently to reschedule appointments, sometimes for one or two days later and others for weeks hence. Over time, I came to develop a theory about his pattern: see Dr. Roberts in the office, stop my medicine immediately for ten days, play in the pinball tournament, restart my medications and take them for fourteen days, have my blood drawn, see Dr. Roberts two days later. It all worked out to a nice rhythm. When I asked him about his pinball proficiency, he would only say he was still playing and was winning some money. He had also found a job working in a local supermarket and had applied to several colleges, hoping to start in the fall.

One of the problems with adolescent invulnerability is the statistical truth supporting it. Johnny Moon had no serious complications from his Graves' disease, and it did "burn out," resolving with medical treatment by the end of his freshman year of college. We stopped the medications at this point, and his thyroid function remained normal for the next few years.

I recall my warring emotions: a deep concern for this highly likeable young man and my intolerance for what I believed was his "irresponsibility" in risking his health and long-term well-being just to play pinball. How varied our ideas of success can be as we each travel along our own life's journey! How alluring fame and fortune can be, even when it comes at our own expense.

As is often the case, the things we feel most intolerant of in others may well be the things we struggle with ourselves. From a certain point of view, it can easily be argued that working seventy hours per week caring for the sick (no matter how noble that avocation may seem to society), at the cost of one's health and relationships, bears a striking similarity to stopping one's medication to win at pinball.

CHAPTER 23

"Be not angry that you cannot make others as you wish them to be,
since you cannot make yourself as you wish to be."

Thomas à Kempis (circa 1380 – 1471), Medieval Catholic monk
in The Imitation of Christ

My awareness of hyperthyroidism all around me had peaked after my encounters with Johnny Moon, and my pursuit of identifying Graves' disease provided me with several lessons shortly thereafter. The characteristics of hyperthyroidism are so immediately recognizable to the trained medical eye that the disease is famous for its "across the room diagnosis" capability. A number of diseases can be diagnosed simply through smelling, hearing, or touching a patient. Generally, one must be close to the patient to do so, as the "hearing" usually requires a stethoscope. Graves' disease occurs more commonly in women than men, by a factor of five to ten times, and may affect as many as two percent of all women during their lifetime.

Consequently, there are a fair number of females walking around with the disorder, and many with the physical signs of the disease. Within a two-month period during the summer after Johnny's diagnosis, I saw two such women, both at the local shopping mall. The bulging eyes and the swelling in the neck can be obvious enough to be spotted thirty feet away. The only diagnostic problem is that patients with treated and resolved Graves' disease may retain their bulging eyes and swollen neck for the remainder of their lives. In other words, the obvious signs mean the patient has had the problem at some point in their life, not that the disease is currently active.

Aspiring to be a Good Samaritan to my Midwestern community, I was ever vigilant for opportunities to make these across-the-room diagnoses. I suppose much of this stems from the admiration that I had for Sherlock Holmes and his ability to accomplish similar feats. In fact, it was the reading of *The Complete Sherlock Holmes*, by the ophthalmologist Arthur Conan Doyle, during my sophomore year of college, which inspired me to become a doctor. The two-volume set had been such a wonderful alternative to studying for my final exams those icy two weeks in December.

In any case, I think I imagined there were numerous unsuspecting souls afflicted with hyperthyroidism, on the verge of simultaneous heart attack and divorce, and were I sufficiently observant, I could save them from these dual disasters. The first sighting was in a restaurant at the local shopping mall.

"Look," I said to my wife, "that woman over there in the red sweater. She has Graves' disease." She followed my gaze to an attractive woman sitting across the restaurant about twenty-five feet away.

"She's going to die?" my wife responded. "From what?"

I briefly updated her on the signs, symptoms, and prognosis of untreated Graves' disease, as well as the history of the name.

"Do you think I should go over there and tell her that she has a thyroid problem?"

"Of course not. What would anyone think if a complete stranger came up to her with that information?" Apparently, my wife's commitment to saving these unsuspecting souls was not as strong as mine.

"But I'm a doctor," I reasoned. It would take me years to outgrow this mid-life professional extension of adolescent invulnerability.

My wife gave me the "I-know-you-are-going-to-do-whatever-you-want-to-independent-of-whatever-I-say" look and started to ready our three small children to leave the restaurant. "I'll meet you outside in the mall," she announced and began her quick getaway.

With complete confidence, I approached the table where the bulging-eyed female was sitting with another woman. The materials on the table suggested they were having a business dinner.

"Excuse me," I began with a smile. "I'm sorry to interrupt you here, but I am a physician and I couldn't help but notice..." I quickly interrupted myself. "Look, I've never done anything like this before, but as I said, I am a physician, and I noticed your eyes and your neck, and I couldn't help but wonder that you have a thyroid problem." I was proud of myself for not using the term Graves' disease.

The attractive lady in the red sweater looked at the woman with her, who obviously was not privy to this information, and then up at me, making it clear that she was about to invoke superhuman strength in order to be barely polite.

"Well, thank you. Yes, I do know about my thyroid, and I was treated last year for it. Thank you again," she concluded, with a tone of voice and body language that said, "Could you please move away from this table immediately, before I call the manager?"

"How did that go?" my wife asked when I joined them outside the restaurant, feigning the remote possibility my conversation could have gone well.

"Well, she already knew about it, I guess," I responded. "She did thank me twice," I explained, "but all in all, I think it might have been a bad idea. I'm not sure that she had told the other lady at the table."

"Hmmm," replied my wife simply, in a tone of voice that made it unnecessary to add, "well, any idiot would have known that!"

Undaunted by this setback, I redoubled my commitment to my community. I decided my idea had been brilliantly conceived but poorly executed, and I kept my eyes open for a second opportunity to rescue a poor and unsuspecting soul with bulging eyes. *The next time you'll do better,* I figured.

Only two months later, at the same mall, while standing in the line to buy movie tickets, I turned around and saw another woman with a very prominent thyroid gland (to my great fortune, she happened to swallow just as I looked at her) and proptosis, those characteristic protuberant eyes. I was alone in line, buying tickets for my family, and did not have any more rational relatives to restrain me. She also appeared to be in line alone, but of course there were plenty of other people within earshot. There was no question she was actively hyperthyroid, with the glistening skin and fine tremor in her hands. After careful analysis of the options, I determined my plan of action.

She became aware of my staring at her eyes and smiled nicely in return. It was just a friendly "hello" smile, nothing more. After I had purchased my tickets, I laid in wait. She obtained hers and began to head back into the mall.

"Excuse me, Miss," I said, tapping her lightly on the shoulder from behind. She whirled surprisingly quickly. *Lightning reflexes*, I thought. *This has to be Graves' disease.* "I'm sorry to bother you, but I am a physician. I noticed when we were in line here that you may have some signs of a thyroid disorder."

"What did you say?" she responded rather quickly. I repeated my speech. "A thyroid disorder? No, I don't have a thyroid disorder!"

"Did your mother have any thyroid problems?" I tried, knowing that Graves' disease has a strong hereditary component. It occurred to me that my question about her mother might seem out of context to her, but it was too late.

"My mother is dead," she said, now angry. I began to have the sense I might be failing to fully communicate the Good Samaritan motives of my mission here. "Are you sure you're a doctor?" she added, confirming my suspicions. "You seem a bit young..."

"Well, yes I am, and I think it would be good for you to see a doctor to have this checked out."

"Let me get this straight. You are a doctor, and you're wandering around the mall trying to drum up business for your practice? Is that it?"

Of course, I was appalled at how she could have reached such a conclusion. In any case, we weren't making any progress on her thyroid problem.

"No, no," I blurted out. "I mean, yes, I am a doctor, and no, I'm not suggesting you see me in my practice. I was just thinking you might want to talk to your own doctor about your thyroid gland, that's all." *This isn't working. She's getting more angry with every word that I say.* "Listen, I'm sorry, I didn't mean..."

"Look, Mister," she barked. *Mister! You've never been called that before.* "Get out of here right now before I call the manager. Okay?"

Now red-faced, I spun around, gasping, "Sorry," as I turned and walked as quickly as possible in the opposite direction. Creating the maximum possible distance between the obviously hyperthyroid woman and me was now my singular mission, the Fleeing Samaritan.

"Sir. Sir!" a male voice cried from behind me, and I felt a hand on my shoulder. It was one of the ushers in the theater. "I need your ticket, Sir." I realized, in my embarrassed haste, I had scurried into the theater rather than out of it. After taking a moment to clarify my current position, I apologized, retreated back to the mall side of the ticket taker, and, after waiting a few minutes for the coast to clear, returned to meet my family for a quick bite to eat before we all went to see the movie.

Having waited for the woman with the goiter while she bought her tickets, I happened to know that she would be seeing the same movie at the same time as my family. I timed our family's arrival to occur in the midst of the opening credits, we sat in the back row of the theater where no sclerae or thyroid glands were visible to me, and exited quickly as the credits began to roll.

I now affectionately refer to these encounters as my personal "Mind Your Own Business" lessons. They have saved me from innumerable additional episodes of humiliation. I have come to learn that minding one's own business, no matter how sore the temptation to do otherwise, applies in all walks of life, and not just in the across the room diagnosis of disease. Yes, I still find people in malls and restaurants with Graves' disease, past or present. Each time, I say a little prayer that they either have already received, or will receive soon, the care that they need.

CHAPTER 24

"It is better to keep your mouth shut and appear stupid than to open it and remove all doubt."

Mark Twain (1835 - 1910), American humorist, writer and lecturer

The small hospital where I pulled those twenty-four-hour emergency room shifts was located within a few miles of a State prison, which provided the fortunate staffing physician with the occasional opportunity to provide emergency care to its residents. Inmates would arrive under heavy guard, with hands and feet cuffed. By "heavy guard," I mean to say there were two guards per prisoner, each guard at least twice my weight.

The prisoner code of silence is held far more seriously than, well, the one often taken by adolescent boys in trouble. One of the very first inmates I provided care for was a thirty-five year old male who came in at about 10:00 p.m., under the above described escort, bristling mad and highly uncooperative. I must confess that I always have a deep curiosity about the reason for incarceration, although I know each time it makes absolutely no difference in the medical treatment I will ultimately provide. Is it morbid curiosity only? Self-protection? Just plain nosiness? I'll probably never know. It does seem like the first thing everyone wants to know when the subject of a prisoner comes up, though. Despite knowing my purpose was solely to satisfy my own curiosity, I pulled a guard aside, and determined this particular patient was imprisoned for second-degree murder.

"Well. Mr. Tiews," I began carefully, wanting to make a good impression, or at least avoid a really bad impression, in case parole was ever an option for this man. "What brings you in tonight?"   *Too cheery, David. Tone it down.*

The patient glared at me defiantly. He was built like a fullback, all muscle from what I guessed were daily weightlifting sessions at the prison, and was about five feet nine inches tall, weighing in at 195. He had dark hair cut about one-eighth of an inch in length, with a five o'clock shadow that had to be three days old. Other than breathing rapidly, he looked fairly stable from a medical viewpoint, and he was not in much distress. I began to feel a vague sense he was not planning to share any of his medical history with me.

"Mr. Tiews, in order to help you, I need a bit of information about how you are feeling here." *Too soft, David.* "Can you tell me what is bothering you, please?"

The continual glare. Rapid breathing. Nothing more. Meanwhile, the guards are glancing at each other and smiling.

"You seem to be breathing a bit fast. Are you feeling short of breath?"

More glare. Every muscle in his body seemed tense, as though he was about to spring at me. I could feel the cold sweat on the back of my neck.

"Have you had a cough or fever or…"

"Doc," one of the guards piped in, "I think you might assume our Mr. Tiews here won't be providing you with any information. We did bring his medical file from the prison if you'd like to review it. You also should take a look at his shirt, right here."

Looking closely at his prison uniform, in the direction indicated by the guard's pointing finger, I saw a small tear, which couldn't have been more than a quarter of an inch long.

A tear in his shirt? They couldn't possibly be bringing him here for this, could they? Just then, I noticed a small tinge of blood soaked into one end of the tear.

"I need to pull your shirt up, okay?"

No response.

The guards didn't seem pleased to have made this trip to the emergency room, and they were unwilling to unfasten the handcuffs to allow complete removal of the inmate's shirt.

Maybe that's for the best, what with him committing second-degree murder and all, I thought, as I pulled up the back of his shirt on the right side to look under the hole. There was a small, clean cut in the back of his chest wall, just exactly the size of the tear in the shirt. Nothing more. Still confused, I looked up at the guards.

"There was a knife fight tonight. John here was tagged. We brought him in because of his breathing," the guard explained, speaking as though he hoped to increase my current speed of diagnostic efforts.

I put my ear next to the wound. "Can you please take a deep breath, Mr. Tiews?" I half pleaded, wishing for just a morsel of cooperation. Apparently, my patient was not currently inclined toward deep breathing. In any case, there did not seem to be any sound of air flowing in or out of this tiny cut.

I began to percuss, or tap, the back of his chest, trying to sense a difference between the two sides. There was none. Next, with my stethoscope, I listened carefully, noting the breath sounds in the lung beneath the stab wound were much softer than the opposite side. I finished my examination, sent him off for a chest x-ray, and reviewed his prison record, which added no additional helpful information.

The chest x-ray showed what I expected: a collapsed right lung from the prison stab wound. Returning to the bedside with the x-ray in hand, I held it up to the light and showed him the fifty percent collapse of his lung. Through the back of my skull, I could feel the guards rolling their eyes at my attempts at patient education. I pressed on.

"This is the reason you are feeling short of breath. You're working off of only one lung instead of two. We will have to insert a tube into your lung to provide suction to re-expand it back to normal."

"Will I have to stay here at the hospital?" he asked, now apparently sufficiently interested in the discussion and his disposition after treatment to honor us with his gift of speech. He sounded neither angry nor curious. It was impossible to determine the underlying tone of his question, and it would be the only time I would hear his voice.

After confirming with the guards the prison's inability to manage a patient with a chest tube, I told my patient he would likely spend several nights in our facility. He seemed pleased; there was more eye-rolling from the guards. I pondered how I might convince him of the need for his complete cooperation during the procedure ahead. When the time came, though, the incentive to spend a few nights out from under the prison roof was sufficient to buy his total collaboration.

His breathing rate slowed, and I could see the muscles in his neck relax once the tube was inserted and connected to the suction machine, which removed the excess air in his chest and allowed the lung to expand fully.

As the two heavy guards backed the gurney out of the curtained treatment area, Mr. Tiews looked me in the eye, and gave a barely perceptible nod that I took to mean, "Thank you, Doctor." *And maybe also, "Don't worry, I won't track you down and kill you if I am ever released from prison." Maybe not.*

While I never would be able to discern who had held the knife that provided Mr. Tiews with his "hospital vacation," it only occurred to me at the end of my twenty-four hour shift that one of the heavy guards might have been the culprit. Not that my patient would have been more forthcoming without his guards present, based on my experience with other prisoners I saw in this emergency room. It seemed there was another system of justice at work at the prison, invisible to the outside world, impervious to the probing questions of a young moonlighting physician.

Albert Einstein once said, "If A is a success in life, then A = x + y + z. Work is x, y is play, and z is keeping your mouth shut." For one who has suffered, and continues to suffer, from speaking too much, too quickly, there is probably something important for me to learn from Mr. Tiews and his impenetrable silence.

CHAPTER 25

"At the core of all anger is a need that is not being fulfilled."

Marshall B. Rosenberg (1934 -), American psychologist and writer

"Now, this one is Dr. Randolph. I don't know how to say this any other way, but, I have a really bad feeling every time I go into his room," Mark cautiously confessed, as he passed the last of his three-by-five-inch inpatient note cards to me at our Monday morning check-out rounds.

It was always the same privilege to have Mark hand the hospital service over to me. He was meticulous to a fault in his care of patients, and he generally planned the care of those he was unable to send home with such unerring detail that they virtually discharged themselves from the hospital one to five days later. There were sixteen inpatients plus ten consult patients, and twenty-five of the twenty-six of them were truly on "auto-pilot," a term Mark had popularized during our residency training, having himself perfectly set each of their controls to fly them home soon. *But Mark always saves the best for last*, I thought.

"But, as you know," he said, looking at me over his frameless glasses with more than a hint of self-mockery, "I always save the best for last! Dr. Randolph is a thirty-two-year-old male associate professor in infectious disease at the university, who was admitted for recurrent, unexplained anemia." He used the formulaic, fully descriptive, one-sentence summary of the patient used by the best physicians to begin their presentation of a case.

I reflected on my luck in landing my position in this practice with Mark over two years ago. The consummate professional, Mark was an extremely hard worker and held himself to the highest standards of clinical care. Joining him, I had been guaranteed a large panel of patients, the overflow of people who could not obtain an appointment with Mark; his schedule was full. After several years together, we began to see what we believed was one of the most positive signs of success: doctors began referring their family members, and sometimes even themselves, to us for care. Being a "doctor's doctor" is considered the ultimate compliment within the ranks of medicine.

So when Mark mentioned the new physician under our care in the hospital, I smiled. *I wonder how he found us?* I thought, waiting for a moment to ask.

"Jim referred him to us. Told him he should check us out, since no one at 'the U' could figure out what is wrong with him." Mark and I had worked so closely together we could answer many of each other's questions before they were asked. "Jim" was the head of the infectious disease department at our nearby, highly esteemed, University of Michigan Medical School, which had been our alma mater as well. He was an incredibly bright teacher with a delightful sense of humor that made learning fun; we loved him dearly. In my nine years in medicine, I had never heard of a medical school professor seeking care at our local community hospital. Buoyed by the certainty their academic institution provided the "best care in America," and absent any actual data capable of refuting (or supporting) such a claim, it would have been a form of academic treason to break ranks and come to our local private hospital. Only eight years ago, the hospitals were just across the street from one another, and competition had been quite intense. Then, when our community hospital facility was rebuilt in spacious river-vista countryside, where patients could, contrary to prevailing unwritten healthcare regulations, find a parking spot, this competition heightened even further. Jim, being more practical than most, and honestly more interested in his faculty member's well-being than internecine squabbles, didn't hesitate to recommend Mark for a second opinion. Or third, fourth, or fifth opinion, whatever it was by then.

"What an incredible honor," I suggested, to which Mark pulled his glasses to the very tip of his nose in order to provide me with an unimpeded view of a gold medal display of eye rolling.

"Just wait until you hear the rest of this," he cautioned, and he returned his glasses to the point on his nose, where he could again refer to his notes on the card.

"Six months ago, he was hospitalized for a spontaneous right knee joint infection with *Staph* sepsis. No trauma." An unusual and quite serious problem with no obvious inciting event, this infection had spread to his blood stream. "*Staph*" – or *Staphylococcus aureus* – is a very bad bug and can be quite difficult to treat. "No initial response to IV antibiotics. He received methicillin directly into the knee joint, and intravenously, for the next four months. Knee cultures are now negative. He's still complaining of severe knee pain."

This sounds ominous, I thought. *A serious infection in an infectious disease specialist?*

"Who was it who said that doctors always contract the diseases of their own specialty?" I asked, hoping to lighten the mood a bit. According to the old saw, the cardiologist would die of a heart attack, a kidney specialist would have urinary tract stones, an endocrinologist would develop some rare glandular disease, and so on, even down to the oncologist. It was the medical equivalent of the urban legend, devoid of any scientific data or research.

Completely ignoring my efforts to cheer him, he pressed on. "He was in the hospital for a different reason this time. This is his third episode of serious anemia." He had very low red blood cell count. "He's had a complete workup for his anemia. Three workups, in fact."

The causes of anemia are legion. The differential diagnosis for anemia is longer than for every other symptom, physical finding, or lab test, with the possible exception of "fatigue." Internal medicine specialists have a time-honored algorithm of sequential testing to narrow down the possible causes of a low number of red blood cells in a systematic way. For example, seven percent of people receiving methicillin will develop an adverse blood reaction, but this involves the white blood cells, and Dr. Randolph was losing red cells. His blood tests had found him to be deficient in iron, which led to many other appropriate tests, each searching for a source of internal bleeding. Human blood is very rich in iron. When a patient loses blood, he loses iron faster than the normal diet can replace it. Speaking of which, he was a strict vegetarian and ate no meat.

"Vegetarians can develop iron deficiency, can't they?" I was interrupting with the intention of being helpful. Really.

"Yes, we thought of that," he snapped, an unusual reaction for Mark. He clearly was taking this case very personally. "But he has been also getting oral and intramuscular iron for the past several months. His blood counts keep dropping." He went on to list the nearly innumerable tests that he had undergone in the failed attempt to diagnose his problem: upper GI, lower GI, small bowel follow-through (x-ray studies in which the patient swallows a chalky solution of barium to highlight the gastrointestinal tract), gastroscopy, colonoscopy (scopes passed into the GI tract from above and below to directly visualize possible lesions), urinalysis, intravenous pyelogram (study of the kidneys using injected dye), iron absorption test, abdominal CT scan, even a bone marrow biopsy (to look at the source of the production of blood cells).

"What about a radioactive-tagged RBC tracer scan?" I proposed. I was suggesting a relatively new test (at that time) in which a patient who is presumed to be bleeding internally has his or her own red blood cells radioactively treated, and then reinjected into their bloodstream. While somewhat non-specific, some minutes or hours later, a few of these (only temporarily) radioactive cells find their way to the problem spot, and a fuzzy glow may be observed somewhere within the abdomen by the scanning camera, in the general location of the source of the bleeding. I had seen another patient with a very rare small bowel tumor diagnosed in this way only two months earlier. Interested, I went down to the nuclear medicine department to review the films. All I could see was a faint glow resembling an iridescent ball of lint.

"This is a diagnostic test?" I moaned to the radiologist. "This fuzz ball here is a tumor? You must be kidding me!"

"Call me after the surgery," he said, undaunted, "just to let me know what you find."

For some reason, I never found the time to tell him the surgeon found a rare, small intestinal tumor in the precise spot the scan had suggested.

The look over Mark's glasses returned, but this time the mockery was aimed my way.

"Already ordered," he patiently sighed. "He'll go right down to nuclear medicine the next time his blood count drops."

"You seem frustrated about this," I offered, thinking there might be a better way for me to approach this case with Mark.

"I am frustrated. How many times are the doctors over at the university going to refer a patient to us?" It was a rhetorical question; the answer was almost never. "We just have to figure this one out. It's a matter of professional pride!" His voice had the same tone as one of those desperate intercessory prayers that begins with, "God, if you'll just grant this one request, I promise that I will…"

I too looked on this case as a challenge. "I'll stop by tonight and read his whole chart, Mark. I'm guessing that the tracer scan will give us the answer, though. He probably has a small bowel tumor." I rose from my chair to see my patient scheduled at 8:00 this morning in the office.

"Um, David. Just one more thing," Mark said with a rather cautious tone in his voice. "This gentleman doesn't get along with anyone. I mean *anyone*. It is unusual for me to dislike a patient, but I really have a problem with this man."

I was stunned. Mark had never, in the ten years I had known him, expressed a negative personal sentiment about any patient.

"So, just take a deep breath and try not to take him too personally. Okay?"

"Sure, Mark, I can do that," I replied, despite being nearly certain that if he couldn't do it, there wasn't an ounce of hope for me.

It was a wonderful day seeing patients in the office. For me, a wonderful day generally meant I had made an unusual diagnosis, found something quite significant that could change a patient's life for the better, someone deeply thanked me for my care for them, or, more simply, most of my patients were either getting better or at least we had stabilized their medical problems. This was a day when all of these things occurred, and as I drove to the hospital, I was positively euphoric about the incredible honor and privilege of serving as a physician. Added to these warm feelings, the crisp late-fall air energized me as I walked into the hospital.

Things suddenly changed when I walked into Dr. Randolph's room. There was a home-made "Do Not Disturb!!!!!!!!" sign that was not official hospital ordinance; there were eight exclamation points, and I figured I had been duly warned. But his door was half open, and I knocked as I walked in. There on the bed was a tall, far-too-thin, obviously uncomfortable, grimacing man with very short brown hair and green eyes. He was fully engrossed in a television news report and did not seem to notice my entrance. I made my move for the remote control unit on his bed.

"Do you mind if I turn off…"

"Yes, I do," he replied quickly, and he snatched the device with his right hand before I could touch it.

While I am aware that the human ability to shoot laser beams from one's eyes is present only in comic books — and is not the result or purpose of laser eye surgery, as the grandson of one of my patient's once thought — I could feel the burning sensation in the center of my chest, where his gaze was directed, shortly after I sat down.

"Hello, Dr. Randolph, I'm Dr. Rob – "

"Shhh!" he hissed loudly. "I'm watching this."

On the screen, the news announcer was reporting the invasion of Grenada earlier that day. According to the report we were watching, President Reagan ordered the invasion to protect an American medical school there.

"Where is Grenada?" I asked aloud.

"In the Caribbean," Dr. Randolph growled, with even greater contempt, just as a map of the East Indies appeared on television with a blinking arrow to highlight the island in question. "See?"

"We have a medical school in Grenada?" I asked, apparently having learned nothing from our interaction this far.

"Of course we do! Where have you been all day?"

"Seeing patients," I offered, apparently not to his satisfaction. As he watched the rest of the report, I carefully studied him for any possible clue to this diagnostic mystery. He had large-gauge intravenous lines in both arms, and an even larger bore central line dressing over his right collarbone. *Probably still there from the months of intravenous antibiotics.* Physicians often place such a large line in patients needing long-term intravenous therapy, as the multiple daily doses of antibiotics or other drugs can cause damage and pain to peripheral veins. These days, the device is called a port.

There was also a large scar on his neck that looked more like a knife wound than anything resulting from a medical procedure. *Ask about that tomorrow. Not a good subject for the first meeting, particularly if it is a stab wound.* The only other noteworthy observation was that there was simply nothing else in the room. Typically, patients who have been in the hospital for nine days, as he had been, accumulate a wide assortment of get well cards, flowers, stuffed animals, books and magazines to read, and crayon drawings from younger relatives. This room looked as though he had been admitted to it ten minutes before I walked in.

Finally, a commercial appeared on the tube, and he turned to me slowly, as if to signal that a brief audience had now been granted. I introduced myself again, slowly and politely, mentioned we were all puzzled by his problem, and explained I had come over that night to see him in order to get a head start on helping him. I then asked if he would mind if I just asked him a few questions.

"Well, that's the third one today, isn't it?" he shot back. Breathing deeply to try and calm myself, I decided to take his response as permission to proceed.

"I'm sure that everything that I ask you will have been asked before, given your extensive workup, but there just might be one thing we come up with together that no one has thought of so far," I offered by way of advance empathy. "Do you mind if we try reviewing your history again?" To put it mildly, he was not at all receptive.

"You are the thirty-seventh doctor I've seen in the past six months," he announced.

He's keeping a record, I thought. *Very meticulous. Also, thirty-seven is a prime number.* I have no idea why the last part popped into my mind. It just did. I have a very mathematical mind, I guess.

"None of you will ever figure out what is wrong with me, will you?" he continued, building up steam. While his words can be read on paper as a challenge, they clearly sounded like a threat. *Like a death threat?* I wondered, although it would be ten more years before I would actually receive one of those.

Despite the hair rising on the back of my neck, my only acceptable choice was to press on. "Well, part of the benefit of having a new doctor round on you each week is that…"

"So you're thinking that as physician number thirty-seven you're going to be the one who has the stroke of genius, are you? You know I've been admitted to the university twice already, right?" He pronounced the word "university" much like one might pronounce the word "God" when particularly awestruck by one's divine being.

"No. I mean, yes." I was completely tongue-tied. "Listen, I'm sorry. I am here because I'm trying to help. I'd like to…"

"Help! Help? Like this, you mean?" he interrupted, and then he dramatically threw the bed sheet off his legs. The sheet sailed towards me but fell to the ground without covering me and revealed a tangled mass of scar tissue around his right knee.

I took a deep breath. *David, you have about thirty more seconds in here until you explode. This man is pushing every one of your buttons. Why is he so angry?* Such flashes of insight were very rare for me back in those days, and they usually only came with extremes of emotions, such as those I was currently experiencing. *Maybe you should just shut up.* This seemed like a promising strategy, particularly since I couldn't think of a single potentially helpful word to say.

He sat staring, boring now nearly visible narrow beams of red laser light into my chest, waiting for me to return his volley.

One. Two. Three. Four. Take another deep breath. Five. Six. This will never work. Seven. Eight. Nine. Ten. Now we're in a staring contest. Thirteen. Fourteen. Fifteen… No, wait, I skipped some numbers. My mind could divine no better approach to him. Clearly, anything I did or said would be quickly countered by additional rage. Even being quiet would be answered by a darker silence. After my long pause, he slowly turned his head away. It appeared that the audience was over.

"Well, Dr. Randolph. I'll see you in the morning," I said as I rose from my chair, offering as much kindness as was possible under the circumstances. "Goodbye." He did not return my parting word, and I drove home wondering that evening whether the anger I was feeling was coming from inside myself or from him.

CHAPTER 26

"The doctor who treats himself has a fool for a patient."

*Sir William Osler (1849-1919), Canadian physician,
considered the father of modern medicine, from* Oslerisms,
an unpublished collection of Sir William Osler's
bedside epigrams, *1903-5, by R. Bennett Bean*

On Tuesday morning, I saved Dr. Randolph for my last patient, *hoping to build some momentum by seeing the nicer patients first*, I thought to myself, instead of simply acknowledging my obvious fear and procrastination. I saw another one of my former teachers and mentors, Dr. Roger Stanley, retreating from Dr. Randolph's room like a soldier escaping an overwhelming line of fire. Dr. Stanley had also been my residency program director for the latter half of my training. He was a brilliant gastroenterologist in a group of three exceptionally good GI specialists. Roger and I often ended up on the same seven-day on-call rotations and spent identical weeks in the hospital.

"Greetings, David," he chirped as I approached him. Then his head fell, and he looked back over his shoulder towards our mutual patient's room in a slow motion double take. Shaking his head, he confessed, "I don't think I have ever felt this uncomfortable with a patient in my entire medical career."

"I know exactly what you mean," I agreed. "It's not easy being doctor number thirty-eight, is it, Roger?"

"Actually, I'm apparently number thirty-nine," he responded crisply. I had never seen him this exasperated.

"I was speechless after only one minute with him yesterday," I offered by way of condolence.

Roger shot me a quick and surprised glance. I had been anything but speechless for my entire time in his training program. "Well," Roger had said to me at the end of a short and particularly confrontational private meeting during my third and last year of residency training under his tutelage, "at least I never have to wonder what you're thinking, David."

"You know," he began rather thoughtfully. "We really need to pay attention to how we are feeling here. My hunch is that it's a clue to the diagnosis." Being generally suspicious of the concept of "feelings," and more than slightly contemptuous of the Morris Albert song by the same name, I let his remark pass.

At that moment, the floor internal medicine resident walked briskly down the hall waving a yellow lab report slip.

"His hemoglobin (red blood cell count) is down from 10.3 to 8.1 in just twelve hours," he reported. (A normal value in a non-anemic patient would have been above 14.5.) In other words, Dr. Randolph had lost about two pints of blood overnight. The three of us immediately agreed, per the existing diagnostic plan, that he needed the tagged RBC scan immediately. The resident, as puzzled as the rest of us and eager to make the diagnosis, didn't even bother to call someone to transport our patient downstairs. He went into the room and simply wheeled Dr. Randolph to the nuclear medicine department himself.

"I think I know what the scan will show," Roger said somewhat cryptically.

"What? A small bowel source of bleeding? A tumor?" I asked.

"No. I think it will be negative." He paused, as if to weigh the alternatives of speaking and silence. "Listen, after he's done with the scan, don't bring him back to this room. Let's move him into any available ICU bed we've got."

"Are you worried that this will be a really significant bleed?" I asked, pressing to understand his logic. In my opinion, Dr. Randolph really didn't seem unstable enough to warrant one of our scarce ICU beds, even with his existing anemia and additional bleeding this morning. He would be transfused two units of blood that afternoon, which could easily be accomplished on the general medical floor.

"No, not exactly. But I think he bears close observation. Very close observation." He spoke the last phrase as though talking to himself.

"For what?" I asked, sensing he was on to something important but uncertain what it was.

"It's just a theory at this point, and I'd rather not share my thoughts just yet." Roger was an unusually private person, and while his reserved approach to this conversation was somewhat unconventional for medical circles, it was in keeping with his character. He had once told me, "I try to never say anything about anyone I wouldn't say if they were right in front of me." My best guess was that he was thinking something very negative about the patient, and he didn't want to say it until he was more certain. He was always very principled in this way, and I respected him for this. Roger walked into the adjacent room to see his next patient, while I headed down to the nuclear medicine department.

Timidly approaching Dr. Randolph in the lab as he rested on his back under the scanning camera, I politely let him know our plan to transfer him to an intensive care unit bed, since he had another significant episode of blood loss.

"We are very concerned about you," I cautiously continued, "particularly since we still don't know the source of your bleeding."

"You and forty other doctors," he countered, glancing at the radiologist sitting there in the room, to make it clear his ongoing list was growing.

The radiologist glared at the patient and then shot me a look, as if to say, "This is exactly why I went into radiology, so I don't have to deal with this!"

Looking at the camera above our patient, I noted no particular "fuzzy spot" on the screen above him that might indicate a source of bleeding. I was no radiologist, though.

"Well, Dr. Randolph, I'll see you tonight around five-thirty, and we can talk some more," I concluded, retreating quickly to avoid my patient's final grenade. But the radiologist had cut off my exit.

"Say," he drawled slowly. "what ever happened to that other patient of yours, a few months ago, with the positive tagged RBC scan?" I was surrounded; there was no avenue of painless escape.

"Oh, gosh. I'm sorry I didn't get back to you. She had a bleeding small bowel carcinoid tumor. Extraordinarily rare," I sputtered, as matter-of-factly as I could muster.

While enough of a gentleman to refrain from actually speaking the words, "I told you so," he couldn't resist an exaggerated raising of his eyebrows and the prolonged sing-song release of a deep, sarcastic, "Hmmm!" as if to say, "Well, who would have ever expected that?" At this point in my day, a quick "I told you so" would have felt less demoralizing.

"By the way," he added, staring over my shoulder at the camera display as I squeezed past him, "this scan will likely be negative. You'll have the final report in six hours, after we repeat the scan this afternoon."

The tagged red blood cell study report was officially negative; no source of bleeding was found. When I returned from the office late the same afternoon to the coronary care unit, the location of the only remaining available intensive care unit bed in our busy hospital, the door was closed, and the six shades covering the glass windows, which formed the full wall facing the nursing station, were fully drawn. I knocked and waited for a response. None was forthcoming.

I knocked again. I had a technical problem here. In a standard hospital room, there is a door to the adjoining bathroom that the patient may close to maintain privacy. However, in the ICU setting, there is just a wall-mounted commode on the far side of the bed. I did not want to compound my relationship difficulties with Dr. Randolph by barging in on him at an inopportune moment.

After another fifteen seconds, he shouted, "Come in."

Hmmm. Up until now, you didn't realize it was possible to say "Come in" in a sarcastic way, did you, David?

I opened the door. The room was almost pitch black, illuminated only by a single narrow shaft of light sneaking past a ragged edge of one of the shades.

You've never been in a patient room this dark. Is this another clue? I have generally found rare, highly improbable, or first time events to bear greater significance than normally attributed to them by others. There were plenty of each type of clue in this case. I just couldn't yet add them all together.

"Sorry," he began, "I didn't hear you knock the first time."

Not really hearing his comment, and wanting a little light, I asked, "Would you like me to turn on…"

"No. I like being in the dark. Don't you?" I was unable to see his face well enough to confirm beyond a reasonable doubt that I was being insulted. *The odds are good, though.*

"The tagged RBC scan…" I began, hoping to fill him in on his test results.

"Was negative. I heard. The nurse told me an hour ago. Any other news?" If sarcasm had the physical properties of a liquid, I knew my white coat would be drenched in it.

"No," I said, repressing a whole menagerie of wild animal emotions. "Do you have any?" I realized I was biting my tongue. Literally. I could taste the blood.

"Nope!"

"I do need to briefly examine you," I said, and I performed the physical examination I hadn't had the opportunity to do earlier in the day. I found nothing new. It was too dark to check the scar on his neck more closely. I was certain I could feel him smirking in the dark.

Utterly defeated, I stepped back from the bed, looking for some deeper inspiration.

"Bye," he offered.

Maybe that's your inspiration, David. "I'll see you tomorrow," I said, struggling to speak in a civil tone, and I slunk from the room, understanding for the first time the true meaning of the verb "to slink."

I stopped at our office on my way home from the hospital to pick up a medical textbook, hoping to find an important needle in its 1,800 page haystack. As I walked into the building from the parking lot, I saw Mark driving out. He pulled over, stopped his car, and rolled down the driver's window. He was far too cheery for my prevailing mood.

"How's Dr. Randolph?" he chortled.

I simply pulled down my sunglasses to the tip of my nose and glared at him over the top of them with as stern of a "Mark Edwards" expression I could contrive, followed by his characteristically exaggerated eye-roll.

"Okay, okay, I get it," he said, amused. Knowing there would be no possibility of consoling me now, he sped off.

After repeatedly opening the textbook to random pages in futile hope of finding inspiration, I settled down for my most fitful night's sleep in the previous twelve months, despite not getting a single call from the answering service. Before dawn, I dragged myself out of bed and lumbered clumsily toward the shower, distracted, and thinking I was simply tiptoeing into the bathroom. I had awakened my wife, who seemed to think I had fallen.

She asked, "Are you all right?"

"Not exactly," I responded, "but I'll be fine. Eventually."

In the shower, I pondered this perplexing case. Next to waking up in the middle of the night with the answer to a vexing problem, for unexplained reasons this very shower was my most reliable problem solving locale.

What is the source of his bleeding? I asked myself, and then I closed my eyes and waited for an answer. *What is the source of his bleeding? What is the source of his bleeding? What is the source of his bleeding?* It was turning into a mantra. The wrong mantra. *The wrong mantra? Yes. Dr. Randolph isn't bleeding from somewhere or something; his problem is this: he's losing blood.*

Sometimes, if I can carry on these internal dialogues long enough, both voices eventually become confused. I had no idea what this conversation meant, since bleeding and losing blood seemed identical to me at the time, but I knew it was true. I felt refreshed. I now possessed the answer. I was confident: it's only a matter of time until I understand it.

On the fourteenth step of the first flight of stairs in the stairway closest to the physician's entrance to the hospital, on my way to the coronary care unit, it came to me. *His central intravenous line.* Everything fell into place after that: the hostile personality, the recurrent episodes of sudden blood loss, the dark room, the forty doctors who couldn't make a diagnosis, Roger's impression the patient needed close observation. It even occurred to me, only then, that the phrase, "I didn't hear you knock the first time," was a lie, unless the speaker had been informed of such a knock, which, I now remembered, he had not been.

Almost running, I popped the wall-mounted, six-inch silver button to activate the CCU automatic doors with my open palm. I found Roger Stanley standing outside Dr. Randolph's room, talking to the night nurse, nodding and smiling. He seemed particularly happy to see me.

"Greetings!" he whispered, and then he paused for what I assumed to be effect. "We have the diagnosis."

I started to speak, but he silenced me with an upturned finger in front of his mouth and a sideways glance toward our patient's door, reminding me he was potentially within earshot.

"Let's go into the conference room." Once behind closed doors, he continued, "Yesterday, I could tell there was something terribly wrong about this whole situation. I just knew it. Here we have an accomplished doctor who seems to be reveling in our failure to diagnose him. I felt like his opponent. The thought just kept nagging at me. The more I thought about it, the more certain I became. I'm sorry that I didn't share this with you yesterday, but I didn't want to slander this unfortunate man in the event I was wrong about him."

I tried to interrupt him, but he held up his hand. He was really enjoying this.

"So," he continued, "I talked with the night nurse last night, at 11:00 p.m. I asked her to 'accidentally' leave a 50 cc syringe with a 14 gauge needle on top of the small sink in his room." He was talking about a huge needle and syringe, the biggest the hospital had in stock.

Unable to restrain myself, possibly because of some deep competitive compulsion, I blurted out, "It was the central line, wasn't it?"

He looked at me as though he was Hercule Poirot, carefully explaining to a roomful of suspects his meticulously crafted conclusions regarding the identity of the murderer, and I was the butler who had stormed into the room, shouting out the killer's name four pages too early!

After a brief moment of deflation, he collected himself and pressed onward.

"Just let me finish here, David."

Be quiet, David, let Roger tell his story first.

"So anyway," Roger resumed, "I asked her to let our patient know at about midnight that he probably really needed sleep and that she wouldn't be bothering him until morning. Of course, if he needed help, he could press the call button. Somehow, she also persuaded Dr. Randolph to keep the emergency light on above his bed. She told him it was a hospital code violation to have all of the lights out in a room in the ICU. Brilliant." I sat there nodding after each sentence, knowing exactly where this story would end.

By now, perhaps because of my feigned patience, he seemed resigned to share the credit for our joint discovery.

"You figured it out too, didn't you?" he finally asked.

"Well, yes, but about twenty-four hours after you did. The diagnostic test was ordered by you, Roger."

We both understood my reference to "the diagnostic test was ordered." In the *New England Journal of Medicine*, interesting and challenging cases are often presented by young doctors in training to medical school faculty experts. The history, often pages long, describes in excruciating detail the patient's presenting symptoms, other medical history details, physical examination findings, preliminary lab results, and imaging studies, which, when summed together, narrow the possibilities for the patient's diagnosis down from hundreds to maybe dozens. Following that, the resident is usually transcribed as announcing, "A diagnostic test was ordered." I always imagine a gong sounding in the distance when I read those words, the musical cue that the portals of truth were about to open.

The resident then yields the podium to the esteemed faculty professor, who walks her physician audience sitting there in grand rounds, and the journal's readers, through each of the remaining diagnostic possibilities, elucidating the pros and cons of each, and ending with her opinion as to the nature of the mystery test and its results. More often than not, the professor's diagnosis is correct, or at least somewhere in the infield, usually within a short bunt of home plate.

Roger smiled warmly. "The diagnostic test in this case was the nurse standing in the hallway, spying on the patient through the tear in the edge of the curtain." He was beaming. Rightly so; it was a brilliant diagnosis on his part. I wished I had a gong.

"And the result of the test," I picked up, not missing a beat, "was the nurse's observation of our patient withdrawing multiple syringes full of blood from his central line and flushing it down the toilet!"

"Well, actually, it was the sink," he said, always a stickler for perfect accuracy. "When you go into the room, stand on the far side of the bed, right next to it. You can see a bit of blood on the side of the drain plug." If he had a pipe, I'm sure he would have taken a long, Sherlock Holmes-like draw on it.

"Did you tell him you knew what he was doing? I asked quickly, with mixed emotions.

"No, of course not, David. I am a gastroenterologist. I am now telling you that I am certain that he does not have a GI problem. That's really all I have to offer here."

It was clear now, from his perspective anyway, that the small sacrifice of sharing this diagnostic victory with me was more than offset by my singular responsibility to explain our final opinion to Dr. Randolph. As we both were acutely aware, this would be no easy denouement.

"Roger, are you also thinking what I'm thinking about his right knee? He actually injected *Staph aureus* into it himself, six months ago? An infectious disease physician's unique version of Münchausen syndrome?"

In this unusual psychiatric disorder, the affected patient either magnifies symptoms or actually creates illnesses in themselves in order to gain medical testing and treatments, attention, comfort, and/or sympathy from medical personnel. In 1951, Richard Asher was the first to describe this pattern of self-harm, where individuals falsified histories, signs, and symptoms of illness. Remembering Baron von Münchausen (1720-1779), who purportedly fabricated fantastic stories about his own exploits, Asher named this condition Münchausen's syndrome in his original case report in *The Lancet*, a prominent British medical journal.

"Nope. Didn't think of that. Not my field. Good idea, though, David. Nice work!"

And then he was gone, leaving me to my solitary journey back to Dr. Randolph, to tell him in a genuine and compassionate manner, and without the slightest trace of irony or sarcasm, doctors thirty-seven and thirty-nine had finally discovered the source of his problem.

CHAPTER 27

"Did you ever hear of a kid playing accountant,
even if they wanted to be one?"

Jackie Mason (1936 -), American stand-up comedian

This was going to be an experiment. As the final chapter of my adolescence, I had made a clean financial break from my family, paying my own way through medical school. "My own way" was in large part a misnomer, since one can only borrow one's way through a medical education; nonetheless, I had managed complete financial independence from my parents through available loan programs and working at least part-time through most of my graduate education.

My wife and I were in the process of building a new house, the first we would own, I had managed to take on increasing levels of commitment in every aspect of my life, and I was now feeling overcommitted and overwhelmed. The practice and the home construction project would have been more than enough to occupy all of my waking moments, but I had also involved myself, usually through the encouragement of others, in the medical staff organization at our hospital and church leadership activities. My three small children were becoming increasingly interested in spending time with their father, whom they primarily encountered on the rare weekends I was neither on call for the practice nor moonlighting in the emergency room.

My father and I had never had the sort of relationship where I asked for, or he provided me, advice on a more than once-every-ten-years basis. Given my frustration with my packed schedule of activities, and the resulting chronic exhaustion, I finally came to a point of desperation: I would ask my father for his perspective. He had always been very busy when I was growing up, with multiple work commitments and community and social activities. We could have been the subject of the song, "Cat's in the Cradle," by Harry Chapin. He had even been the president of the school board during my senior year in high school, and I figured he could likely shed some light on my predicament, given the commonality of our DNA and our mutual decisions to create exceedingly busy lives. As it turned out, he did.

In late November, I took him to lunch before a Saturday college football game he and my mother had come into town to attend. Despite being over thirty years old, I felt nervous about this whole concept of asking for advice, and even more so given it was from my father. In fact, it wasn't until the waiter brought the check, and I picked it up, that I said, "Dad, I need some advice."

I explained to him all the various commitments I had, their ability to consume my every waking hour, and the exhaustion I felt at the end of every day as I attempted to fit thirty hours of activities into each twenty-four hour period. He didn't interrupt and simply listened to all I had to say. Eventually, I had talked myself out. I ended with a question.

"Dad, how did you manage all of your commitments when I was growing up? You were always very busy, always had a lot going on. How did you do it?"

After a short pause, he leaned back a bit in his chair, put his hands on the armrests, looked directly at me, and said, "Well, I guess I always figured if I needed something to work out the right way, I had to take charge of it myself. I could never figure out any other way to do it."

I waited for a full minute for his follow-up comments, his exposition on his own learning, and how he finally managed to balance his life, but nothing more was forthcoming.

Well, I reasoned, *this doesn't help me much with solving my problem, but it sure does make it clear how I have maneuvered myself into my current predicament.* We did have nearly the same DNA.

Our practice business meeting with Paul Schurz fell between Christmas and New Year's Day that same year. It had now been three and one-half years since Mark had incorporated the practice and thirty months since I had joined him. Paul arrived, as always, fifteen minutes early for the meeting. He would talk with the front desk staff to assess how our collection efforts were proceeding, while Mark and I attempted to finish up with our last patients in order to attend this important year-end business discussion.

By now, Paul's attire had become a continual source of mirth in the practice. I had met with him every two months since my arrival, but Mark had seen him even more often, and he was certain he had never seen Paul wear the same pair of shoes twice. As we both rushed from our patients into our desk area to meet him, we passed over his green blazer, Christmas tie, red slacks, and fixed our gaze on his boldest fashion statement to date: red crushed velvet loafers with green holly sprigs on top, replete with bright red berries.

I can't speak for Mark, but I immediately became obsessed with the shoes. *Are those real holly sprigs? Real berries? Or just plastic, imitation holly? Did he assemble them himself? Would anyone actually manufacture shoes with holly already attached? If yes, would anyone buy them?*

Mark was distracted too, and he suppressed laughter each time I pretended to drop my pen or other object to take a closer look at Paul's loafers. The first close-up was awkward, and I came away with no additional information regarding the authenticity of the holly sprigs. At one point, he crossed his right leg over his left knee, bobbing the leg as he talked a bit. Both hypnotized by the bobbing Christmas foot, Mark and I heard nothing he said. By then, we were accustomed to his manner of reporting our financial performance: there would be ten minutes of preliminary, very detailed information, which we would probably never understand and could, therefore, virtually ignore, followed by the two-sentence summary telling us how we were doing, which commanded our rapt attention. The only skill needed was to recognize when the summary was coming.

In minute nine of the detail, I dropped my pile of papers from my lap to the floor, getting down on my hands and knees to pick them up. I sniffed the holly deeply, confirming it was indeed real and not plastic. Mark began laughing audibly at the absurdity of my position, as did I. Returning to my seat and attempting to restore my own decorum, I looked directly at Mark, an unfortunate mistake. Tears welling up in his eyes, he was visibly shaking with waves of laughter. I nodded, as if to say, "Yes, it is real holly," and then our guffaws began.

Paul looked up, confused and wondering whether his financial analysis of our practice was the object of our laughter.

"You probably think I was making a bit of a joke about the cash flow situation," he ventured, "but I wasn't kidding. This is a serious problem."

"I'm sorry," Mark rushed to say, "it's been a hectic week, and we're both a bit punchy. Please continue."

Paul began to summarize his preliminary numbers for the year, saying we weren't quite breaking even, we needed to lower our physician salaries by about five percent for the coming year, and if we were each willing to see just two more patients per day, we would probably be fine.

"Paul," I interrupted, "in the two and one-half years I've been here, you've recommended this 'two more patients per doctor per day' strategy to me three times. We both feel like we're working harder than most of the other doctors in town. Are there any other approaches we should consider, other than just seeing more and more patients? I've already added two more hours of work per day to the ten to twelve hours I have been putting in here daily."

Paul initially seemed surprised at my question. Perhaps he had not been counting the number of times he had proffered this approach to us, or, more likely, this was the advice he gave every doctor every time there was a financial shortfall. In any case, he uncrossed his legs, rested his palms face down on his thighs, and took a slow deep breath with his eyes closed, as though practicing by rote a stress reduction technique he learned in a seminar entitled, "How to Deal with Difficult Doctors." Over these past thirty months, I had become more and more direct with our accountant, challenging his conclusions, despite my own lack of any financial background beyond the balancing of my own checkbook.

"Well," he began cautiously, "we can consider the wages you are paying your staff." Mark and I were each shaking our heads from side to side. "Well, last time we met, we looked at staff salaries, I guess. They are comparatively low, aren't they?" Both of us nodded.

"Or we could take a closer look at your collection processes." Mark and I both nodded.

He repeated the stress reduction technique one more time. While his eyes were closed, I pointed to the shoes and mouthed to Mark, "Real holly." Mark began shaking again silently, holding his sides.

The official portion of the meeting ended soon thereafter, with Paul promising to do some further research and get back to us. Somewhat frustrated at the prospect of adding another four hours to my workweek, I did the only thing I could do.

"Say, Paul," I began, in the friendliest tone I could muster, "those are really some unique shoes. You certainly don't see something like those every day."

He smiled broadly, taking my neutral statement as a compliment and a potential opening to reestablish his declining credibility after the prior forty-five minute discussion.

"Well, I don't usually talk about my clothes, but, you know, my wife teases me about how I'm the one in the family with the obsession with shoes, not her."

Hearing this, Mark spun away quickly, his facial expression now hidden but his convulsing sides still quite visible, hands wrapped around each side holding them. Paul stole a quick look at the old, resoled, scuffed black wingtips Mark and I were each wearing, in an apparent effort to gauge our potential sympathy with further discussion. Mark needed new heels on his, I noticed. He slowly turned back to face us, his face now composed.

"We all have our passions, don't we?" I said, egging Paul on. "But those particular shoes you're wearing, those are really unique. Did they come with the holly already attached?" I had obviously touched on a source of great pride for him, and as he straightened up to provide the important details, Mark coughed and again turned around.

"You know, you're the first to ask. These are my Christmas shoes. I found the red shoes after last Valentine's Day, fifty percent off. I saved them until this month and attached some real holly with a glue gun."

Mark was coughing violently now in an effort to conceal the loud guffaws uncontrollably emerging from his throat. He was actually making barking sounds.

"Real holly? Wow, what a unique idea!"

We were walking out toward the waiting room. Mark peeled off into the bathroom, slamming the door quickly without saying goodbye.

"Well, we accountants aren't usually considered a very creative lot, as you may be aware," Paul said in a confiding tone. "I guess it's just my artistic side coming out."

"Very artistic, indeed, Paul. Well, goodbye, and Happy New Year. Let's hope we can be just as innovative with the financial health of our practice in the coming year."

The following morning, Mark failed to notice the alteration I had made in my scuffed black wing tips for several hours, while we were each seeing patients. Despite my exaggerated leg crossing, dropping items on the floor, and even pointing out carpet stains right next to my feet, he remained oblivious. Which, as it turned out, was an even better set-up to my holiday practical joke.

One of Mark's predictable habits was to remove his shoes during the lunch hour. With the help of Cynthia, who called Mark out of our little office into the hallway, I was able to transfer my "modification" from my shoes to his in about twenty seconds. Then, it was simply a matter of waiting until his first patient was ready, at 1:00 p.m., for him to discover the shiny green leaves and bright red berries attached to the laces of both of his shoes.

Ever economical, I had purchased plastic holly, which would be used on an annual holiday basis to break the future tensions of our busy medical office and its attendant winter glut of patients, many of whom were suffering from their holiday-acquired upper respiratory infections.

CHAPTER 28

"What we see depends mainly on what we look for."

Sir John Lubbock (1834-1914), English banker,
biologist, archaeologist, and politician

It had been an unusually busy Monday, especially for two physicians whose days were always packed too full. Always the busiest day in a primary care doctor's office, we seemed to be running faster from patient to patient than usual, all day long. The deep grey of our Michigan winter was now in its fifth month, with no sign of sunshine on either horizon, or overhead for that matter. Our patients, also residents of the third cloudiest state in the nation, were just as serotonin-depleted as we were, and a general air of depression hung in the air like the continuous drab ceiling hanging low overhead outside.

As it turns out, human beings become ill all seven days of the week at roughly the same frequency, with recreational injuries being much higher on weekends. Sports injuries were on the rise, as we were now well into winter. So Monday mornings always begin with the calls from the people who became sick or were injured on Saturday and Sunday but didn't want to go to the emergency room, thinking they could "make it" until Monday morning. I had been seeing patients since 8:00 a.m., including a number of got-sick-or-injured-on-Saturday-and-Sunday ones over the "lunch hour," and my next and final appointment was a consultation for Dr. Williams, the obstetrician/gynecologist in solo practice whose office sat directly above ours, on the second floor of our four-story medical building. While I thrive on the time I spend in the examination rooms with patients, getting to know them, taking a history, performing a medical examination, I have less enthusiasm for some of the clerical aspects of my profession, and dictating the office note for each patient is one of them.

I often find it difficult to tear myself from an exam room when spending time with a patient in need. Surreptitiously glancing at my watch, I thought, *Well, it's 3:55 pm. My next patient is at 4:00. If I end this visit now, I'll have time to dictate the chart note and still be on time for my four o'clock.* This seemed like a logical plan, except for several issues. First, the patient I was with at that moment still seemed skeptical about his need for lifelong medication for his newly diagnosed hypertension, and spending an extra five minutes with him might make an important difference. Second, I could picture the stack of charts of the seventeen patients I had seen already today, every one requiring a dictation as well. I usually scribbled and scratched out brief notes when meeting with patients and then used those hieroglyphics as a guide to my recorded version of each visit, which I would dictate at the end of the day. On Monday morning of each week, I would vow to leave two minutes free at the end of each appointment to dictate a note, so I could go home on time, but this had never actually happened. Not even once. Sitting in front of my doubting patient, I thought, *Why start now?* and spent the remaining five minutes persuading him about the benefits of antihypertensive therapy. At the end of the appointment, he seemed genuinely convinced.

I added his chart to the growing pile, now eighteen, and went into see Mrs. April Wilson, my last patient, who was scheduled for an hour-long visit to evaluate some gastrointestinal complaints her gynecologist was unable to diagnose when she saw him the previous week. A pleasant forty-five-year-old woman, she looked "older than her stated age," as we say in medicine, but at the same time she brought positive energy into the room. She had short, dark hair, bright green eyes, was dressed sharply, and greeted me with a broad smile and a confident handshake. A bit less under the spell of our dark Midwestern days, she was nonetheless tired and frustrated with her symptoms.

"This is the first time in my adult life I've actually been able to do whatever I want to," she began, "and I feel worse than I have in years. I have no appetite, feel bloated whenever I eat anything, and my ankles are swelling a bit. I'm exhausted all the time! I haven't been this tired in as long as I can remember."

Chronic hepatitis. Stomach cancer. Colon cancer. Pancreatic cancer. Celiac disease. Giardia infection. My mind began its automatic listing of various possibilities, but most of them failed to explain her complete constellation of symptoms.

We went through a very detailed medical history, which disclosed only a few other areas of concern. She had gained eleven pounds in the past six months or so, despite exercising regularly, being nauseated, and eating less. *That certainly makes cancer less likely.* She had given birth to a son named Terry with Down syndrome when she was twenty years old. He was severely disabled from birth and required twenty-four hour direct care and supervision. The doctors had told her and her husband that Terry had a serious heart condition and would not likely live for more than one year, or two at the most. They had decided to keep him in their home, despite the recommendation from the doctors that he be institutionalized. Terry went on to live another twenty-three years, and he had died twelve months ago.

Depression? I wondered to myself, and I queried her about symptoms, such as loss of interest in usual activities, waking in the middle of the night with trouble getting back to sleep, constant sadness, and even suicidal thoughts, but she was not really experiencing any of these. She did not feel depressed, she said, just tired. *This does not feel like depression.*

In fact, she was rather excited. She had been in school for nine months and was really enjoying her study of art history. She glowed as she spoke of her new endeavor, but then frowned deeply when she said she kept falling asleep while studying and had trouble getting out of bed in the morning. *Hypothyroidism?* The opposite of hyperthyroidism, sometimes people with a gradually failing thyroid gland will develop difficulty with concentration, fatigue, and will sleep longer hours. She didn't have other typical symptoms of a low thyroid state.

"I'm really at a turning point in my life, Dr. Roberts," she explained. "I wasn't even sure I wanted children in the first place. Terry was a joy, but he also required twenty-four hour by seven-day by twenty-three years of supervision. He never went to school. He couldn't be alone. I was with him almost every minute. I've never said this to anyone before, but to be honest, if I had ever known he would have lived to be twenty-three years old, I don't think I would have decided to take him home when he was born. He was so severely disabled."

Tearful, she looked up at me intently to gauge my judgment of her confession. I have seen this look often, and it is virtually guaranteed when the patient prefaces his or her remarks with the phrase, "I've never told anyone else this, but…" Now, I know that up to this point in my life, I had done far more than my fair share of judging others, but behind the closed examination room door, I never felt anything but a sense of honor and privilege when my patients trusted me enough to tell me their deepest secrets. I had given serious thought in college to pursuing a life in the ministry; instead, I felt called to be a physician. As it turned out, my career choice had enabled me to do both.

Maybe there were some "clerical" aspects of medicine I did enjoy after all.

I just smiled warmly and took a deep breath. She seemed relieved. "I have no idea how you managed all those years," I said quite honestly.

She paused and looked at me, understanding I accepted what she had offered without criticism.

"Maybe I just need to accept that these feelings are normal," she concluded. I nodded, and we continued our medical history conversation.

After about an additional one hundred questions and answers, I hadn't learned much more. She had some swelling of her face, her breasts, and abdomen, and she had been a bit more irritable lately.

"This is probably just menopause," she offered. "My menstrual periods have been very irregular over the past two years. My mother was forty-five when she went through menopause."

Through further questioning, I learned her periods had been rather heavy the prior year, scant for the first three months the current year, and for the previous six months she had only occasional spotting. *Fairly typical for menopause, except she is not describing any hot flashes.* Her gynecologist had not done any blood tests to confirm she was indeed in menopause, she reported.

We then proceeded with a complete physical examination. I didn't find anything on examination other than the abdominal bloating and ankle swelling she had mentioned. Since she had seen her gynecologist six months ago for her annual pap and pelvic examination, I did not repeat this. Mrs. Wilson had been told everything was normal, and I made a note to check with Dr. Williams to confirm this.

I excused myself to allow her to dress and went to my office to page through my huge medical textbook, hoping for some inspiration. There on my desk lay a copy of *Harrison's Internal Medicine*, a more than 1,800 page book, which was larger than anything else made of paper in the office, other than the stack of charts on my desk waiting for dictation. Something in my book scanning process prompted the thought that her symptoms might be explained by an endocrine tumor, an abnormal growth of one of the various glands in the female body: pituitary (in the brain), thyroid or parathyroid (in the neck), or adrenal or ovary (in the abdomen). I finally formulated a hypothesis that she might have an estrogen-secreting ovarian mass or maybe an adrenal tumor. Either of these could be quite benign or quite serious. Both would be exceedingly rare.

Well, you can't diagnose a disease you don't consider, I thought, recalling some good advice I had received as a third-year medical student on my internal medicine rotation, and I went back into the room to wrap things up with April Wilson.

"My primary concern is that you seem to be experiencing symptoms of some sort of hormonal excess or imbalance," I explained.

She nodded. "I've talked to my friends who are going through menopause, but other than my periods, I feel like I have the opposite of menopause, whatever that is!" she laughed.

I laughed too. "Well, I'm not sure what it would be either, but I would like to order a number of blood tests and see what they show. I'm going to check quite a few different hormonal levels to see if we can find some clue to what is going on here."

"Dr. Williams said you would probably order an upper GI and a lower GI." She spoke the names of these tests with a grimace, and her face took upon the expression of a guilty prisoner awaiting sentencing.

"No, I'd like to wait until we see what the blood work shows. We'll have a better idea when those tests come back, and then we can decide together what to do next."

I did not want to put this poor woman through any unnecessary, unpleasant experiences. I really wanted to help April Wilson find out what was wrong with her, so she could move forward with the life she was so excited to pursue. I was also worried, as I knew something was wrong here. This was not a psychosomatic illness.

"So, you don't think this is all in my head?" she cautiously asked, in a manner that made it clear that either someone close to her did, or that she was herself worried about the possibility.

"Well, the pituitary gland is in your head, and I will be checking some of the hormones it produces. But, no, I think something is off-kilter with your endocrine system, your hormones, and I promise you we'll get to the bottom of it." I really wanted her to feel reassured.

After writing the names of about a dozen blood tests, which today are quite readily available but back then had to be sent away to more than one reference lab across the country, I handed her the paperwork, and I told her I would see her in about ten days to review all of the test results.

After working through my eighteen charts with my trusty Dictaphone at the end of the day, I mentioned to Mark that I thought I might have seen a patient with an estrogen-secreting tumor.

"But I've never seen one myself, and according to Harrison's, they are pretty rare," I cautioned.

Mark seemed impressed I had even thought of it. "Well, you can't diagnose a disease you don't consider!" I quipped as we both walked out the door at about 6:30 p.m.

"What was your theory about rare diseases you told me when we were residents together on oncology?" he asked.

Mark was a brilliant physician who had taught me a great deal, so I was surprised he had remembered one of my own approaches to diagnosis. It was something I had observed in medical school a few times, then tested out myself, and then began to teach others. The theory developed out of the discussions that followed the many case presentations on medical rounds I attended as a student. A case would be presented to the attending physician by an intern or student, and then the other students and interns would be asked to generate a list of the various diseases that might explain the patient's symptoms. Some students would try to come up with simple and straightforward answers, and others would focus on more esoteric possibilities. I had noticed what I thought was the best possible approach and emulated it with success in my own internship.

"Well," I replied to Mark, "any time somebody asks you for your differential diagnosis on rounds, always guess the rarest possible disease that still fits the patient's symptoms. If you are right, which will almost never happen, everyone will think you're a genius. If you are wrong, which will be ninety-five percent of the time, your colleagues will think, 'Wow! I'm impressed. I wish I'd have thought of that! What a smart answer!'"

"David," Mark confided, "I never would have thought of an estrogen-secreting tumor. So I'm already impressed, either way."

Until that moment, it hadn't occurred to me that Mark might be impressed with me, despite the fact he took me into his practice when he was barely making ends meet. His comment made my day, though, and I sang out loud with the radio all the way home in my car.

CHAPTER 29

"We must make the choices that enable us
to fulfill the deepest capacities of our real selves."

Thomas Merton (1915 - 1968),
American Catholic writer and Trappist monk

The following Monday, Mrs. Wilson's esoteric laboratory test reports began to appear on my desk. Most everything was normal, except for several tests, true to her prediction, showing what might be called "the opposite of menopause." In the female climacteric, as it is also known in medicine, the ovaries gradually fail to make estrogen, and sensing the absence of this hormone, the pituitary gland sends progressively higher levels of stimulating hormones into the bloodstream to coax the ovaries back into production. The ovaries, having failed, are unable to effectively respond to these chemical messages. So, in menopause, blood tests show very low estrogen levels and high stimulating hormone levels. Mrs. Wilson had the opposite: very high estrogen levels and very low stimulating hormones.

It was worrisome that her estrogen levels were about fifty times higher than normal. While levels vary throughout the menstrual cycle, a normal value might be in the range of 100, and her estrogen level was 5,000.

I showed Mark the lab result and said, "I can't believe this but I really think she does have an estrogen secreting tumor."

"I told you I was impressed," he quickly responded. "What do you plan to do next?'

"Well, I called her Ob/Gyn last week, and he said her pelvic exam had been completely normal six months ago. But I still think we need to do an ultrasound to check."

This was back in the days before the invention of magnetic resonance imaging (MRI), and computed tomographic (CT) scans were still only being performed on the head. Mark agreed the ultrasound was the next step. We both had some bad experiences with ultrasound and were not generally impressed with its diagnostic abilities. The images in those days were very fuzzy and non-descript, "Like a polar bear in a snowstorm," we would say when reporting the results of the test on medical rounds. Obstetricians ordered the vast majority of ultrasounds in this era, when some assessment of a fetus during pregnancy was needed.

In addition, Errol Santini, M.D., a colorful, bigger-than-life emergency room doctor with whom we had worked in our residency training, had fueled our skepticism of the test. Of course, we called him "the Great Santini." When we cautiously suggested the test on one of his patients, he would stiffen to his full six-foot-six height and bark, "Ultrasound? Ultrasound? Why, they couldn't find a submarine in the Huron River."

We would always laugh, mentally visualizing the lazy and relatively shallow river that runs through our town, knowing it could never conceal a submarine, even to the naked eye. Mark later informed me our ER teacher had good reason for his skepticism: his wife had an ultrasound in her third trimester that showed a single, small but healthy baby. Two months later, she delivered twins!

"Mrs. Wilson, I have news about your blood work," I began after she answered the phone. "Your pituitary, thyroid, and adrenal hormones are all normal. Everything looks good there. But you do have, well, as you put it, 'the opposite of menopause,' with very high estrogen levels."

"What can cause that?" she quickly asked, sounding frightened.

"There are a number of possibilities," I replied guardedly, "and we can discuss them all when you come in on Thursday. But I think it would be a good idea for you to have an ultrasound of your ovaries before then, so we have all of the information we need for your visit."

While there was evidence to strongly suggest an estrogen-secreting tumor, I try never to use words like "tumor" or "cancer" over the phone, as patients have a difficult time hearing or understanding anything after either of those words are spoken. This phenomenon also occurs when using such words in a face-to-face encounter with a patient.

We were able to schedule an ultrasound for late Wednesday afternoon. The first thing Thursday morning, I received a call from the radiologist, who had read my concern on the requisition slip about an estrogen-secreting mass and wanted to personally let me know the result. Personal calls directly from radiologists were rare, so I knew the ultrasound had found something abnormal. He confirmed my suspicion by providing me with the test results. The call was perfect timing, because Mrs. Wilson was due in the office in about thirty minutes, and I could discuss the diagnosis with her then. He asked if I wanted him to fax over some images from the ultrasound, and I said, "No, thanks." *The only thing in medicine more blurry than an ultrasound image would be a faxed copy of one*, I mused.

I thought about calling Dr. Williams first. My discussion with him was going to be one of the two very challenging conversations I had ahead of me today. I decided to start with Mrs. Wilson first, then I could tell Dr. Williams about my visit with her afterwards.

Mrs. Wilson appeared quite nervous when I entered the examination room. This was going to be one of the most difficult sessions to review a patient's test results I had ever experienced, and I really wanted to be able to present the information in a helpful manner, so she could effectively cope with what was going to be life-changing information. I also carried some existential questions into the room with me that morning, which weighed me down more than the continually grey sky overhead. *What sort of universe allows a woman who had devoted more than half of her years on earth to caring for a severely disabled Down syndrome baby to face news this difficult, just when she is beginning to experience the life she had originally hoped for? How can I possibly help her with a situation this challenging?*

She immediately saw the sober look on my face and understood, I believe, my news was not going to be good. I sat down in the chair next to her, turned toward her, and tried to explain.

"Mrs. Wilson, do you remember last week when I said I thought something was going on hormonally?" I was recapping this history as much for my benefit as I was for hers. "We also talked about this Monday, on the phone. I was worried about your ovaries secreting very high levels of estrogen. We ordered the ultrasound because of that." She nodded, following each step in her workup.

I paused and took a deep breath. "Well, I was right. But I was wrong too. I thought you might have had a tumor of your ovary."

This is going to be really hard to say to her, after all she has been through. "What the ultrasound showed was that you are five-and-one-half months pregnant."

"Oh, no, Doctor! I was afraid of that." She looked at me with the same look on her face as her "confession" the previous week. "You know, I'd rather have ovarian cancer." Tears began flowing down her face, and as I found a tissue for her, I noted the moisture building in my eyes as well. "My religion does not tolerate abortion, and I have no idea what I am going to do," she confided bravely.

I couldn't think of anything to say and just remained still.

"I also know I can't go through another experience like the one I had with Terry. I loved him. I loved him very much. But I cannot do this again." She was staring at her lower abdomen, and paused and wiped her eyes. "I can't even guess my chances of having another Down's baby. I've already had one, and I'm way past forty years old now. There's a very high risk, isn't there?"

"Yes," I softly replied, nodding. I took her hand. "I just want you to know that I'm here for you, and I do want to help. I know you've been very honest with me, and I really appreciate it. I'm honored that you feel comfortable expressing your feelings."

"Thank you. Sometimes it is hard for me to accept my own needs and feelings as being important."

Gently, I suggested to her a possible plan. "You know, given where you are in your pregnancy, you don't have to make a decision today. Why don't you take time to think about it and discuss this with your husband? We can meet again on Monday and talk some more. I'll call Dr. Williams and let him know right away. I know he will also be happy to speak with you, if you would like."

Now more openly weeping, she nodded her head twice and barely whispered, "Thank you. That's a good idea." She glanced at her watch.

"Do you mind if I just sit here for a few minutes before I go? I just need some time alone."

"No, I don't mind at all. That would be fine," I replied and quietly left the room, closing the door behind me. I explained the situation to Cynthia, and five minutes later, she gently knocked and went in the room, while I walked up the stairs to talk to her obstetrician.

Of course, I was embarrassed I had come to the diagnosis in such a roundabout fashion, ordering about seven hundred dollars worth of blood tests instead of a simple ten-dollar pregnancy test, which, in those days, were only available in doctor's offices, hospitals, and laboratories. But I wasn't as embarrassed as Dr. Williams was. In his early sixties, he was at least twice my age, with jet black hair except for his slightly graying temples and a roly-poly, but not quite obese, look about him in his tightly buttoned white coat. There is simply no elegant way for an internist to explain to an obstetrician that the patient he had sent to me for what he had described in his referral note as a "bizarre set of GI symptoms" had the single most common condition he saw in his practice. He sputtered, shook his head, began to speak at least five times, and stopped after only uttering a few words.

"I just…," and "She didn't…," and "Well, if I…" were three of his attempts.

"Well, it didn't occur to me, either, until the radiologist called with the ultrasound result," I confessed, attempting to provide some comfort.

It gradually became clear to me that not only was my physical presence at this very moment an extremely painful reminder to him of his embarrassment, but that every time he ever saw me for the rest of his life, he would experience similar pain. He was now staring at the ground in front of his shoes, shaking his head and his arms, exhaling deeply, caught up in some personal exorcism of whatever demons needed release before he could walk back into an examination room to see his next patient.

I mumbled some completely incoherent phrase, intending to signal my departure, and actually began to run towards his office door.

Still staring at the floor, completely and utterly despondent, he said to anyone who had ears, "Well, I guess you can't diagnose something you don't consider."

Still attempting to absorb the two previous and so completely different conversations, I talked to Mark when I returned to our joint office. Here

I was, the young, brilliant internist who had so impressed him with my astute diagnosis of an estrogen-secreting tumor, now sheepishly handing him a small stack of lab results – very expensive lab results – and telling him the ultrasound had disclosed a five-and-one-half-month-old fetus.

One of my favorite things about Mark is his ability to see many different levels of both seriousness and humor in any given situation and express them simultaneously. He was aware of the incredibly difficult situation Mrs. Wilson faced, and he was quite empathetic.

Pausing for a moment, he confessed, "I have absolutely no idea what I would do if I were her. I wouldn't even know where to start." Tilting his head downward, he shook it slowly from side to side. After a pause, he started to smile, and said, "What did... Never mind. I'll ask you later."

At the end of what had been another very long day for both of us, we were sitting in our joint office space, finishing our dictations.

Mark turned around toward me in his swivel chair and said, "Look, you might not be in the mood to talk about this right now, but what did Dr. Williams say when you told him his patient was twenty-four weeks pregnant?" He started to chortle a bit and, as he did whenever he was about to laugh heartily, held his sides.

Despite my own embarrassment, I regaled him with every detail of the conversation, without any disrespect intended. We both deeply respected Dr. Williams, who had been one of our teachers in medical school. As I parroted all five of Dr. William's aborted sentences, Mark was now laughing hard enough that his chair was bouncing. I thought it might be an opportune time to use some self-deprecating humor in an effort to absolve myself of my own guilt over how the workup had proceeded.

"I still can't believe that I thought of a rare estrogen-secreting tumor before I considered pregnancy. Coming from Dr. William's office, I guess that I just figured she was..."

"David, your theory still works perfectly," he interrupted. "I remain impressed." He spun his chair back around to finish his dictations, but I noted by the rattling of his chair that he had to pause for a few seconds each time he started laughing again.

That night, I had trouble drifting off to sleep. I thought about the joy that most, but not all, women feel when their doctor's office tells them that, yes, they are pregnant. Today, with home pregnancy tests universally available, the dynamic has changed greatly. I also thought about how difficult life had been for Mrs. Wilson, and how she had given everything she had to give. But mostly I thought about her saying, "I'd rather have cancer." I realized that she had made an enormously difficult decision to take her son home twenty-five years ago, based on the information she had at the time, information that proved to be inaccurate. As a result of the dilemma she and her husband had faced, the entire course of their life changed. Now, she faced a moral question that was more challenging for her than the first one. I knew she didn't really want to have cancer, but I understood why she felt it would be easier if she did. Ovarian cancer would be a life changing, if not life ending, event, but she would not have to confront the depth of doubt she now faced about her second pregnancy.

God, help me to find some way to help her when I see her next week, I prayed. Realizing my complete inadequacy, I added, *And please help and guide her yourself.*

CHAPTER 30

*"The better work men do is always done under stress
and at great personal cost."*

*William Carlos Williams, M.D. (1883 - 1963),
American pediatrician and poet*

Immediately after the "Christmas Shoes Incident" with Paul, I took a more active role in the business aspects of our practice. More of a "numbers person" than Mark, it finally became clear to me we both needed a better understanding of the economics of patient care. Besides, we were both fed up with the chronic financial shortfall, without any clear understanding of its source. I had informally surveyed some of our colleagues and learned Mark and I had longer patient office hours and lower incomes than the other primary care physicians in our town. At that time $40,000 per year was a lot of money to each of us, and a third more than our residency program salaries. It was also thirty-five percent less than the prevailing salary for a primary care internal medicine doctor.

Comparing notes with just a few other physicians really helped. They each said the single most important thing we could do was to "become personally involved in the accounts receivable process." Eventually, we learned this meant one of us, namely me, needed to review our daily cash collections and weekly revenue from insurance companies to be sure we were on track.

I called Paul and asked him to bring the relevant reports to our next meeting. Mark and I met with those office staff involved in checking patients out, explaining the need to collect from each one at the time of service. Most people assume a doctor's office would have no problem with cash flow, our office staff included. Once they learned we were not making ends meet, they took matters into their own hands and became extremely effective in assisting patients meet their own financial responsibility on their way out of the office.

Kathleen, the most compulsive of our office staff, was particularly effective. Whereas the previous week she had cheerfully sent patients on their way with an upbeat, "That's okay. Just send in the money when you have time," the following week she was singing a very different tune. Standing up, looking into each patient's eyes, she had developed a speech that was so persuasive it made me want to hand her fifteen dollars of my own money each time I overheard her.

Soon, Kathleen was providing a daily report of the success of cash collection efforts. Initially, she estimated they were collecting about forty percent of the money due; now they were at ninety-four percent. But, she explained to Mark and me, there were some tough cases, some patients who never paid their bills. She needed our help.

"Sure," I replied immediately.

"What do you want us to do?" Mark asked, a bit more cautiously.

"Well, I'd like to just write a number on the charge slip for those patients. So, if you see $200 written on the slip, it means the patient owes us that much. When you see the number there, could you just ask the patient to pay it on their way out?"

"I don't know if it is a good idea for the doctors to be talking about patient bills," Mark said. "I couldn't explain their account to them if they had questions."

"Well, it's either bringing it up to them or seeing two more patients per day," I countered.

After some discussion we agreed on an approach where we would each say, "Mrs. Jones, I notice you have a balance here of two hundred dollars. I'd really appreciate it if you'd take a few minutes to work out the details with Kathleen at the desk on your way out."

Both of us began the new approach that same afternoon. While I was initially very uncomfortable even bringing up the subject, it was easier each subsequent time. Most patients seemed a bit embarrassed at first, but after a month or so, we had very few people for whom repeated "encouragement" was necessary.

Kathleen continued to lead the charge, taking pride in each dollar she collected. One weekend on call, I stopped at the office to pick up my stethoscope and found her there on the phone in the reception area. From our office, I could hear snatches of her conversation.

"Yes, I know, Mr. Briggs, but we have to pay the lighting bill and the phone bill just like everyone else does. I know, and I understand it can be difficult, but you know we have to collect from our patients in order to keep the office open. I just want to be sure you bring your checkbook to your visit on Monday."

I marveled at the tremendous difference a single employee could make when just armed with the information she needed to help the practice to succeed. I wished we had brought them in to help solve our dilemma a year earlier.

Our next meeting with Paul occurred at the end of February. He had brought the requested materials, but he seemed a bit puzzled at the same time.

"You know, I was going to bring these reports to this meeting anyway, so I am glad you both asked for them," he began, full of confidence. A brief but understanding glance passed between Mark and me, suggesting we were not fully convinced the appearance of these new statements was coincidental.

"You're both probably wondering whether I've gotten to the root of your problem, and I believe that I have," Paul began, with his usual inaccurate mind-reading demonstration. "Your cash collections were dangerously low most of last year," he continued, "but I do have a bit of good news. We have your front desk staff doing an excellent job now, and we're bringing in more than an additional five thousand dollars per month, just from their efforts alone."

Mark and I again exchanged glances. Paul seemed to be talking about this improvement as though he had been the primary engineer behind it.

"What about insurance collections?" I asked.

"Well, I'm not sure. Let me just look through these statements." He fumbled briefly through the documents, paused, and then said, "Well, it looks like there could be a big opportunity here as well." He held up a single page out of a thick packet of reports. "As you can see here, over sixty-five percent of your accounts payable are over one hundred twenty days old."

Mark frowned, uncomprehending.

"Can you please explain that to us again, in English?" I requested.

"I'm sorry. I mean, of the money owed to you by insurance companies, almost two-thirds of it is for services the two of you provided to patients over four months ago."

"And that's bad, right?" Mark asked, testing our understanding.

"Well, actually, for a physician office, usually we consider anything over one hundred-twenty days uncollectible," he replied matter-of-factly.

We knew our office staff collected the information regarding services provided and forwarded them to Paul every week. I was embarrassed to realize I had no understanding of what happened after this.

Desiring to better comprehend the process, I asked, "What is the source of the delay, Paul?"

"Well, actually, physician billing is a complex process with many steps. There can be delays in each one, or all of them. For example, if your office takes a month to send your charge information to us, then that would be a thirty-day delay right there." He was sounding just a bit condescending now, and Mark and I both began to bristle.

"Just a minute," I said, and I left the room to find Kathleen. Returning with her in less than twenty seconds, I explained, "I've asked Kathleen to join us so she can hear this discussion. She's done a great job with our cash collections, and I think she may be able to help with the insurance end as well."

Paul nodded, but he appeared uncomfortable.

I continued, "Kathleen, we were just talking about delays in insurance payments. Paul was saying if we send in our charges to him late, then we might not be paid by the insurance companies."

Kathleen, who normally sat bolt upright anyway, grew somewhat flushed and somehow added an additional three inches to her height in the chair.

"Well," she began, appearing to be containing herself, "if we did submit them late, then that would be true. We were submitting everything on a weekly basis until about six months ago, when Paul told us we didn't need to send the charges in quite that often. He said every two to three weeks would be fine. So I've been sending in the information every other Friday."

Up to this point, I had been unaware of what was a now a clearly obvious tension between Kathleen and Paul, but between her icy stare, her tone of voice, and their body language, a longstanding feud was revealing itself.

Paul jumped in. "Kathleen, I was just giving a hypothetical example. In fact, Doctor Edwards and Doctor Roberts really ought to know you do a better job sending us the charge information than any other office does. We can go back to weekly submissions if you all want to."

"So," I suggested, "we don't need to spend any more time on this part of the process. What happens, Paul, after you receive the charge information from Kathleen?"

"Well, our office converts the information into claim forms, and we send those to the insurance companies."

"How long does that take you, Paul?" I was aware I had begun a cross-examination, but I no longer was trying to be polite.

"Well, you know, it can vary, depending on the complexity of the services."

"Then, how long, on average, does it take you to submit a claim?"

Mark was now nodding, encouraging me to continue.

"Well, I don't have the data with me…"

"Can you send it over this afternoon, when you're back at your office?"

"Well, it might take some time to pull together. Maybe at our next meeting I could present it." Paul seemed to feel cornered and was now trying to claw his way out of the conversation.

Mark, who had been silent up to this point, finally erupted. "Look, Paul. We've been having these meetings now for over two years. Your only suggestion to our financial challenges has been to see more patients. The improvement in cash collections was our idea. You had nothing to do with it. Now I'm hearing we may not collect two-thirds of what's owed to us, and I'm not happy."

Paul was beginning to panic. Being cross-examined by me was one thing. Perhaps he considered my opinion of less importance because his primary relationship had been with Mark all along. While ordinarily somewhat docile in business matters, Mark was aware of Paul's attempts to placate us, and he had simply had enough. Ever calm and collected, Mark had erupted about the same number of times as Mt. St. Helens in the time I had known him: once. Paul and I both sat with our mouths agape in complete surprise.

Mark continued, "Look, I never see my children during the week anymore as it is. It's time to do something different. I'm asking David to take over for the practice on this collection issue. You'll work with him, and you will collect the money from the insurance companies. Is that clear?"

Despite my surprise at his anger, I was pleased with the stand he was taking. In retrospect, it was the economic turning point in our practice.

Again employing his relaxation technique, with eyes closed and palms down on his legs, Paul appeared to be attempting to teleport himself from the room. When he opened his eyes and saw us still staring at him, he finally spoke.

"Well, I'll prepare those reports as soon as I can, and I'll come back and go over them with you. I'm not sure if we have an opportunity to improve our billing practices or not, but I promise you, I'll…"

I interrupted him. "Paul, how much money are we talking about here? How much is the amount older than one hundred twenty days, exactly?" The dam of our pent up frustration had obviously broken.

Kathleen was now clearly smirking, feeling deeply vindicated by both of her physicians.

He fumbled nervously through his reports, searching through tables of numbers, stopping when his index finger reached the particular object of his search. He frowned deeply.

"Well, remember here, I've said that we don't consider this amount collectible."

"How much, Paul?" Mark demanded. Paul clearly appeared trapped.

He sighed. "Sixty-three thousand, eight hundred eighty-two dollars and forty-seven cents."

We were speechless. The number was fifty percent more than either of our salaries.

You should have known this from the start, David, I began my self-critique. *You and Mark have sensed something wasn't right for over a year.*

I was angry with Paul too, but I realized my anger with myself was my main issue.

Mark was just staring at me. "Take over here," he said without speaking, his eyes peering over his glasses with a piercing gaze and his head slightly nodding.

"Paul, let's sit down together for a few minutes right after this meeting and talk about our next steps," I began. "I think we need to agree on an approach today."

Paul did not seem pleased with this suggestion; it was clear he preferred to work with Mark, but he smiled and said he would be happy to meet with me. After Kathleen and Mark left the room, Paul and I agreed to meet weekly to go over insurance collection reports to help me better understand the business aspects of our practice.

Looking back on it, this was probably the first moment of what would be my future business career. Our practice hired an outside consultant, who confirmed our entire financial problem was related to our poor collections, and we relieved Paul of his accounting duties. Over the subsequent weeks, I started posting hand-drawn graphs over my desk, which I prepared using the data our consultant provided. It took three months, but the line representing "insurance debt aged greater than one hundred twenty days" slowly trended downward to a number less than six thousand dollars. While some of the debt was indeed uncollectible, we managed to find over forty thousand dollars of our lost money.

Back then, the practice economics were painfully simple. Take the total practice revenue, subtract all of the expenses, including taxes, and the remainder goes to the doctors. Near the end of our third year together, Mark and I were looking for the first time at a very positive checking account balance for our medical practice. Eager to please our families, who had not seen much of us over the prior seven or eight years, the temptation to just split the money and spend it on elaborate family vacations was quite strong.

At one of our Monday morning check-outs, Mark said, "You know, I'm working a lot more hours than I ever expected to. My family is not very happy with the situation, especially since I spent three years telling my wife our life would be much better after internship and residency. But it isn't. I don't need the extra money, I need time with my family."

I told him I had been thinking exactly the same thing. "I'd rather spend our practice savings adding a new partner, who could share this increasing workload, than to continue our current pace."

We figured between the two of us we were doing the work of about two and one-half doctors, or twenty-five percent per person more than we could sustain. The new partner could immediately be busy half of his or her time without adding a single new patient to the practice.

"Of course, Paul wouldn't approve," Mark quipped, knowing we wouldn't need Paul's opinion anymore. "He didn't approve of me adding you, either," he continued, raising his eyebrows and then looking at me over his glasses, this time with his signature look of eye-rolling sarcasm.

"The extra forty-five thousand dollars will pay a new person for a whole year," I added. We both nodded; the decision had been made.

We both felt a tremendous weight lift from our shoulders even though the actual pressures of patient responsibility would continue for months before we could finally see the light at the end of the tunnel and know it was not another oncoming train. Over the next three months, we were fortunate to find a new partner, Alan Dennison, who had a background in geriatrics, an emerging branch of internal medicine specializing in the care of the elderly. Alan was a tall, jolly, gregarious man with the necessary excellent sense of humor needed to survive the practice of primary care. His deep sense of optimism, his boisterous laugh, and his even deeper understanding of, and love for, seniors would each prove to be a tremendous practice asset.

This was an important time for me as well, as it would be the official end to my junior partner status in the practice. I had spent my first three months working off a folding metal table, waiting for the moment we could afford a new wooden desk. I had spent two years facing the disappointment of new patients who had learned Dr. Edwards was not available, but a new partner would see them. I had spent three years doing some of the more mundane practice tasks, like updating our *Physician's Desk Reference* and making certain we had enough toilet paper in the office. Now, all of these responsibilities could be passed along to our new junior partner.

In Alan's case, though, the card table would be a permanent fixture, as long as we remained in that first office suite. There would never be room for a wooden desk in that small space. He soon came to realize that the "privileges and responsibilities" of being the new junior partner were very short on the former and rather long on the latter.

CHAPTER 31

"Red meat is not bad for you. Now blue-green meat,
that's bad for you!"

Tommy Smothers (1937 -), American comedian and musician

Amanda Polowski had never been to our practice office. When she came to the emergency room one winter morning with fever of 103.5 degrees Fahrenheit, muscle aches, and severe diarrhea, pretty much everyone thought she had influenza. She was so dehydrated the ER couldn't refill her with fluids in less than eighteen hours, and the decision was made to admit her to the hospital. Her sister-in-law was one of my patients, and on her recommendation, Mrs. Polowski asked to be admitted to my service.

By the time I arrived at the hospital after office hours, the intern and resident had each completed their work-up, collectively reaching two diagnoses: influenza and eosinophilia. One need not be a Latin scholar or a medical doctor to discern the meaning of the latter word. Merriam-Webster's tells us that it derives from the Latin for "abnormal increase in the number of eosinophils in the blood that is characteristic of allergic states and various parasitic infections." Of course, we are still left with the root, the word eosinophil: "A granulocyte readily stained by eosin that is present at sites of allergic reactions and parasitic infections." We're getting closer, but what is eosin? "A red fluorescent dye ($C_{20}H_8Br_4O_5$)

obtained by the action of bromine on fluorescein and used especially in cosmetics and as a toner; also: its red to brown sodium or potassium salt used especially as a biological stain for cytoplasmic structures."

By now, you probably have a headache; so did Mrs. Polowski. All the reader needs to know at this point is her number of eosinophils – white blood cells dedicated to handling allergic reactions in the human body – was much higher than expected. For extra credit, you might also memorize the fact that these eosinophils stain bright red on a blood smear stained with eosin. Eosin – ophil: eosin loving.

In the Midwest, doctors find such elevated levels primarily in patients during the typical allergy seasons. Parasite infections, while common in third world countries, are quite rare in Midwestern college towns. Typically, the average human being will have a total white blood cell count of about 4,000 to 10,000 cells per cubic millimeter. Of those, usually one to five percent of them are eosinophils. The vast majority of circulating white blood cells fight off infections, with granulocytes focused on bacteria and lymphocytes focused on viruses. In Mrs. Polowski's blood stream, thirty-five percent of her cells were eosinophils. Her white blood count was well above normal, at 15,000, so all together she had about twenty times more of these bright red-staining cells coursing through her veins than you or I might have at this moment. This was clearly more than a simple allergic reaction. Besides, eosinophils have nothing to do with influenza.

"So, why all this fuss about eosinophils?" the discerning reader may be wondering. Because they hold the clue to Mrs. Polowski's diagnosis, that's why.

The winter flu season is a busy time for hospital interns and residents. It was apparent my new patient did not really hold their interest; their work-ups were both quite perfunctory. The resident on the floor approached me to give me an update just before I walked into her room.

"Temp is now 101. She's received a total of three liters of IV fluid since she hit the ER. No urine output yet, but I think it is coming."

"Thanks, Jim," I replied. "I haven't seen her yet, but I'm bothered by her eosinophil count. I haven't seen one this high since medical school."

"Yeah, it's high all right. It may have something to do with her influenza, but I haven't had a chance to read up on it. We're swamped. Seven admissions in the past four hours, and it isn't even six o'clock yet."

A bad night on call would be seven admissions between noon and six o'clock the following morning. They were far ahead of this pace.

"Whoa! I'm sorry," I empathized. It wasn't all that long ago I had been in his shoes. I was still recovering, almost three years after completing my training program. *Never forget, David. Never forget.*

"That's a big load. Listen, why don't you let me track this down, since you're so busy?" It was rare for an attending physician to volunteer to take on the resident's work, and the unwritten protocol required Jim to refuse the favor.

"Sure," he replied, but then he suddenly looked apologetic. "I mean, we are so busy, I'm not sure I will be able to circle back to her until tomorrow." As if suddenly summoned by some inaudible alert, he sped off without a word. I turned to enter my new patient's room.

"Good evening, Mrs. Polowski. I'm Dr. David Roberts. I believe you have a sister-in-law named Sally Wisniewski, who is also my patient. Is that right?"

She smiled and nodded. In her early forties, she was a pleasant woman with short cropped brown hair, five foot three inches tall, about twenty pounds overweight, looking quite exhausted. She tried to sit up a bit in bed, with partial success, groaned in pain, adjusted her hospital gown, and brushed back her bangs from her forehead.

"I think I'm feeling better," she offered, although the adjustments she had made really hadn't made her appear any less sick. "The IV seems to be helping me."

"Do you mind if I turn off the television?" I asked her, already having the control box in my hand and preparing to begin the sixteen button-push series that I had calculated would turn the screen to black. She seemed wrapped up in the five o'clock news, but nodded "yes," and as I picked up the control box, I couldn't help but watch the picture on screen of a very tall British comedian wearing a red fez, of all things, who sat slumped on the ground while performing live on a BBC television program. Despite the reports of laughter and applause from the audience as he collapsed, I looked at his photo and said, "That guy is having a heart attack." I feigned unfamiliarity with the television control long enough to hear the announcer confirm that Tommy Miller, the man in the fez, had been pronounced dead shortly thereafter. My new patient seemed impressed with my diagnostic ability.

"To our knowledge," the youthful British correspondent concluded, "this is the first death ever witnessed on live television."

"Apparently, he hasn't heard of Lee Harvey Oswald," I piped up. Sixteen clicks later, the room was quiet.

I asked her if we could go through a number of questions about her current illness, and told her I would also need to examine her as well. She groaned and shifted uncomfortably in her bed.

"Listen, Dr. Roberts, I really appreciate your coming to see me tonight. But you're the sixth person who has done this 'history and physical thing' in the past four hours. Could we possibly wait until morning?"

I was used to this plea and really felt sorry for her. She had experienced the usual sequence of inquiry, starting with the emergency room nurse, then the physician there. Once transferred to the general medical floor, her floor nurse completed a full nursing assessment, a forty-five minute experience. Then, an intern performed a complete history and physical, which lasted a full hour. Next, the intern's supervisor, the internal medicine resident, stopped in for about twenty to thirty minutes to confirm his intern's findings. That was five so far.

"Well, I understand you feel very sick and you've had a very long day. I don't want to make this worse for you. At the same time, I do need to ask you some additional questions. I'll try to focus on the things my five predecessors haven't already covered. Okay?"

She shifted again in bed and sighed deeply, while simultaneously nodding.

"Besides," I added, with an impish grin, hoping to cheer her up, "no one ever died of an extra history and physical."

The remark caused her to laugh out loud, and, sensing her agreement to proceed, I dove right in with my questions. I told her I wasn't convinced she had influenza, and the initial round of questions confirmed this. Her symptoms had started over two weeks ago with an episode of viral gastroenteritis. Her muscle pains and fevers commenced three or four days later, and her diarrhea had continued since then. This was not the typical story for a patient harboring the influenza virus. So we turned to questions concerning her abnormal blood count. There are dozens of causes of eosinophilia beyond seasonal allergies and parasites, and I focused my questions on each of them, hoping to exclude as many possibilities as I could.

By the time we were finished, we were both quite tired. I felt confident that we had excluded prescription and over-the-counter drugs as the cause of her abnormal blood count. She hadn't travelled outside of our state and wasn't at risk of having contracted an unusual parasite infection. She answered "no" to my basic questions related to various forms of cancer or immune deficiency disorders. We similarly excluded endocrine diseases and another half-dozen even more rare causes of eosinophilia.

Only one of her answers gave me pause, and that was because of the pause she herself inserted before answering "no" to my question about raw pork consumption. I proceeded to the physical exam, which did disclose a few additional findings. First, she had periorbital edema, or swelling around the eyes. An unusual finding, it can be seen with low thyroid conditions and kidney failure. She also had significant muscle tenderness, particularly in her jaw muscles and over her ribs. *This really looks like a parasite infection,* I thought. But she has no travel and no exposure.

After bidding her goodnight, I went down the hall to the charting area and recorded my findings. *Something isn't adding up, here. Something important is missing.* I hated to go back and bother Mrs. Polowski again, as she was nodding off when I left her. *Waking her up might be for her own good,* I argued with myself, and then I walked back down the hospital corridor and into her room.

She stirred as I re-entered the room and opened her eyes. I apologized for what was now round seven of her medical interrogation, and she laughed again briefly.

"I couldn't help but notice, when I asked you the question about eating raw pork, you hesitated for a second before you said, 'No.' I am wondering if you have given this a bit more thought since I asked you the question."

She looked intensely uncomfortable, this time on an emotional, rather than physical, level.

"Well," she began, and then paused. I just looked at her and waited. "You know, about four weeks ago, I was making some homemade Polish sausage. It's a three-hundred-year-old family recipe. It does contain pork. We make it every year near the end of Lent."

"Do you think you might have..." I interrupted, thinking I was on the threshold of a brilliant diagnosis.

"Doctor Roberts, I know better than to eat any raw pork. My mother has made that point clear since I was a little girl. I even have it written on my recipe card: 'DON'T EAT PORK BEFORE COOKING.' My mother had it on her recipe card too. I copied it word for word. No, I'm fairly sure that I have never done that."

"All right, thanks again. Now, you have a good night's sleep, okay? Well, as good a night's sleep as one can have in a hospital," I added with an air of realism. "I promise you I won't bother you again."

I found an internal medicine textbook in the conference room and immediately turned to the chapter on parasite infections, locating trichinosis quickly. In 1835, James Paget, then a twenty-one-year-old, first-year medical student at Bartholomew's Hospital in London, was an observer at the autopsy of a middle-aged man who had died of tuberculosis. The post-mortem exam revealed extensive tuberculosis in the lungs. Apart from this finding, the young medical student noted numerous tiny chalky spots in the corpse's muscles. He borrowed a scalpel and verified the bony texture of these lesions, which his professors dismissed as irrelevant. (I suspect the tradition of dismissing medical students as being irrelevant likely predates the 2,400-year-old Hippocratic Oath.) After borrowing a microscope from the nearby British Museum, and with careful dissection, Paget concluded these lesions consisted of tiny calcified cysts, each surrounding a coiled and threadlike worm. A pathologist at the medical school verified Paget's new discovery and gave it the genus name *Trichina*, from the Greek term for hair, and the species name *spiralis*.

Trichinosis, the disease, is caused by eating meat contaminated with these parasites. The parasite infects over one hundred fifty species of mammals, with pigs being the most common. Some scholars believe that the Old Testament prohibition of dietary pork was based on the practical observation that this food-borne illness was most common in pigs.

Patients with trichinosis, I relearned as I refreshed my medical school-populated memory bank with my current textbook review, typically develop symptoms of mild abdominal discomfort and diarrhea within the first week of ingestion of the offending food. Fever, muscle discomfort, and periorbital edema usually begin ten to fourteen days after ingestion. There was no question in my mind: Mrs. Polowski was infected with the trichinosis parasite.

Some readers may find this detailed exposition of parasite infections to be tedious. Please keep in mind that I have spared you the details related to the method by which the cysts "hatch" in the stomach and how they burrow into the bloodstream through the small intestines, setting up their new homes in muscle tissue throughout the body. If, at this exact moment, you feel a slight twitching in one of your muscles, let me assure you that it is not trichinosis. Unless you've been to a third world country recently or have eaten raw pork, that is.

"Mrs. Polowski. Mrs. Polowski," I whispered, gently touching her shoulder in the hopes of softly awakening her. After all, I had promised twice to leave her alone. When she stirred and then opened her eyes, I jumped in again. "I've been doing some reading, and I am absolutely convinced you have a trichinosis infection. Can you think back to that day you made the sausage, just one more time? Are you *certain* no uncooked pork passed your lips?"

She could not have looked more guilty. "I was going to tell you in the morning," she began. "I was in the kitchen, and my son, Edgar, came in and asked about the sausage. It's his favorite. He wanted a taste of it. I gave him my mother's stern speech about never eating raw pork. The speech is also a family tradition. I was salting the pork and other ingredients and mixing them in the bowl with my hands. After my son left the kitchen, I think I may have taken just a small taste of the sausage, to see if it was properly salted."

You *think* you may have?" I asked, not to be pushy, just to be certain.

"Doctor Roberts, I know I nibbled a small bit of that raw sausage mixture. I'm sorry I didn't tell you earlier. I haven't been thinking clearly with this high fever."

"Well, that is certainly understandable, Mrs. Polowski, and very helpful too. We have the information we need to help you feel much better. I'll see you in the morning." Leaving the room, I ran into the resident in the hallway.

"Jim, Mrs. Polowski has trichinosis," I stated dryly. He looked stunned, taken aback. He actually did take a step or two backwards. "We'll need to have an infectious disease specialist see her in the morning. Let's start appropriate anti-parasitic treatment tonight."

"But, but, how did you know it wasn't influenza?"

Traditionally, internal medicine residents pride themselves in always being at least one step ahead of the attending physicians. It was clear he was deeply wounded, not just by being scooped, but because it was such a rare disease and a great diagnosis.

I described to him my version of the time course of her symptoms and my findings of periorbital edema and muscle tenderness.

"Also," I concluded, saving the most important historical fact for last, "she has a history of eating raw pork."

"Raw pork? She told you she ate raw pork?" He was agitated now. "I asked her about that, because of the eosinophilia. She denied any ingestion of raw pork."

"That's what she told me too, the first time I asked. And the second."

"Wow. What a great case," he said with admiration and exuberance. I could tell he was already starting to become excited about presenting Mrs. Polowski's history in the morning to his faculty physician, building suspense, and finally revealing this unusual diagnosis. He was defeated tonight, but he would be a hero tomorrow.

Everything from this point on proceeded as expected. The muscle biopsy showed the same calcified cysts coating the spiral-like worms seen by James Paget more than one hundred fifty years earlier. She responded nicely to treatment and was discharged only forty-eight hours after admission to complete her course of medication at home.

CHAPTER 32

"One of the most striking differences between a cat and a lie
is that a cat has only nine lives."

Mark Twain (1835 - 1910), American author and humorist,
in Pudd'nhead Wilson

Amanda Polowski called our office early the next morning after her discharge from the hospital. There is truth to the contention that doctors treat their patients who have rare diseases with a special level of attention, at least in my case. I immediately returned her call. She was fine, she said, but was concerned about her son, Edgar.

"Do you see children?" she asked hopefully.

"How old is Edgar?" I asked, knowing that our practice only accepted patients twelve and over.

She said he was thirteen. He was complaining of muscle pains and had a fever of 104 degrees. "And no," she volunteered, anticipating my next question, "he hasn't eaten any raw pork."

She was able to bring Edgar to the office within an hour. His symptoms were identical to his mother's. So were his physical findings, although the swelling around his eyes was quite subtle. I was certain he had trichinosis.

Hmm. You've now seen one case of trichinosis and you're the world expert, are you? I teased myself silently. Nonetheless, I was quite confident in my diagnosis.

"Now, Edgar," I asked him after we had finished the history and physical examination. "I know you know you're not ever supposed to eat raw pork sausage, right?" He nodded seriously. "But in order to help you feel better, I need to know, did you eat any of the sausage your mom made before it was cooked?"

"...No." There it was. The one and one-half second pause preceding his answer, exactly the same length as his mother's. "I didn't eat any of the sausage." I wonder whether denial was hereditary or just environmental.

"Edgar," I said patiently, knowing where this was going, "I know you think you'll be in trouble if you ate any sausage. But your mother is right here. Mom, do you promise that Edgar won't be in trouble if he tells the truth here?"

"...Yes," she replied with great ambivalence. That pause again! Despite her actual answer, it was completely clear to both her son and I that Edgar would be in enormous trouble if he had ingested even the smallest amount of raw pork.

"Edgar, in order for me to treat you with the right medication, I need to know if you ate the raw sausage. This is really important."

"No," he blurted out, now in tears. He was speaking directly to his mother, ignoring me completely. "I promise I didn't."

"Mrs. Polowski, would you mind if I talked to Edgar alone here for a minute?"

"...Well, no, that would be fine." She left the room quickly.

I pulled up a chair right in front of where the boy was sitting and placed myself in it, occupying his entire field of view.

"Okay, Edgar, I know this is difficult for you. Tell me what happened with the sausage. I promise I will not tell your mother."

"I asked Mom for a taste," he answered quickly, attempting to glance over my shoulder at the door in anticipation of his mother's sudden return. "She said, 'No,' and gave me the whole speech I've heard ten million times. As I was leaving, I saw her put a bit of the raw sausage right into her mouth."

"Yes, she mentioned that to me when she was in the hospital."

He looked at me in wide-eyed surprise. "She did?" he exclaimed.

I was beginning to suspect the level of seriousness of the verbal warnings about avoiding raw pork were only surpassed by sanctity of the family oath of silence taken by transgressors.

"So anyway, when she turned around to wash her hands in the sink, I snuck back into the kitchen and took a taste of my own." His guilt was only vaguely detectable beneath his teenage hubris. "It tasted pretty good."

The urge to deliver the stern lecture welling up inside of me was nearly irresistible. But at that instant, I briefly recalled several of my many acts of subtle "civil disobedience" from my own teenage years, and I held my tongue. Besides, trichinosis is a reportable disease, which means that the Department of Health would be making a call to his home in the very near future. I felt it likely that Edgar would discover this to be a meaningful life experience by the time it was over.

I retrieved his mother from the hallway. When we were all seated again, I said, "Well, it doesn't really matter whether Edgar remembers eating any raw pork or not. You, Mrs. Polowski, have biopsy-proven trichinosis, and your son has the identical symptoms. I think we need to begin treatment today." They were both nodding their heads. "We could do a muscle biopsy, just to be certain." Now both heads were shaking side to side.

"Should everyone else in the family be treated too?" Mrs. Polowski asked. Edgar had six siblings. I pictured a long line of Polowskis in the waiting room, each with florid symptoms of trichinosis, high fevers, muscle pains, gross swelling around their eyes, each adamantly denying any consumption of the parasite-laden sausage mixture. It was tempting to ask if any of them had eaten the raw pork concoction, but by now, even I had learned something from my experience with this family.

"Do any of them have symptoms of trichinosis?" I asked instead, knowing she was intimately familiar with the subject.

"No, not yet."

"Let's just watch and wait," I said. I wrote out the prescription and handed it to Edgar. "I'll see you both back in two weeks. Be sure to take this medication until it is gone," I reminded them both.

Two weeks later, they returned, without any report of additional stricken family members. Each felt much better, both still had mild muscle soreness, but their fevers were gone. Follow-up blood tests still showed eosinophilia, but at much lower levels than when they had each presented with their illness.

At the end of the visit, Mrs. Polowski reached into her purse and pulled out a package wrapped in aluminum foil, with an additional outer layer of plastic wrap. Accustomed to occasionally receiving gifts of food from patients, I took it from her, thanked her, and stood up to go.

"Aren't you going to open it?" she asked, looking hurt that I wasn't already peeling back the plastic. Her periorbital edema was gone, and there was a bright twinkle in her green eyes.

"Sure," I responded. I never knew if I should open these packages in front of the patient or not. Some patients seemed to prefer that I save their gift until later. Peeling back the clear plastic covering with some difficulty, I began to feel the general nature of the contents beneath the foil. They felt like sausages! *She wouldn't actually bring me those original sausages, would she?* Now peeling back the foil, I could hear Edgar hissing, his last and final effort to contain his amusement.

"Sausages!" I exclaimed, smiling warmly but deeply perplexed. Mrs. Polowski was now shaking with laughter.

"I'm sorry, Dr. Roberts. I just thought… Well, you seem to have a wonderful sense of humor, and I thought you'd think this was pretty funny."

It was funny. Very funny. The funniest joke a patient had ever played on me. I was now laughing with them heartily. They both stood up and made their way to the exam room door.

She turned and started to speak, "…Oh." That pause, again! "In case you're wondering. These aren't from home. They're not the famous three-hundred-year-old family Polish sausage recipe."

I suspect I must have looked visibly relieved as she continued. "I picked them up at the grocery store last night. The plastic and aluminum foil wrapping were just to provide the homemade appearance," she explained.

Kathleen, our office secretary, was also of Polish descent, so I gave the sausages to her. I knew she would enjoy them, knowing nothing of the story behind them. Until the next day, that is; I thought it would be best to tell her after she had eaten them.

CHAPTER 33

"There is nothing so strong or safe in an emergency of life
as the simple truth"

Charles Dickens (1812-1870), English novelist

Every doctor, if asked, can tell you the most difficult or challenging moment she or he has ever experienced in their career. Mine occurred in this small, rural hospital emergency room, where I continued to moonlight to help make ends meet at home and also to fill in some of the gaps in my internal medicine training, where the opportunity to perform certain procedures had been lacking.

I had arrived about ten minutes early one Saturday evening for a twenty-four hour shift, which started at 7:00 p.m. Passing the waiting room, I saw a large group of people intently absorbed in the television broadcast of the opening ceremony of the Summer Olympics in Los Angeles. As I passed the door, President Reagan announced, "I declare open the Olympic Games of Los Angeles."

Gretchen, the head nurse there for over twenty-five years, met me in the hallway.

"Ambulance arriving in seven minutes, and Dr. Lee can't stay. He has another shift at the ER across town. There are two ambulances heading there too."

Dr. Lee, the most experienced emergency medicine physician in this small city, was making his way out of the department and called out, "Sorry," as he ran to his car. The rural but mid-sized Midwestern town had two emergency rooms, and he was headed to the larger of them, fifteen minutes away.

Behind him, on the 24-inch waiting room TV screen, a man in a white suit was flying into the Olympic Stadium wearing a jet pack on his back. Dr. Lee, Gretchen, myself, and the other 2.5 billion people watching worldwide stopped and gawked. When I looked up five seconds later, Dr. Lee was gone.

Turning to Gretchen, I quickly asked, "Is it an MVA (motor vehicle accident)?"

"Yes, car hit mother and daughter on bicycles, from behind. Mother coming here, driver and daughter to the other hospital."

The consummate professional, this head nurse could pack more medical information into fewer words than anyone I had ever met. I found myself omitting articles, adjectives, and adverbs in response to her when she was talking this way.

"Got it," I replied, and I immediately went to work setting up the crash cart in our largest bay, the one we used for trauma. My initial responsibility once the ambulance arrived was to intubate the patient, using a scope to visualize the vocal cords and pass the breathing tube through them under direct observation.

"Two minutes out," called Gretchen. "Mother getting CPR. No pulse, flat-line monitor tracing. No major external wounds." The patient appeared to be clinically dead to the ambulance crew.

I checked the equipment one last time.

"Ambulance here. CPR still in progress." I picked up the scope in my left hand and the tube in my right as the patient came through the double doors, heading directly to my bay. One paramedic continued chest compressions as the ambulance gurney pulled up to within inches of my position. She was a large woman, wearing a neck brace, both of which could make the intubation more difficult.

"Stop CPR!" I called out, and I quickly opened her mouth, inserted the scope, visualized the cords, and watched the tube pass neatly into the trachea. Inflating the balloon, I called out, "Resume CPR!" and the team responded immediately. Instantly, a breathing bag was attached to the breathing tube, and the patient's chest expanded as air filled her lungs.

"IV sub-q," announced the nurse, indicating the intravenous line placed by the emergency technician in the field was no longer inside the vein, where it could be used to deliver medications to the heart. We needed an IV line immediately.

"We had trouble finding veins," said the paramedic apologetically, without need. Nurses were checking both of the patient's arms; no veins were visible.

The central line kit was immediately to my right, and while the paramedics continued CPR, another nurse and I sterilized the chest for the placement of the central line. Sometimes a complicated procedure where the large central veins can be difficult to locate, particularly in a cardiac arrest situation, this effort was immediately successful, and we had established, within minutes, the airway, breathing, and circulation that make up the "ABCs" of CPR.

During all of this, one of the paramedics was relaying as much medical information as possible. "Forty-six-year-old woman on bicycle sideswiped by a car approaching from behind. Unconscious on scene. Severe abrasions right arm and right leg. No obvious head trauma. Cervical collar placed because patient was unconscious."

Gretchen walked into the bay. "Daughter arriving by ambulance in three minutes!" she shouted. "Closed head injury, jaw fracture, multiple contusions. Pulse 120, BP 90/60."

What? Coming to this hospital? I thought to myself. *Didn't Gretchen say she would be going to the other one, where they have a pediatric unit?*

Apparently reading my mind, Gretchen continued, "There's another wreck, the interstate. They're getting those folks."

Our patient before us showed no signs of life. We quickly ran through the protocol to see if we could "awaken" the heart, including the use of adrenaline and a series of electrical shocks. Nothing was working. We paused CPR again for a few seconds in order to obtain a portable chest x-ray, and then we resumed.

As the x-ray machine rolled out of the bay, Gretchen announced, in the distance, "Ambulance here with girl!" and shortly thereafter, the next gurney rolled in with my non-responsive patient's daughter. Behind them, I could now see the tiny but unmistakable image of Aretha Franklin leading a huge choir in "When the Saints Go Marching In" on the waiting room television.

The paramedic announced our new patient's history. "Eleven-year-old girl, bicycling, hit directly from behind by a car, went over the top of the car, rolled off the back. Multiple head and face injuries. Unconscious at scene but moved all extremities in ambulance. Probable jaw and skull fractures."

I saw her thin body as the cart rolled in, blood covering her face and parts of her hair. Prepared as before to insert the endotracheal tube, this time with a scope designed for children, I opened her mouth to clear the airway for the scope and found teeth in the middle of the back of her throat. Her upper jaw had been fractured, and it was necessary to fold back her upper left row of teeth to their original position in order to pass the scope further. Once this obstruction was cleared, it was easy to pass the smaller pediatric tube between her vocal cords and into her trachea and connect the tube to a breathing bag. Her heart and blood pressure were not only compatible with life, but reasonably good.

The nurses were gently palpating her arms and legs for signs of obvious fractures; miraculously, all but the child's left ankle seemed intact. With gloved hands, I was carefully palpating the patient's skull, attempting to find what seemed to be her only source of continued bleeding. Feeling underneath a clump of blood-soaked, matted hair, I felt a defect in her scalp. I peeled back the mass of hair to reveal a half-dollar sized hole in her skull, with bright pink brain tissue glistening in my direct view. I had never before seen anything like this in a living patient.

"Please call a neurosurgeon immediately!" I called out, now barking orders in the typical and well-accepted manner of a serious emergency.

"Clarity and volume," Gretchen had taught me, "are the two things we need from a physician during a cardiac arrest situation. Don't be afraid to yell, as it's better than not being heard."

I moved back quickly to the mother, only eight feet away. Still no response to our efforts. I was reluctant to let a forty-six-year-old woman go without some sense that there was no reversible process here we were missing. The developed chest x-ray was placed on the view box. She had multiple broken ribs on the right, but her lungs and heart looked just fine.

The contrast between mother and daughter could not be missed: the eleven-year-old girl, with life-threatening injuries like an open skull fracture, who seemed perfectly stable from a cardiopulmonary (heart and lung) point of view, and her mother, with some minor abrasions and no heart or lung function whatsoever.

What am I missing here? I kept asking myself, not really sensing I would find an answer to my question.

"Ambulance with driver who hit mother/daughter three minutes out!" a voice called out. "Intoxicated sixty-seven-year-old female, no major trauma evident, possible concussion."

Lord, have mercy, I thought reflexively as I heard the news of yet another arrival. Then, taking my quip more seriously, I thought, *Lord, I really do need some mercy here. Some help.* During my training, I had heard emergency room physicians gripe about another unexpected patient in such a situation. As the team leader, other ER staff looked to the physician for inspiration. This complaining approach had always seemed counterproductive.

"That's okay," I said. "We can do this." *I hope. I've never done this before.*

We had continued CPR on the mother for thirty minutes now, after thirty minutes performed at the accident scene and en route. The presence of the severely injured daughter only eight feet away made me reluctant to let go of her mother, but it was clear there was nothing more we could do.

"Let's stop now," I told the team. "We've done everything there is to be done." Quietly, we removed the tubes and lines from the mother and closed the curtain behind us as we left the pod.

Gretchen pulled me aside. "Dr. Roberts, the husband/father is on an airplane flying back here right now. He will be instructed immediately to come to the hospital on landing. We anticipate arrival in three hours. He doesn't know what is happening." She watched me suppress a grimace. "I'll set up a conference room. Would you like me to join you?"

"Absolutely, Gretchen," I replied. "Not only would I like you there, I need you there."

The flashing lights of the next arriving ambulance painted the corridor walls behind Gretchen in blue, red and yellow tones. Over her shoulder, I saw eighty-four white tuxedo-clad pianists playing "Rhapsody in Blue" on the television. The irony was killing me, but I didn't have time to dwell on it.

"Your plate is full, and you can't be away long," Gretchen concluded. "I'll come find you when we're ready," she said, with confidence and reassurance.

The double doors swung open, and the third gurney from this horrible accident burst through the opening. I raced back to the third bay to meet the patient. The emergency room treatment area was amazingly quiet, the only sounds being the steady and reassuring beeping of the daughter's heart monitor, backed by the slower rhythm of her respirator. Somehow, the nurses had managed to relocate all of their other patients elsewhere in the hospital. I never figured out where.

The driver of the automobile that struck the mother and daughter was a sixty-five-year-old woman who was very thin, almost emaciated, and clearly inebriated. The intensity of my anger at this woman was overwhelming, knowing what lay only eight and sixteen feet to my left, one and two curtains away.

Easy, David, easy. Take a break. You're not ready for this yet. However, I chose to ignore this wise internal counsel and opened my mouth to speak.

"Dr. Roberts, we have the university on-call neurosurgeon on line one for you," interrupted the clerk mercifully, saving the patient from my anger. As I followed her back to the desk she added, "Neither of our neurosurgeons here in town are available this weekend."

I quickly supplied the critically injured girl's relevant medical history, emphasizing the open skull fracture, our hospital's comparative inability to care for a complex patient like this, and her stable cardiovascular condition. There was no question, I said, that she should be transferred immediately.

"You're absolutely right," the on-call neurosurgeon at the university hospital immediately replied. "Unfortunately, we don't have any ICU beds available. You're the third transfer I've had to say no to tonight. I'm sorry."

"Do you have any other suggestions? I asked, now panicking. "This young woman's transfer is her only hope."

"I'm afraid there aren't any open neurosurgical ICU beds within three hundred miles. I've spent all afternoon calling around. If you can keep her stable tonight, we might have something for you in the morning. I promise I will call you back."

"Thanks, I appreciate your effort, but this is an eleven-year-old girl with an open skull fracture. We don't even know where to start." From the

TV behind me came a striking trumpet fanfare, loud, clear, and moving. I learned later that evening it was the "Olympic Fanfare and Theme" composed by John Williams for that very night. Throughout that hectic evening, I would hear the refrain over and over, my still, clear, and inspiring personal call to remain calm and focused in the midst of this storm.

The neurosurgical resident on the phone really did want to be helpful, and he walked me through the orders I needed to write regarding antibiotics, dressings, and monitoring. He convinced me the open fracture could work to my young patient's benefit, as to a certain point it would prevent excessive pressure buildup in the skull. He also promised to have a neurosurgical ICU nurse call our emergency nurse as soon as possible. That call came in five minutes later, with more helpful advice regarding nursing care.

While still frustrated, the phone call break had given me a chance to refocus my mind and energy on providing the best possible patient care, and I was ready to meet the driver. The police had already administered a blood alcohol breath test. She "blew a three-point-zero," the officer told me, which was three times the legal limit.

When I made my way back to the third pod, she was sleeping. Gently tapping her shoulder, I introduced myself and asked her to tell me what had happened.

Confused at first, and appearing surprised to be awakening in a medical facility, she paused. Then with slurred speech, she said, "I was inna acshident. A car acshident."

"Do you remember anything about the accident?" I asked, with as much patience as I could muster. The woman looked incredibly thin and chronically ill.

"No, I don't, I guessh," she softly replied, and she began to cry.

Through a number of sources, including her prior hospital records, we were able to piece together her story. She was a past heavy smoker who was diagnosed with lung cancer about ten months ago. After surgery to remove the mass, she had undergone an aggressive course of radiation and chemotherapy, with no appreciable benefit. The tumor was aggressive, had metastasized to her lymph nodes in the lungs, and she now had five golf ball-sized masses visible on her chest x-ray. According to her husband, who arrived later, it was only the previous afternoon that the doctors had told her they had nothing left to offer.

Her examination was normal, other than the observations that she was twenty pounds underweight and intoxicated. She was also under arrest, and as soon as our medical evaluation cleared her as being fit for discharge, she was taken by the police to jail.

The daughter remained unconscious but stable. From time to time, the nurses observed movements of her legs and arms, and she seemed to have short periods of slightly improved awareness. She also resumed breathing on her own, which was a favorable sign. We were able to transfer her to our hospital's intensive care unit, stable from a cardiac point of view, but in critical neurologic condition. I had written a detailed note in the chart regarding my conversation with the university neurosurgeon and the desirability of transfer when a bed was available, and I could now only hope for the best.

As I finished my admission note, Gretchen came up behind me, put her hand on my shoulder, and squeezed.

"He's here now," she said calmly.

"Who's here?" I asked, the past four hours a blur.

"The girl's father. The woman's husband. He's in the conference room."

As we walked into the hall, she explained she had informed him of the accident and of the desperately critical condition of his wife and daughter, but nothing more than this. She learned from him that there were no other children.

"Just the three of them," she said. "He kept apologizing to me for being out of town, saying he should have never gone on his business trip."

The live coverage of the Olympics had ended, and the day's highlights were being replayed on the screen. As I turned to follow Gretchen, President Reagan, speaking to the assembled athletes, was encouraging our country's team. He then quoted himself from one of his own movie roles, smiling and concluding with "Do it for the Gipper."

Okay, I thought, this one's for the Gipper.

We walked into the room. There sat a man in his early forties, desperately searching my eyes for clues as to the fate of his family.

This is going to be incredibly difficult. Where do I even begin? How would I want to hear this kind of news if I was in his shoes?

After introducing myself, I jumped right in. "Sir, I know it must be terrifying to walk off an airplane and be told to come immediately to the hospital. I can't imagine what you must be going through right now."

He nodded quickly as if to encourage me to speak faster.

"Your wife and daughter arrived here about five minutes apart, four hours ago. You already know they were hit by a car while riding their bicycles. They both had very serious injuries when they arrived. Your wife's heart had stopped beating at the scene of the accident, and despite every possible effort, we were unable to save her. We were not able to restart her heart. I am so sorry there was not more we could do for her."

Gasping, he held his head in his hands, tears streaming down his face. Composing himself, he looked up again, asking quietly, with his eyes, "And my daughter?"

"Your daughter has serious injuries as well, including a skull fracture and a broken jaw, but her heart and lungs appear to be strong. She is upstairs in our intensive care unit. We're working on transferring her to the university hospital as soon as a bed opens. We will keep you posted on our progress."

"Thank God," he sighed. Obviously torn between grief and gratitude, he was unable to speak. He needed time to sort through all of this, just as anyone would.

"I have to go back into the emergency room for a while," I explained. "I know this is more information than you can possibly take in right now. I can't even imagine how difficult this must be for you. Gretchen will stay with you, and I'll be back later. You'll probably have more questions then."

He and Gretchen both nodded, agreeing with this plan. I did return in less than an hour, but the room was empty. Early the next morning, I found him in the ICU, at his daughter's bedside, holding her hand. She was still only minimally responsive, but enough so to give her father hope.

Seeing him there, I could not help but wonder how I would manage, were I in his place.

"Is there anything more I can do to help you, sir?" I asked him.

He had a few simple questions, mainly about the equipment in the ICU and the meaning of various tracings on the monitors. He was attempting to more clearly understand his surroundings as a way to help his daughter;

being the best possible father was his remaining family role. I explained in as much detail as he seemed able to grasp, which was a great deal.

Finally, I said goodbye, shook his hand, and turned to go back downstairs to finish my twenty-four hour shift.

"You know," he said softly, looking up at me as I turned to meet his gaze, "we never really know. We never really know if it's our last day, do we?"

"No," I whispered hoarsely, "we don't."

CHAPTER 34

"Despair is the price one pays for setting oneself an impossible aim."

Graham Greene (1904 - 1991), English author

The ponderously slow nature of our legal system has a way of wearing down even the most innocent of defendants. While never feeling very innocent myself, I was growing increasingly weary under the weight of the proceedings in my malpractice lawsuit.

Two and one-half years ago, six months after the death of Roger Redmond, a tall man in a nondescript suit and tie appeared at our office one day asking for me. I went into the waiting room, and he asked, "Are you Doctor David Roberts?"

"Yes, I am," I replied, completely oblivious to what was happening.

He pulled out an envelope with my name on it and placed it in my hand. "Here you go," he said. "Can I also please speak to Dr. Edwards?"

"Sure," I said, and I sent Mark out to the waiting room.

The envelope was heavy and thick. I went back to our office, sat down at the desk, and extracted the folded eighteen-page document. I had never seen a subpoena before, but at first glance, I knew I was holding legal materials. It took another second to find the line: Regarding the Estate of Roger Redmond vs. Dr. David Roberts. Also on page one were the words "medical malpractice."

Reading on, I found seventeen additional pages describing of all of my perceived failings as a physician. Had they all been true, I had no business practicing medicine. I was devastated.

Do they really think I did all of this? I wondered.

To make matters worse, Mark had also received a subpoena. His supposed crime was being my employer, and as the president of our professional corporation, our practice, he was being held liable for my actions. I honestly felt worse about his subpoena than I did my own.

At that time, the body of literature on the physician experience of being sued could have been contained on one of our three-by-five index cards. Despite my efforts to find some information to help me "normalize" my feelings, none was available. Today, there are numerous studies documenting physician experiences of being sued. For example, the day I received the subpoena, I felt surprise, shock, outrage, anxiety, and dread. A number of studies in the ensuing twenty years would document these identical feelings to be common in most physicians. Feelings of intense anger, inner tension, frustration, and insomnia are frequent throughout this period. Ninety-five percent of physicians feel ongoing emotional stress as the result of a lawsuit, which frankly leaves me more concerned about the remaining five percent.

We also now know that after being sued, a quarter to a third of doctors will experience symptoms of a major depressive disorder, and between two and fifteen percent will experience the onset or exacerbation of a physical illness. Fewer than two percent of physicians acknowledge drug or alcohol misuse during the time period of their lawsuit.

The next day, Bill Stout, the defense attorney assigned to me by my medical liability insurance carrier, would explain such subpoenas are routinely "exaggerated."

"The plaintiff's attorney wants to paint the most horrible picture possible of the acts of negligence on the part of the physician. Don't take it personally," he cautioned. "They're all like this."

"How could I not take something like this personally?" I asked him. "This says I'm the worst doctor in the world."

I was not at my best that morning; I had been up all night, replaying the subpoena's accusations in my head and trying to match them to my version of the facts of my care for Mr. Redmond, now almost three years prior. Coming into the office the next morning, I wondered whether I even deserved to be there.

"Well, everyone does take it personally, at first," Bill clarified. "It sounds like you've never been sued before."

"No, I haven't. I had only been in practice for four months when I first saw this patient."

"Well, that's good. That certainly will help your case. Most physicians do get sued, eventually," he continued, in an effort to reassure me, but I was feeling worse.

At the closing of my medical school graduation ceremony, I rose with my classmates and, as a new physician, took the Hippocratic Oath. The central message of the oath is encapsulated in this line: "I will prescribe regimens for the good of my patients according to my ability and my judgment and never do harm to anyone."

"*Primum non nocere*," the medical school dean proclaimed, four years before my graduation day, as the opening line of his address to new matriculates on our first day of medical school. None of us was a Latin scholar, and there was a great deal of anxious rustling throughout the room while the dean paused for effect.

"First, do no harm," he continued, translating for us, explaining the primacy of this phrase of the oath. "Everything you learn here in medical school will be an extension of these words."

In stark contrast, this subpoena outlined every possible way I had violated this oath. All of the classic emotions of shock, anger, outrage, and denial welled up inside of me as I read and reread the subpoena.

According to Sara C. Charles, M.D., in an article in 2001:

"These reactions are related to [two] major factors: the personality characteristics of physicians and the nature of tort law. Physicians are self-critical and, therefore, have a tendency to doubt themselves, be vulnerable to feelings of guilt, and to possess an exaggerated sense of responsibility. These personality features render them particularly vulnerable to the demands of tort law because fault must be established for compensation to be paid. In medical malpractice law, fault is based on a deviation from the standard of care that resulted in the injury. As a group, physicians are acutely sensitive to any suggestion that they have failed to meet the standard of care or are not "good" doctors. Their honor—that sense of personal integrity that most people cherish—is at issue, and the threat of its loss is devastating. This accusation of failure represents a personal assault: the central psychological event that generates the stress that gives rise to the symptoms and reactions described."

"Failure to diagnose" was the central issue, according to my assigned attorney. I had "failed to meet the standard of care."

I asked my attorney, "How does the court establish the standard of care for a patient who was not truthful about his symptoms?"

Bill said he understood my frustration, but we could get to that discussion later. During this first phone call, he outlined the legal process in medical liability cases and duly warned me that it would go on for years.

And it did. There was the discovery phase. Photocopying all of the records and sending them in. Requests for more information. Meetings with my attorney to prepare me for my deposition, which provided me with guidelines on how to answer questions.

The one that I now recall most clearly was my attorney's instruction, "Now, if the plaintiff's attorney asks you, 'Did your attorney tell you what to say in answer to this question?' you should immediately answer, 'Yes, he did.'" He paused long enough to allow me to look shocked. Seeing the expected response, he continued. "Of, course, the plaintiff's attorney will appear appalled, and then ask you, 'He did, did he? What did he tell you to say?' Take a moment to gather your thoughts, and then say, 'My attorney has clearly instructed me to answer every question with the absolute truth.'"

I told my attorney I actually liked the whole idea of participating in an interchange like this, having been very involved on my high school's debate team, but it seemed improbable Mrs. Redmond's attorney would leave himself wide open to such a rejoinder.

He smiled broadly. "You'd be surprised." I felt comforted.

The deposition itself was another matter. It occurred more than two and one-half years after Mr. Redmond's fateful and fatal hunting trip to Montana. The plaintiff's attorney, my attorney, a court reporter with her little transcribing machine, and I were all crowded into the smallest patient exam room in our medical office. It was a grueling, four-hour interrogation by Mrs. Redmond's attorney. I had rehearsed in my mind various ways of being detached and non-defensive, and I came into the room believing

I could withstand almost anything. So, after the preliminary introductions, in which everyone was cheery and pleasant, I spelled my name for the court reporter, was sworn in, to "tell the whole truth," took a deep breath, and waited confidently for the first question from Mrs. Redmond's attorney.

"Dr. Roberts, do you acknowledge that we would not be in this room today had you correctly diagnosed the nature of Mr. Redmond's severe heart disease, because he would still be alive?"

I had the actual physical sensation of having the wind knocked out of me, despite the absence of any direct physical blow to my chest. Bill and I had not rehearsed an answer to this question.

"Objection," interjected my own attorney, "conjecture."

The other attorney nodded. That seemed to be the end of it. Bill then looked intently in my eyes. I'm not a believer in mind-reading, but I could distinctly hear him convey the thought, sucker punch. He then took a deep breath, as if inviting me to do so as well.

As I did, it occurred to me I had already survived the worst part of the deposition, without having to say a word. Somehow, my confidence was bolstered, and I was able to use the simple and straightforward "tell the truth" strategy over the subsequent four hours. My years of high school debate team experience proved valuable as well.

"Before you answer any question, anticipate the next question, and answer accordingly," Bill had coached the day before.

"So, the second time Mr. Redmond left your office, you were so confident he was healthy, you didn't even schedule a follow-up appointment for him?" quizzed the plaintiff's attorney, early in our fourth hour together.

"I told Mr. Redmond, both verbally and in writing, he should return to my office immediately after he came back from Montana. But he stormed out of the office without following my instructions to make such an appointment," I answered. *I hope I answered his next question, too.*

"You instructed him in writing?" the attorney countered, smiling. "Do you have a copy of the note you gave him in this regard?"

"Well, no, I don't. As I said, he stormed out of the office, taking the note with him." Holding up his medical record and pointing, I continued, "But this chart entry describes word-for-word the information contained in the note I gave him."

"Are you aware that you are the only living person who claims to have seen this note, Dr. Roberts?" He pronounced the word "claims" with the clear implication I was lying.

Don't take the bait, David, I imagined hearing Bill's voice, inside my head.

"I didn't know that," I responded as casually as I could above my rage. I am not particularly fond of being called a liar. I have several little buttons people can push, but this happens to be my big one. "Mrs. Redmond did inform me her husband had told her about the note I gave him and that he never showed it to her. I'm not sure why he would say something like that to her if such a note did not exist."

"Conjecture," countered the plaintiff's attorney over the top of my answer.

"No," Bill quickly responded, "Dr. Roberts' observation is completely in keeping with the intent of the question." Again, the two nodded, as if each had said what they were required to say for the court reporter.

Some secret language, I thought to myself, not unlike the one we have in medicine.

After four hours, I had been asked, and answered, about a dozen questions, each posed in ten different ways. Apparently satisfied with his one hundred twenty questions, the plaintiff's attorney shifted into a posture suggesting a conclusion to our marathon was at hand.

"I have just one last question, Dr. Roberts. I'll come right to the point. Mr. Redmond is dead. You have told his wife you believe he was misdiagnosed. Do you admit full responsibility for his death?"

Another more tactful version of the opening question. I was tired and had been feeling the need to go to the bathroom for the past hour. Bill and I had not covered bathroom breaks in the briefing; absent clear knowledge of protocol, I defaulted to the "holding it in" strategy, which was a poor decision. While the similar question had enraged me four hours before, I had become somewhat numb to the ongoing personal assault and could now think more clearly.

"No, I do not," I began firmly. "I believe…"

"Thank you, Dr. Roberts. I have no further questions."

"Just a minute," Bill asserted. "Dr. Roberts didn't have the opportunity to finish his statement. Let's allow him to continue." *Okay, David, make this good,* Bill's subliminal voice was prompting.

"As I was saying, I believe that Mr. Redmond, or any patient for that matter, has a responsibility to provide his physician with factual information concerning his symptoms. In my meeting with Mrs. Redmond in this very room after her husband's death, she confirmed her husband had repeatedly misrepresented the truth to me about his smoking, his drinking, and his chest pain. I believe I am responsible, as a physician, to take the information provided by the patient, combine it with the results of any tests obtained, and reach logical conclusions based on this information. I strongly believe I did this in Mr. Redmond's case."

Throughout these final words, the other attorney shuffled his papers and appeared anxious to leave. Less than half a second after I finished, he was on his feet. Then, his countenance changed, he smiled, and he casually sat back down. No one else had moved.

"Just one more thing, Dr. Roberts," he said rather slowly. "Did your attorney tell you in advance how to answer my last question?"

CHAPTER 35

"And to kill time while awaiting death,
I smoke slender cigarettes thumbing my nose to the gods."

Jules Laforgue (1860 –1887), French poet

Nothing of consequence seemed to happen in the Redmond case for another six months. Bill Stout would send letters from time to time announcing tentative trial dates, followed by other letters cancelling and rescheduling them. His short notes told me he had conducted depositions: Mrs. Redmond, Mr. Redmond's brother, and three of Mr. Redmond's hunting partners. One letter stated he was headed to Montana to talk to the hunting guide. Each communication rekindled the denial, anger, bargaining, depression sequence in my brain. I never seemed to make it to acceptance.

"Please don't hesitate to call me if you'd like to discuss the case further or would like to hear the details of the depositions," his letters would always end. I never called, apparently more often stuck in the denial phase than any of the others.

The most recent trial date had been set three months earlier, and had not changed. I was to appear in court in one month, over three years since Mr. Redmond's first visit. My competence as a physician was to be the focus of a public proceeding. My confidence in my actions now exceeded my doubts; physician expert witnesses had testified in depositions in a very positive manner regarding the appropriateness of my medical care given the information I had at my disposal.

Bill and I met in my office at 6:00 p.m. one evening to go over everything in detail.

"Maybe I should start with a complete update of all of the depositions, just to equalize information, since we haven't really discussed them," he began. He started with the testimony of Mrs. Redmond and Mr. Redmond's brother. They had been very consistent, and they focused on my admission that I had misdiagnosed Mr. Redmond in their visit to my office shortly after his death. They seemed to recall less about Mrs. Redmond consistently pointing out the inaccurate information her husband had provided, but that was to be expected, Bill said.

The three hunting partners, his longtime friends, provided rather different versions of his death.

"Very inconsistent," Bill reported, "but not in a way what would help or hurt us in court." I was frustrated at hearing all of this. I had assumed the purpose of this slow legal process was to discover the truth. Of course, at this point in my life, I was assuming the truth to be my own version of it.

"The key to the whole case, though," Bill continued after kindly addressing my frustration, "is the testimony of the hunting guide in Montana. I've never heard a story quite like this."

Neither had I.

About two days into the trip, the hunting guide explained, Roger Redmond had become completely despondent. Rather than join the hunting party on its daily excursions, he decided to remain in camp. The hunting guide testified he looked angry and hostile and literally stopped talking to anyone in the group. This went on for days. Each day, the group would come back to find him sitting in a camp chair, heavily intoxicated, with an empty pint whiskey bottle and three or four empty cigarette packs at his feet. Initially, the group laughed it off, saying that Roger was "in one of his moods," but after he had stopped eating food for four days and appeared to be subsisting only on alcohol and nicotine, his friends decided something needed to be done. At a campfire, they selected the one among them who was closest to Roger to talk to him.

"The details become sketchy here," Bill explained. "The hunting guide says the friend talked to Mr. Redmond for about an hour, but the friend says it was a one sentence, one-sided conversation. 'I just told him to shape up,' the friend says. 'He didn't say anything.'"

"So, we'll never know what happened exactly," Bill continued, "although it probably doesn't make any difference. Now we come to the strangest part of the whole story."

"The next morning was the last full day of the trip. The group had a successful day the day before, killing one elk, and had one additional permit available. Despite it being his birthday, Mr. Redmond didn't get out of bed that morning, and he ignored the pleas of his friends to join them on their last hunting day. The group was gone until late afternoon, and they returned to find him missing from the camp. A brief search did locate him, locked inside one of their large rented sports utility vehicles. The hunting guide testified the car was full of blue smoke, and the group could barely see inside the vehicle. 'It was eerie,' Bill now read from the deposition transcript. 'All we could see was the glowing tip of his cigarette in the haze. We could tell he was breathing, because the tip would glow bright red each time he inhaled.'

"The group now surrounded the car, pressing their faces to the glass to locate him. On the right rear passenger side, one of the hunters started pounding on the window and calling out, 'Roger! Roger! Open the door!' But he did not respond. There was only one set of car keys, and they were presumably inside the car, as the radio was playing softly in the background.

"After about twenty minutes, and three additional cigarettes, each signaled by the bright flame of his butane lighter, most of the group headed back to the center of camp for dinner. One of his friends remained, intermittently calling out to him to open the door. The sun was setting when the friend called out to the others, 'He looks like he's having a seizure!'

"Somebody broke the window with a camp shovel, and with some difficulty, the group, now reassembling at the vehicle, opened the door and pulled him out onto the grass. He wasn't breathing. He had no pulse. The group attempted to perform CPR for about forty-five minutes, with no success. In their remote location, there was no hope of any rescue. The guide distinctly recalled one of the hunters muttering at the end, 'He killed himself,' but that individual had no recall of such a comment in his own deposition."

I was having trouble taking this new information in all at once. Mr. Redmond's path of self-destruction had begun at least twenty-five years ago, and it had ended in Montana, with only a brief passage through my office. Whatever the remaining weight of responsibility I still felt, it was clear to me he had died by his own hand.

"Surely, a jury would see it that way, too, wouldn't they?" I asked Bill, feeling quite optimistic.

There was a long silence. "Well, you never know," he replied quite tentatively, and he went on to explain the vagaries of jury selection and composition, venue, and the influence any given judge might have on a case. I was incredulous.

"How could anyone see the truth differently than I do," I asked him. He said something about every person having his or her own truth, including jurors.

"What percent of people smoke cigarettes?" he asked.

"About thirty percent in this country," I responded, with a statistic then current.

"Okay, that's four jurors. What percent of people drink excessively?"

"Maybe fifteen to twenty percent of men and five percent of women, here in our state."

"So we're up to a total of six jurors, unless some of them do both, in which case they'll be even more entrenched." I winced at his mathematics; he was exactly right. "Of course, you also have to decide if you want to be in the middle of this public display. Sometimes these cases can have pretty extensive newspaper coverage." He went on to explain the pros and cons of a jury trial in a case such as this.

I was feeling even more flustered now. "So, what is the alternative?" I asked.

"Typically, parties in a case like this may reach a settlement. Particularly when the patient dies. At forty-five years of age, Mr. Redmond was a relatively young patient, with at least twenty years of income-producing potential ahead of him. This really increases our risk here," Bill pointed out.

I was so angry I couldn't even hear him. I wanted my version of the truth to prevail. I wanted to be vindicated.

"But wouldn't settling the case be tantamount to admitting I was guilty of killing him?" I asked.

"No, in legal terms, when a settlement is negotiated, it specifically states that no guilt for wrongdoing is being asserted. The parties have just agreed on certain terms rather than carrying the case forward." Experienced with taking other doctors through this critical point in malpractice cases, he was patient and kind to me in his explanation. "The plaintiff's attorney knows that they are on shaky ground here and that Mr. Redmond's behavior was extreme. While some malpractice cases involving the death of a forty-five-year-old man could involve millions of dollars, I believe this one could be settled for less than $100,000."

"One hundred thousand dollars! That's more than two years of my salary!" I was appalled.

He went on to explain to me the various dynamics of a settlement. It would be confidential and not a public document. Once it was signed and sealed, I could not be sued over this case again. I would have to report the suit every time I applied for medical staff privileges for at least ten years, describing the "failure to diagnose coronary disease" aspect of the case, and then just state the case was settled for "less than X dollars," with X being just above the final number.

"It's your decision, David," Bill emphasized. "Your insurance company is willing to take this case to trial. While they understand the advantage of settling the case, they also know the importance of going to court in strong cases for the defense."

By now, it was 7:45 p.m. Bill wisely let me off the hook. "Look, you don't have to decide anything tonight. We can meet again and talk it through some more if you like. You now have all of the information in this case, you know everything I know. Go home, get some rest, and think it over. Call me when you're ready."

He left the office, and I returned to my desk and sat motionless for about twenty minutes, unable to reach any conclusion. I reflected on a passage from the Gospel of John I had read in my early morning time of reflection that week, where Pontius Pilate, at the trial of Jesus, says, "What is truth?" *Indeed, David, what is truth?* It was dawning on me that mine was not the only truth, but at this point, I was only becoming more confused.

Finally, I recognized I was not in the proper frame of mind to make a good decision, locked up the office, and went home.

I am unable to explain adequately how my mind resolves complex questions and problems when I am deep in sleep. I am probably afraid to admit, even now, that the absence of my conscious mind, and more specifically my ego, enhances my brain's ability to weigh the concepts of "truth" and "justice" in a much more objective manner. Despite my confusion about this complex issue when falling asleep that night, I still believed myself to be an expert at determining my own truth and my own sense of justice. *I want to be vindicated* was my last waking thought.

CHAPTER 36

"Of all strategies, knowing when to quit may be the best."

Chinese proverb

My thoughts apparently drifted with me into my vague, dreamlike state. "Why is it so important to be vindicated, David?" Looking around, I realized I was on trial, in a poorly lit courtroom, at dusk. The room was packed, and every person in every seat was someone I knew. The jury sat to my left, each with their piercing gaze pointed toward me. I was sitting on the witness stand in my white lab coat, shirt, tie, suit pants, socks, and polished black wingtips, attempting to answer the difficult questions fired at me by a hard-edged prosecuting attorney, who just happened to look exactly like me. As I tried to formulate an answer to this first question, I had the odd sense I was looking in the mirror. One of the ways we can interpret our dreams is to imagine each character as some unique part of ourselves. What part of me was represented by this fervent prosecutor?

"I went into medicine to help others," I began. "I thought I was going to make a difference for people, helping them heal, helping them to care for themselves. Obviously, I didn't do that for Mr. Redmond, did I?"

"I'll ask the questions here, Dr. Roberts," my twin corrected me. "Your job is to find the answers."

"Sorry."

"So, Dr. Roberts, was it really a life of selfless service you were seeking in medicine? Of helping others, expecting nothing in return?"

These questions are getting harder. "Well, I thought so, anyway," I replied, realizing I was falling into some sort of trap.

"Then why the need to be vindicated? You say you did your best. Isn't that enough for you? Or do you have some deeper need here?"

I thought about the odd relationship between my efforts as a physician and the feedback I received from patients and families. On the one extreme, I had stayed up all night in a young mother's room in the coronary care unit, resuscitating her multiple times from what would have been otherwise fatal cardiac arrhythmias, ultimately watching her leave the hospital under her own power. On the other end of the spectrum, I had been awakened dozens of times in the middle of the night by patients who just wanted reassurance. (My favorite was the friend of mine who called me at three in the morning, recited his symptoms, and then asked me if I thought they were serious enough that he should call his doctor.) Somewhere in the middle, were the trips from the holiday dinner table into the hospital to see a patient who could have obtained appropriate care had they been seen a few days earlier. Not to mention all of those Saturday morning phone calls from people who just noticed they had run out of their prescription medication. *Well, how many pills were in the bottle yesterday, after you took the last one?* I always thought, but I never actually asked.

I realized the one thing all of these cases had in common was my anger about them. These patients, or their families, never bothered to say, "Thanks for staying up all night and repeatedly saving my life," when they left the hospital to return to their families. They never began their phone call with, "Look, I am really embarrassed to be having to call you on the weekend about my prescription," or, "I'm so sorry to be bothering you on Christmas Day."

My opposing counsel interrupted my litany of "doctor as victim" examples. "Does this life of selfless service you have chosen, David, require every patient to thank you for everything you do?"

"Well, no, but it's nice when..."

"Could it be that what you are searching for in medicine, beyond the legitimate desire to serve others, is the appreciation they provide you for the work you do?"

"Objection, your honor!" chimed in my defense attorney. I hadn't noticed him before now. He also looked exactly like me, but he was not wearing a white lab coat. "Let Dr. Roberts answer the previous question without interruption."

"Overruled," replied the judge, quickly. He, too, bore a strange resemblance to a much older and perhaps wiser version of me.

"Could you repeat the question?" I responded meekly, confused by all of the new characters in the courtroom.

My prosecutor took a long slow breath, as if impatient with my reluctance to face this critical challenge. "Could it be that what you are looking for in medicine, beyond the legitimate desire to serve others, is the appreciation they provide you for the work you do?"

I had two answers to his question. *Of course not*, first came to mind. The primary benefit of this answer was its ability to preserve my aura of sainthood, if not near martyrdom, and give legitimacy to all of my suffering in my never-ending fight to heal humankind through my life of selfless service. The only possible downside to this answer would be this: it isn't actually true.

You do want to be appreciated, David. Everyone does. For every patient who didn't take the time to express their gratitude for some perceived sacrifice on my part, there was always another who brought food, or sent a card, or made me something with their own hands, most often in return for the simplest act on my part, one that never seemed to me to be the slightest inconvenience at all. I had a systematic way of discounting these heartfelt and appreciative acts, though. At the same time, I think I amplified my frustration and anger when the bigger sacrifices I thought I had made went unrecognized.

I swallowed hard. Intuitively, I knew this dream was about finding the piece of truth I needed. The fact that it was being played in a courtroom was apparently not lost on me, even in my unconscious state.

"You're right," I began, feeling a bit lighter as I unburdened myself, "I want to help people, but in the end, what I really want is for them to appreciate me for what I do. To recognize the sacrifices I make. To affirm my identity as one who cares." There, I had said it.

"So, if I understand you correctly, you are saying your happiness in medicine is dependent not so much on the work you actually do, but upon the response you receive from your patients?" It was clear my prosecutor was nudging me slowly towards the edge of some nearby cliff, but I didn't mind. It had felt refreshing to confess my own selfish motives.

"Well, yes, I guess that's one way to put it. Of course, I still derive a great deal of satisfaction from helping them."

"No doubt you do. But this is often a very sick group of people, and you see them at critical junctures of their lives. Some of them are barely hanging on to life itself. Do you really think it is wise to stake your own personal happiness and professional satisfaction on their ability to say, 'Thank you?'"

Now that was a very good question. "Well, no, I guess not. But if this sense of appreciation doesn't come from my patients, then where will it come from?"

"Just another reminder, Dr. Roberts," said the prosecutor in the mirror, a bit more kindly now, "I'll be the one asking the questions here. You're the one providing the answers."

He then paused for what seemed like dramatic courtroom effect. I shifted in my seat nervously, sensing the edge of the cliff immediately before me.

"Dr. Roberts, I have only one final question, but it is the most important one you will answer. In fact, it's the question you just asked me. So tell me now, if that sense of appreciation you need doesn't come from your patients, then where will it come from?"

I now paused, too, but not for any dramatic effect. I was digging as deeply as I could within myself to discover the truth.

"I suppose it has to come from deep within me," I confessed, now feeling lighter than air. "I need to be confident about my calling in medicine and the life of service I have chosen. I need to believe this with certainty."

"So, if you can know this, really know your purpose in this world, then from where will your vindication come?"

Hey, I thought he said he had only one more question, I protested internally. However, I knew it was not only the primary question of my dream, but the answer as well.

"My vindication can only come from inside of me," I answered softly.

"No further questions, your Honor," he concluded, and he returned to his seat.

* * *

I awoke the next morning feeling certain about my best course of action. I explained my reasoning to Mark, who completely agreed. I called Bill at lunchtime and instructed him to settle the case on behalf of myself and our professional corporation.

"Whatever vindication I need will have to come from within me, and not the legal system," I told him.

"Well, that's something I've never heard a physician say before," he said, surprised. "But I think you're right."

Some weeks later, a final settlement document arrived in the mail. The amount, ironically, was about a whole year's salary for a primary care physician, and well less than the $100,000 Bill had set as the upper limit. Suddenly, I felt as free to talk about the medical aspects of the case privately with friends and colleagues as I had been mute before. I could not speak about the actual terms of the settlement, which were confidential. Surprisingly, almost half of the physicians in whom I confided returned the favor by telling me of their own malpractice suits. I was surprised, having felt so alone the past several years, to learn of the number of excellent physicians named in legal actions.

The debate about whether "defensive medicine" resulting from malpractice suits raises the overall cost of healthcare has been raging in America for forty years. Defensive medicine is defined as a deviation from sound medical practice, induced primarily by threat of liability. One interesting study has shown that forty percent of over 1,400 malpractice suits involved no medical error whatsoever. There are convincing studies showing physicians may increase their test-ordering frequency for a time after a suit and then return to their prior practice. Other researchers estimate that the United States spends over one hundred twenty-five billion dollars annually on the excessive tests and procedures ordered by physicians hoping to cover themselves in the event of a poor patient outcome. With such conflicting evidence, it is difficult to determine definitively whether tort reform, the most frequently suggested remedy to the malpractice crisis, will in fact lower national health care costs.

I can say with certainty that to this day, I maintain a higher index of suspicion in any patient who has symptoms even remotely consistent with cardiac disease, and I also know I still order more cardiac studies than I would had I not been sued. In addition, I take more careful medical histories from patients with chest pain, perform more thorough examinations, and am more likely to pick up the phone and go over a case with a cardiologist if I feel some level of uncertainty. I must admit, the individual patient benefits in each of these cases, whereas the cost to society is clearly higher.

Interestingly, this extended level of caution I experience in relation to each patient with possible heart disease has not extended to patients with other types of problems, a personal observation in my own practice that has been confirmed by sound research. Physicians who have been sued become more careful and order more tests with similar subsequent patients, but they don't change their patterns of practice with other types of problems they face daily.

As I now reflect on the curious death of Roger Richmond, I can't help but wonder whether he is an archetype of our consumption-oriented American society. For example, we know the cost to this country of the health consequences from cigarette smoking is in the neighborhood of two hundred billion dollars annually. This amount of money would be sufficient to provide an excellent insurance policy for over sixty million people, more than our actual number of uninsured Americans. The costs of obesity are likewise greater than the cost of covering our uninsured.

On an even deeper level, Mr. Redmond may also symbolize the tendency in our society to expect that medical science can somehow save us from ourselves, no matter how badly we abuse our bodies. I have seen so many people behind the closed examination room door who seem unable to acknowledge the cause and effect relationship between their poor health behaviors and their failing bodies.

CHAPTER 37

"Live as if you were to die tomorrow.
Learn as if you were to live forever."

Mahatma Gandhi (1869 - 1948),
political and spiritual leader of India

As I entered the double-wide trailer for what was to be my very first house call in over four years in internal medicine private practice, I beheld a surrealistic sight. There were three people in the room: my patient, his son, and his daughter. The living room in which I stood appeared to comprise over two-thirds of the square footage of this trailer, with a kitchenette to the right. Sparsely decorated, probably unchanged in any detail since wife and mother Alma Clark's death four years earlier, the room had a sad and neglected appearance. The light played off the kitchenette table at an angle revealing the greasy swirls from forty-eight months of masculine cleaning.

Chuck Clark, who had been in reasonably good health only four months earlier, now lay dying in a hospital bed situated to my left. His son and daughter, twenty-one and eighteen years old, were each ensconced in the farthest corners of the dimly lit room, she appearing terrified, he seemingly bored. I could physically feel the oppressing senses of fear and uncertainty as I entered their cold home. The children's eyes turned toward me, looking as though I was their family's personal angel of death; they were right. No one spoke.

I had received a call from the hospice nurse an hour earlier to inform me Mr. Clark had a very low blood pressure and appeared to be failing. I was on call that night for our medical group and had stayed late in the hospital finishing the day's work. I was already more than two hours late for dinner at home. Having taken care of the Clark family since my internship eight years ago, I knew this illness was devastating to his children, and I felt that perhaps I could help in some small way by driving over to his trailer.

It was dusk when I left the hospital. On the western horizon, the fading light looked like a black and white photo. Everything was grey, and a deep chill settled into me as I ran to my car through the cold, damp wind. On that seven-mile drive to the Clarks' trailer from the hospital, under the blackening cloud ceiling, I reviewed my eight years of history with the Clark family. Alma, Chuck's wife, had died in the hospital emergency room four years ago. I had walked out to the waiting room and told the family she was gone. That was my debut as the Clark family's angel of death. Now, or at least sometime in the next several weeks, I knew I would be having a similar conversation with the two children about their father.

Five years earlier

Chuck had a sixth-grade education and had worked in a local auto factory sweeping floors for the past twenty years. An incredibly hard worker, he would do anything to avoid missing a day at the plant. He had also been a hard-living man. Exactly five feet tall (the same as Alma), weighing about 140 pounds, he had square features, a kind and generous smile, and an always-appreciative response to the medical care he received. There are ways in which each of us believes that we have had hardship in our lives; Chuck clearly had more challenges than most. Yet he retained a certain optimistic quality, which at times put me to shame. I would be feeling a bit sorry for myself about getting only three hours of sleep on-call the night before, and Chuck would arrive in the office with his winning smile, in the face of the inordinate obstacles he faced as a single parent in a minimum-wage job, and suffering from serious heart disease.

He freely confessed he had little to no understanding of his two teenage children. Alma had almost exclusively managed those relationships in their more traditional division of labor. To Chuck, Adrian and Maija might just as well have been aliens from another universe.

"I took my daughter shopping for a bra yesterday," he began, and then looked deep into my eyes, smiled, shook his head in long slow strokes, shrugged his shoulders, and finally sighed, as though nothing more needed to be said. It didn't.

Having unconsciously chosen to invest more of my time and energy in medicine than in my own three children, I could vicariously experience this terror, and I felt the chill run up my spine as I imagined myself in his shoes. I suddenly felt more refreshed; my poor night's sleep now seemed like only a trivial inconvenience.

Through the years, I developed a real affection for him and looked forward to his visits. He seemed to be such a simple and straightforward man; I felt I was so complicated. There was something so poignant about his "my life is a disaster, I am lost in this world, and I have so much to be thankful for" philosophy, something I would eventually understand I needed to learn myself. One day, I mentioned to him how much I admired his ability to find the small ray of light in every patch of darkness and that I had learned a great deal from him. He looked up suddenly, completely surprised by what I said. Then he smiled again. There was a moment of understanding: we both not only admired but loved each other like family. Being men, of course we said absolutely nothing about how we were feeling, but we knew.

He had smoked two to three packs of cigarettes per day for forty years, but he had quit at the time his wife spent her first week in the medical intensive care unit, about one year before her death. He came to see her just after she had a tube placed down her throat and was connected to the breathing machine. He had never been in an ICU or seen a ventilator. As soon as he saw her attached to the machine, he started to panic and then hyperventilate. I ran over from the office to see him, and by the time I arrived, he was complaining of chest tightness. Had I not known Chuck for several years, I would have assumed, as the ICU intern had, he was having a panic attack. But there was something about the look of a deeper, more primordial fear in his eyes, the slightest bluish tint to his lips, and, to be honest, the sense of impending doom that I was feeling inside of me, which told me to rush him down to the emergency room.

His electrocardiogram showed that he was having an acute myocardial infarction, a massive heart attack. Thirty minutes later, the cardiologist was catheterizing his heart and visualizing on the fluoroscopic monitor what we call in medicine "the widow-maker": a ninety-five percent stenosis, or narrowing, of the left main coronary artery. The flow of blood to most of his heart ran through a narrow channel about the width of a thread! He didn't know it at the time, but he had just smoked his last cigarette.

Only forty-five minutes after his heart cath, he was in the operating room having four different bypass grafts sewn in place to restore flow to each of the major arteries of his heart. The next morning, making rounds at the hospital, I first saw Chuck, and then Alma, each in their respective intensive care units, both in critical condition, and both, as it turned out, on their way to recovery. True to form, Chuck had found a way to smile at me around the ventilator tube that coursed between his lips and down his throat to his lungs.

I've never seen anyone smile around an endotracheal tube, I remember thinking at the time. *Only Chuck!* I gave him the "thumbs up" sign with my right hand and returned his bright greeting. He recovered rapidly, and he and Alma were home within the week.

When Alma died the following year, Chuck struggled to manage his job and family responsibilities on top of his new, surgically imposed, healthy lifestyle. He actually did better than I imagined possible, quitting smoking "frozen turkey style," as he called it, claiming it was "much harder than just regular cold turkey." I laughed heartily at his play on words. He beamed, recognizing the pleasure he had given to me. It was at that moment I noticed that Chuck never actually laughed aloud. Sometime early in his life he had found a way to express all of his joy in his smile, and that was enough for him, and for those around him.

Chuck also began a daily program of walking for exercise, at a time when factory workers never took their lunch break to make four laps around the huge parking lot. He lost some weight, and his cardiac function improved much more than I guessed was possible.

The recent progression of events in Mr. Clark's case had been unbelievably rapid, leaving me still searching for some clue as to how I might help him. I remembered the day in August, four months prior to this trip to his trailer, when he called me because he became very short of breath at work, in an area of the plant permeated by strong paint fumes. It was hard to say what might be going on over the phone. *Low blood oxygen levels? Worsening emphysema? Lung damage from organic vapors? Lung cancer?* In any case, he needed evaluation and came into the office that day, right after his shift at the auto plant had ended.

In the exam room, he mentioned again that his wheezing started after being in the midst of dense clouds of paint fumes. His chronic tension headaches were more severe too, sometimes waking him up at night. Did he have migraine headaches? A brain tumor? Perhaps this was just the stress of parenting? When I examined his lungs, I noted he was wheezing, probably from the paint fume exposure, on top of the damage from his forty years of smoking that not even his past five years of abstinence could fully repair. His heart sounded fine. From a neurological point of view, he was normal, and there was nothing in his examination suggestive of a brain tumor. His blood oxygen levels were adequate, and other lab work was normal.

As was the case any time Chuck missed work to see me, something was clearly wrong. But a chest x-ray and a CT scan of his head had both been normal just three months ago, and Chuck did not want to repeat them now, so I prescribed additional medications for his wheezing and headaches, and I asked him to come back in a week for a reassessment. On the way out of the exam room, he tossed the slip restricting his work activities that I had just penned into the trash can.

His condition progressed rapidly downhill. Five days later, he was admitted to the hospital with internal bleeding from two stomach ulcers. He also had what appeared to be a mild left lower lobe pneumonia (lung infection) on his chest x-ray and a urinary tract infection.

After going home from the hospital, Chuck's headaches became much worse, and he came back to the office in early May. Usually a very stoic individual, Chuck had tears in his eyes. He was having trouble walking, getting dizzy when he rapidly turned his head, was selecting the wrong words (saying "feet" when he meant to say "feel," for example), had fallen four times, and was unable to remember his home phone number. The last symptom bothered him more than the sum all of the others. This time, his physical examination showed multiple abnormalities. He couldn't see anything in his right peripheral vision, and he staggered when he walked. He could not remember any of the digits of his phone number.

Alarmed by his symptoms, I admitted him to the hospital and ordered another a chest x-ray and CT scan of the head. The results were quite startlingly different from the studies we had obtained less than four months earlier. Where there had been a "suggestion" of a possible pneumonia only two weeks ago, there was now a robin's egg-sized mass in his left lower lung field. The CT scan, normal only ten weeks earlier, now showed an apricot-sized mass in the left posterior portion of the brain, with massive swelling of the surrounding brain tissue. As I reviewed the films with the radiologist, he kept checking the names and dates on each of the studies.

"I can't believe these are the same person, only three months apart," he said sadly, shaking his head.

Mr. Clark had what we presumed to be a rapidly growing lung cancer that had already metastasized to his brain. A CT scan of his chest showed characteristic findings of lung cancer, which had spread to many lymph nodes in the middle of his chest. One of our pulmonary specialists passed a scope into Chuck's lung and obtained a biopsy that showed "poorly differentiated adenocarcinoma of the lung," in other words, a very aggressive tumor with very few available effective treatments. His prognosis was exceedingly poor.

As Chuck and I sat and talked in his hospital room, I tried to explain what was happening to him and why it all seemed to be occurring so rapidly. I told him there were some available treatments, including radiation for the brain tumor, which could help his vision, his emotional state, and his growing confusion.

"Will I be able to remember my phone number again?" he asked innocently, as if this were his only problem.

"Well," I cautiously responded, "I can't promise you it will, but I sure hope so." As I began my explanation regarding his lung cancer, he held up his hand to stop me.

"Doc, we both know that I can't be cured, right?" he asked, point blank.

"Well, I'd like to have the oncologist see you and tell us whether…"

"Look, I know I'm dying. I know I don't have that much longer here. Alma felt the same thing just a few weeks before she died. Can I just go home and be with my children?"

While he had phrased his last statement in the form of a question, it was clear this was his decision. We were able to start him on his radiation therapy treatments, and he was discharged to his home two days later.

It was almost dark now, and I missed my turn into the poorly lit trailer park. Backtracking, I found the entrance and tried to read my hastily scribbled directions I had received from the hospice nurse. "The trailer park is like a maze," she had told me. "It took me twenty minutes to find his trailer my first time here."

It had now been three months since his last hospitalization. Walking from my car to what I hoped was Chuck's trailer, the events of these past two weeks flowed through my memory. His even more rapid daily decline. My failed efforts to persuade him, and the neurosurgeons, to remove the brain metastasis. More internal bleeding. Blood clots in his legs. Bleeding into the wall of an abdominal aortic aneurysm we had been following for years. Every day it seemed something else went wrong with him. I was seeing him in my office two or even three times per week.

Usually, his first words to me when I entered the exam room were, "Hi, Doc. I still can't remember my phone number." Then he would smile again and raise his eyebrows, as though one of us was in the process of winning some sort of wager.

At one of these office visits, I pondered his consternation about this. What was the big deal? Why was he so upset about his phone number with everything else he was facing? Incurably curious, I finally asked him.

"Doc, I call my children at home after school every day, just to make sure everything is okay. It just kills me when I can't call them." Of course, he added, he now kept a copy of the number on a scrap of paper in each of his socks, so he didn't have to remember. At this point, though, he had only worked three days out of the previous four weeks.

Every possible treatment for each of his new problems seemed to conflict with his other conditions or treatments. If we put him on blood thinners for the blood clots in his legs, it might make the bleeding in his stomach or aorta worse and could cause bleeding in his head around the tumor, which was more fragile in light of the recent radiation. There was no right answer for anything, it seemed. We general internists tend to look for clear solutions, but what was clear was there were no absolutes for Chuck other than the one we eventually all will face.

There was a single, momentary bright spot in the rapid downhill course over those four months. Seven days prior to my visit, I had found a note on my desk from Cynthia, my nurse: "Mr. Clark called. Wanted you to know he can remember his phone number now. Said you'd be glad to hear the radiation and steroids worked. ☺" Chuck's simple optimism was inspiring, and I smiled to think of his focus on something positive, while buried in the avalanche of his medical problems.

CHAPTER 38

"There are, aren't there, only three things that we can do about death: to desire it, to fear it, or to ignore it."

C.S. Lewis (1898 - 1963, English author, in Letters to an American Lady (7 June 1959)

It was about nine o'clock as I walked up the two aluminum steps to Mr. Clark's front door that Thursday night. The poor outdoor lighting in the trailer park lot and complete darkness of the cloudy, moonless Midwestern night served as a prelude to what I would find inside. I knocked and waited but received no response. After trying the door handle and finding it open, I let myself in to see Mr. Clark and his two children, all located in a geometrically maximum distance from each other.

Keeping on my jacket to ward off the chill inside, I approached the bed.

"Mr. Clark. It's Dr. Roberts. How are you doing?" He looked up, unable to speak, but had a warm and welcoming look in his eyes. He was a ghost of the man I had known so well, having lost at least thirty pounds, and was deathly pale from his cancer-induced low blood count. I thought of how gregariously he would have provided the grand tour of his trailer had he been well. He lifted his right hand an inch off the bed in an effort to shake mine, in the manner we always used to greet each other, but he lacked the strength to do so. I took the cool hand in mine, shook it firmly, and then held it.

"Are you in pain?" I asked, knowing the hospice nurse had last given him an injection over four hours ago. He gently and barely shook his head from side to side and then smiled in a way that brought peace into the room.

The scene that night could not have been a starker contrast to Alma's death in the cacophony of the emergency room four years prior. The trailer was deathly quiet; all was still. The only sound was Chuck's deep and slow breathing. Inhaling and exhaling along with him, I began to feel an air hunger. He was breathing only about eight times per minute, far too slow for a man as sick as he was. The breaths were mostly deep gasps, in the slow crashing rhythm of waves, about one every seven or eight seconds, less than half the rate I would have expected. Through my stethoscope, his lungs sounded clear and without wheezes, except for the area affected by the tumor. His heart examination was normal.

"Dr. Roberts, why is this happening to my father?"

I turned to see his daughter almost cowering in the kitchenette, her small head and shoulders framed between the counter and the cabinet. Maija was her mother's daughter: small, frail, expressionless. Her short brown hair appeared to have been last groomed months ago, and the drab colors of her clothes appeared to have drained away any color in her face.

She seems so afraid. What she's really asking is, "Why is this happening to us, his children?" I have no idea how to answer that. As I began to speak, I became acutely aware of my own helplessness in the face of her fear.

Her brother, in the opposite corner, stared intently at the floor just below his father's bed, appearing to be indifferent to all that was happening, ignoring death. Adrian looked as much as the former image of his father as his sister resembled their mother: short and stocky, with angular facial features and his father's square jaw. I was sure I had seen the flannel shirt he wore on his father at his last office visit.

"I know this must be incredibly difficult for both of you, having already lost your mother," I began, swallowing hard, searching for some way to bring them an ounce of comfort. Behind me, I noticed the rhythm of the breathing waves had started to become more irregular, some loud crashes, some soft ones, no longer at a constant interval.

Over the past few months, I have done nothing to help your father, I thought. I was struggling mightily to think of something that I could do to help his children.

I recalled an experience in the medical intensive care unit during my internship. One of my patients was dying; her family and our hospital priest were in the room. I was so inspired by Father Tim's gentle and loving approach in the patient's hour of death. Maybe something similar could help this family tonight.

"Come over here and sit on your Dad's bed," I began, watching the children for a response. Maija, his daughter, began to walk towards me. I took her hand and had her sit on her father's left side. "Hold his hand," I continued, as I placed his hand in hers.

Adrian wasn't moving, though. I walked over to him and held out my hand, suspecting I was emblematic of all of the authority figures he had battled through his adolescence, including his father. He would not take my hand. I stood there facing him directly, still holding it out. After a brief standoff, he did get up, shuffled slowly toward the bed, sat on his dad's right side, and held his hand. There were now gaps between Chuck's breaths that lasted as long as twenty seconds, but a soft smile appeared on his face, and it now broadened.

"Maija, Adrian, your father is dying," I began, slowly and softly. "I can only imagine how difficult this must be for you, but this can also be a wonderful moment for him. He can't talk right now, but I know he can hear us." Both children were looking directly into their father's beaming face. "I realize he may not have always been the easiest man to talk to. I, too, had a hard time talking to him sometimes, but this is your chance, while he is still alive, to say anything to him you haven't yet said."

The awkward silence was only interrupted by Chuck's deep gasping breaths. I realized I, too, had so much to say to him, but this was really the family's time to be together. *Maybe you can help them start this, though, David.*

"Chuck," I whispered, "thank you for teaching me to smile in the face of my troubles."

"Dad," Maija immediately added, "I love you so much." With her confession, all emotional dams in the room burst, and both she and her brother began to talk to their father in the way they had always longed to.

"I'm sorry I couldn't talk to you much after Mom died," she continued, weeping.

"Dad, I know I have been a royal pain in the ass for the past ten years," Adrian said. Hearing this, Maija let out a combination of a laugh and a sob. "It wasn't you. Honest, Dad," Adrian continued. "It was me. I have just been so angry I didn't know…" His voice trailed off in his sobs. "I love you, Dad."

As their heartfelt and pent-up confessions of love and devotion poured forth, there was a transformation occurring in the room I will never be able to adequately describe. Standing at the foot of the bed, I watched Maija move closer to her dad and begin to stroke his face. Adrian gave him a hug. Chuck opened his eyes and gazed at both of them in wonder, looking as though he wasn't sure if he had just arrived in heaven or was still on earth. An even deeper smile filled his face, and then it seemed to inhabit the entire room. The atmosphere of love and peace at this moment was far more powerful than anything I had ever experienced.

My eyes also filled with tears, and I thought of all of the deaths I had attended during my medical training. Almost every one of them had been a "code," where a patient experiences either a cardiac or respiratory arrest, and the code team is paged to respond immediately. After running at top speed down halls and up stairs, the team members arrive, breathless. Each resuscitation effort involves near-violent compressions of the breastbone of the dying patient, sometimes breaking ribs, not to mention the progressively stronger electric shocks delivered to the chest. All of this generally occurs in the patient's hospital room, crowded with doctors, nurses, respiratory technicians, and usually with me, at that time the internal medicine resident on-call and code team leader, shouting orders for more intravenous medications or additional electrical shocks. Rarely, our efforts were successful, at least in the short run, but most often, they were not. When the patient could not be resuscitated, usually after thirty to sixty minutes of extreme effort, we would all leave the room with a deep sense of failure. Death is failure, we were taught, and so we believed.

I thought about Mr. Harandi, the angry man with the ruptured heart, recalling his cardiac arrest, the violent resuscitation effort there on the hospital hallway floor, and the much greater sense of failure I had felt due to my personal role immediately before his collapse. While his rage had carried him to his own death, here in this room, Adrian's anger seemed to be melting away in the light of his father's smile and in his dying.

Here before me was Chuck Clark, lying in the arms of his children, looking the happiest I had ever seen him, likely experiencing here on his deathbed the most wonderful moment of his difficult and challenging life.

During my daily reading time, at five o'clock that very morning, I had come across a challenging and thought provoking quote by C.S. Lewis, the English author: "There are, aren't there, only three things that we can do about death: to desire it, to fear it, or to ignore it." Sitting quietly on my couch at home, only sixteen hours earlier, I had quickly (and rather superficially) concluded I could completely understand why people fear death and how they choose to ignore it as a result. In that early morning moment, though, I couldn't fathom how one could desire death itself, having been such an involved participant in the attempted, and failed, resurrections of so many deathly ill patients. I could imagine the desire for what might await us on the other side of death, but this was not Mr. Lewis' subject. He was talking about the act of dying itself.

Standing there in the trailer, I thought, *What is it that makes death in the hospital so antithetical to what is happening here? What it is about being physicians that causes us to miss this? That universally compels us to deny the finality of death and to try to reverse it almost every instance? Has it ever even occurred to each, or any, physician that there is an alternative to fighting, fearing, or ignoring death?*

I also stood in wonder at all of the improbabilities of my being present for this sublime moment: my very first house call in five years of practice; my patient dying during my visit; my also being present at Alma's death. Who was I to be so privileged to be there, to witness this miracle of death?

Startled by what seemed to be a new sound, I returned from my reflection to the scene before me. What I heard was not a noise, but rather complete silence. Maija and Adrian, resting their heads on their father's chest, were quietly crying. Chuck – eyes closed, face still faintly smiling – was no longer breathing. Deep peace and warmth now permeated every corner of what had been a cold and distant room an hour earlier.

After helping the children make the necessary phone calls, they each hugged me goodbye, offering their sincere thanks. I wandered back to my car, the clouds now dispersing, the gibbous moon now rising. Driving home late at night, I fanned this mysterious and previously not understood spark of feeling growing in my heart: the desire for death.

EPILOGUE

"Care more for the individual patient than for
the special features of the disease...
Put yourself in his place...
The kindly word, the cheerful greeting, the sympathetic look --
these the patient understands."

William Osler, M.D.

"You know," Mark commented one evening in the middle of June, as we were packing the very last box of medical texts for our upcoming moving day, "it is sort of a minor miracle we have made it to the point we can move to the new professional office building."

In several weeks, we would add two more physicians to our group of three, making our existing office suite impossibly small. As it was, there had been three physicians inhabiting the twelve-by-twelve-foot space containing our two desks and one folding metal table for two years now, and, with only three exam rooms, it had required very creative scheduling to allow all three doctors to see patients in what had become a tiny office.

"Our partnership will have added three new physicians in the five years we have been together," Mark calculated. This was an incredible growth rate for a primary care group in those days. We had excruciatingly high standards for new partners, but as teachers, we also had regular contact with the best residents from our own training program, and we had been able to lure the best two graduating residents into our group.

"I'm so glad you were willing to take me in after only one year of practice," I said. "Given our collective lack of business acumen, I think our basic sense of frugality is what saved us."

"Or almost killed us," Mark said, laughing, as he emptied his bottom file drawer into the last packing box.

We spent a few minutes recalling the many attempts we made to save money during the early years of the practice. There were the usual strategies, like buying necessary office supplies in bulk, and the expected consequences, like not having room in the examination room cabinets to store the one hundred rolls of toilet paper I had bought on my first office shopping trip.

We recalled one of our favorite practice history stories about the time we needed to create a space in the office for our typist to transcribe our dictated notes. The space was not a problem, but there was no proximate electrical outlet for her equipment. We had tried various extension cord solutions, all of which caused someone to trip at least once. Besides, the landlord told us our solutions each were fire hazards.

Preliminary estimates from the building contractor suggested it would "only" cost $1,400 to wire a new plug, clearly an amount we could not afford at the time. Having received my electricity merit badge in the Boy Scouts fifteen years prior, I could not see any reason to pay such an exorbitant amount for such a simple task. "Let me handle this," I said.

Mark was skeptical, but he knew I was likely to try it anyway. He didn't exactly give his approval, nor did he say no.

"No," did say our landlord, "I can't turn off the electricity so you can do the wiring yourself. It has to be done by an approved electrical contractor."

"No problem, Mark," I assured my doubting practice partner the next day. "I can attach the wire with the electricity still on, then easily run it through the wall. Total materials cost will be $4.50, maximum."

Flash-forward to the following Friday at about 7:00 in the evening. The ceiling tiles had been retracted, the electrical junction box opened. Flashlight in my mouth, pointing towards the exposed electrical wires, I was standing on the six-foot aluminum extension ladder, my shoeless feet carefully obscuring the label reading, "CAUTION SAFETY HAZARD: Do Not Stand On Or Above This Step!" I was apparently unfamiliar with the concept of foreshadowing.

So far, everything is going according to plan. I can't believe we were going to have to pay $1,400 for this, I laughed to myself, just before the bright flash of light. Immediately following that, I simultaneously heard the loud pop and felt the sense of electrical current running down my arm, through my torso, and down my legs into the ladder. Something smelled funny. The white electrical cable flew by my face, and I felt my legs giving way.

Of course, the next logical step was to grab the white ceiling tile support frame as the ladder fell over sideways, crashing onto the secretary's desk. Not surprisingly, my own weight greatly exceeded that of the four ceiling tiles normally suspended by this intersection of flimsy aluminum. Fortunately, I had the overturned ladder to break my fall. I am not certain whether or not there is such a thing as an acrobatics merit badge, but it was clear that if it did exist, I would never have earned it.

Now lying on my back, with the fallen ladder acting as my cradle, I opened my eyes. My flashlight, still in my mouth, pointed directly at the electrical box above, illuminating a remaining trace of smoke.

Well, I'm conscious, I realized, as I began my own personal medical review of systems. I could move both arms, both legs. *That's good.* My back hurt, but nothing was broken as far as I could tell. Struggling to my feet, I reset the ladder in a vertical position and began to climb it again.

Then, out of the blue, a bolt of rationality broke through. *Go home, you idiot! A trip to the emergency room will cost you a lot more than $1,400!* It must have been the dawn of the sort of good judgment one develops after an experience such as this, an experience deeply rooted in bad judgment. I packed up my things and went home.

Sixteen hundred seventy-six dollars and twenty-seven cents later, our new office dictation station was ready to go. It had cost a bit more than we had expected due to the repair work needed on the ceiling tile frame. As it turned out, the junction box I had opened carried 220 volts of current, which would have instantly fried the dictation equipment the moment it was plugged in. Perhaps it was just as well to have the contractor do the wiring after all.

"You know," Mark said, pulling the last item out of the drawer while looking at me over his frameless glasses, "I think this is an appropriate time for an official review of 'The Humor File.'" He held in his hands a three-inch thick tattered manila folder, which was full of a special category of practice heirlooms. This sacred file was the repository of anything we had found funny over our five years in practice together, with a particular emphasis on medical humor. I believe Mark had started the file during my second week in the practice, a particularly humorless time in my tenure with him. Patients brought us cartoons and we put them in the file. An unusually ironic picture appeared in our hospital newsletter, and one of us added thought balloons above each face, with inappropriate and sophomoric, but humorous, labels, and we put it in the file. Bizarre articles from the lay press or even stranger pharmaceutical ads in medical journals were always deposited in the manila treasure box. Review of the Humor File during the darker and more stressful times of our practice life became a ritual between Mark and me. It was impossible to page through the bulging file of hilarity without laughing hard enough to produce another forty-eight hour supply of endorphins, chemicals produced by the human brain that create a sense of euphoria. We judged the best contributions to be the most subtle ones. The deeper the irony, the harder we laughed.

The first item, on office letterhead (Edwards, Roberts, and Dennison, M.D.s, P.C.) was a script the office staff had written for a song in "honor" of their "beloved doctors" for our most recent office holiday party at my home. The medley, sung to the tune of their favorite songs from *The Sound of Music*, contained a verse highlighting the personality foibles and behavioral quirks of each of the three practice physicians in the way that only overworked, underpaid, and hopelessly dedicated employees in an overcrowded office can produce.

(To the song, "*The Sound of Music*")
The phones are alive, with the sound of ringing
With gripes we have heard for a thousand days

(To "*Sixteen Going on Seventeen*")
Mark Edwards, you started it all
Now there's so many of us, we're hanging on the walls

Files line the hallways, charts fill the air
And when you want relief, you can go nowhere

(To the tune of *"Edelweiss"*)
Dr. Roberts, Dr. Roberts, every morning we greet you
Paste in our ears, notes on our backs, how we love to work here
We'd always hoped you'd bloom and grow,
      bloom and grow much taller
Dr. Roberts, Dr. Roberts, we always jump when you holler.

(To the tune of *"My Favorite Things"*)
STAT venous dopplers with six lumbar punctures
Front desk went crazy with three lines on hold
Then Dennison flew by, yelling at Cynth (Pelvic in 1, EKG in 2)
These are the things that make some of us wince…

The lyrics sheet closed with a commentary on our practice's diverse, and sometimes unusual, patients.

"We certainly have had some interesting cases, haven't we?" I said, and then I asked him about two or three of his most interesting patients, how they were doing, and whether they were still alive.

Mark updated me on each of their histories quickly, using medical jargon and acronyms to provide ten minutes of information in only two.

"You had some real doozies, too, David," he opined.

"Remember the lady who wrote thirty-seven of the Top 40 songs?" I responded eagerly. "I haven't seen her in over a year, but she is doing well. She continues to follow regularly with her psychiatrist. She was still teaching school and taking her lithium daily when I saw her last year."

"How is Mrs. Wilson doing?" Mark wondered. He had an uncanny way of remembering my patients' names many years later, even when I had long forgotten them. After laughing, as we always did, at the very thought of the referral from an obstetrician to an internist to diagnose a pregnancy, I became more serious.

"I never saw her again in the office, since it was just a referral, and the diagnosis had been made. I received a note from her last fall, though. She told me she had obtained her undergraduate degree and had begun teaching art history in our local community college. She's never been happier, she said."

I went on to update him on Johnny Moon, the Pinball Wizard. He had majored in computer engineering, at the time a new field, and moved to California to finish college while working for a new software firm, where he helped to develop some of the earliest and most successful computer games.

"Well, the Roger Redmond case is behind us, anyway," Mark mused. He rapped his knuckle on the Formica wood-simulated top of his desk. "Knock on wood. I hope we are never sued again. What a mess that was."

Never one for being superstitious, I was not sure his Formica tapping would provide much benefit. Nonetheless, in the many years we each continued to practice, neither of us would ever again need to avail ourselves of our medical liability insurance coverage.

"Here's a classic," Mark said, now chortling as he pulled another historical document from the Humor File. A fifth-generation photocopy of an article from a well-known tabloid, headlined, "Lonely Agony of the Man Allergic to 20th Century Living," it featured a picture of a man who looked exactly like Burt Reynolds at age forty, wearing a plastic mask and holding an oversized oxygen tank in his lap. According to the article, tap water, synthetic materials, additives, pollens, dusts, and animals could kill him. Apparently, newspaper and magazine ink was also lethal, which was the piece of irony Mark and I found most entertaining. Originally, the article had been brought in by one of Mark's patients, wondering if this could be her problem. At the time, we had been seeing a minor "epidemic" of patients believing their fatigue and loss of energy were due to environmental toxins, an apparently more desirable diagnosis than simple anxiety or depression.

Mark briefly scanned the article, looked at the patient, and said, "Well, I haven't heard that printed media could be lethal. However, if there was a fatal newspaper, it would be this one."

After the patient left, he showed me the article, then immediately deposited it into our humor file. We had ranked this "number one" in the category of Interesting Health Fads, edging out other contenders like the story about Cher almost choking on a vitamin pill (Robert Altman saved her life) and an actual article from the *Journal of the American Medical Association* entitled, "Deaths Related to Coffee Enemas." Not that either of these subjects were humorous in the sense of reveling in the tragedy of others. It was the irony we appreciated deeply.

Mark reflected, "You know, our patients are so diverse. When you think about the kindness and the hostility and everything in between our patients give to us, it's just amazing we know where to start with any of them. Like the professor who came here and wouldn't just come out and tell you he was eating two crates of lettuce per week. What other profession has the opportunity to deal with that?"

"You, know, Mark, I think I figured him out. I was so frustrated when he would come in, and what I finally understood was that he wasn't the problem. He just had a highly unusual diet. My frustration was really just with myself, with my own reaction to his choice of food, my own ridiculous tendency toward over-responsibility."

Mark smiled at my words. We both knew what a tremendous opportunity medicine offered us to learn more about ourselves.

"Remember the drunk driver I told you about who killed the mother and daughter on their bicycles?" I asked.

"Yes, but I didn't know the daughter had died," he replied.

"They never transferred her to the university. According to the ER nurses, she actually recovered well, and two weeks after the accident, she was scheduled to go home. The night before discharge, she had a massive aspiration. Her stomach contents had flowed up her esophagus and flooded her lungs. She developed pneumonia and died three days later from the resultant overwhelming infection. What a tragedy," I reflected.

"Getting hit by an automobile couldn't kill her, but the hospital could," Mark wryly observed. His comment predated research on medical errors causing hospital deaths by more than a decade.

"You haven't heard the rest of it. The drunk driver was tried on two counts of manslaughter and found guilty. The nurses told me the judge felt sorry for her, given her diagnosis of terminal lung cancer, and he suspended her sentence immediately after the jury delivered their verdict. I can't imagine how the husband and father must have felt at that moment, can you?"

He did not reply and just shook his head slowly.

Mark took a few minutes to talk about some of his own patients. Dr. Randolph, the physician with the septic knee who was suffering from his own bloodletting, had disappeared from our practice, and then our

Midwestern town, within a year of his diagnosis. Neither of us had heard anything from him since.

"I wonder what makes some of us decide to provide care as a profession, and others decide to receive care as their life's work?" he asked. "Is it genetic? Environmental? Both? Neither?"

I loved these rare moments when we both had time to talk with each other about something more than our immediate practice responsibilities. Mark had a deep philosophical bent, and conversations between physicians about what it feels like to be a doctor are all too rare.

"You know," he continued, "the best decision I made was to ignore Paul and to bring you into the practice. We would have gone out of business three years ago if it wasn't for you. Even through the rough patches, like your first week on hospital rounds and the lawsuit, I still always knew we could make this work."

I was now feeling uneasy, unworthy of Mark's direct compliments, yet another of my underlying shortcomings. I felt so indebted to him.

"Thanks," I replied, anxious to end my own discomfort and not really understanding his need to say these things. "You know," I replied, "I don't think I could have made it in private practice without you. I can be so brash, so quick to move, and we both know the results. You've been so steady, so supportive."

Mark shuffled a bit uncomfortably in his chair and slowly shook his head ever so slightly.

"Well, that may be how you see it. I feel like I've been too indecisive, too slow to react. I really appreciate your energy. Most of the time, we were both thinking the same thing. You were willing to stick your neck out, though, and actually say it."

"I was always taught that telling the truth was always the right thing to do. I was always so crushed when it didn't seem to work, when I communicated poorly and offended someone," I replied, frustrated with myself, but not quite understanding a better way.

There was a comfortable silence lasting a minute or so as we both reflected on all we had been through together.

"You know," Mark said somewhat tentatively, as he shifted in his chair, "I think it will be good for both of us to be part of a bigger practice. There are some things I'd like to explore, but I haven't had the time because of how busy we've both been."

"Like what, Mark?"

"Well, you know I've done some research in the past, and I really enjoyed it. I've wondered if there might be a way to spend some of my time back in academic circles. I've thought about doing some work in biostatistics."

I panicked. "You're thinking about leaving practice, Mark?"

"No, not quitting. But I do think there might be something beyond patient care in my future." He paused, as though thinking deeply. Mark was a brilliant physician, and I was certain he would do well in this endeavor should he make the decision to pursue it. "What about you, David? You certainly have enjoyed your involvement in the teaching program. Do you think you could continue just practicing full-time the rest of your career?"

Mark had touched on my principal challenge over the previous twelve years, since my first day of medical school: the all-consuming priority I had given medicine in my life. I had not yet found a single clue as to how to better balance my career and my family life. I was often exhausted from the emotional burden I carried with me, the very weight of life and death our vocation seemed to place as a mantle on our shoulders. I knew something needed to change, but I wasn't sure what it was. My general approach was to believe that if I could just change my circumstances, things would improve. It didn't occur to me for quite a few years that the necessary change needed to begin inside of me.

We both were aware I had been sounding an alarm about what I thought could be the impending implosion of the very residency training program from which Mark and I had graduated. Not having much tolerance for department politics, I had put our department chairman on the spot in several public venues. His response was understandably defensive. Someone once said, "People who are brutally honest get more satisfaction out of the brutality than out of the honesty." While I hate to admit it, that may have been the essence of my failure to communicate more effectively.

"Well, the residency program certainly does need help," I cautiously replied. "We didn't fill all of our positions this year, and I know there is talk about finding a new program director."

"You'd be great at it, David," Mark said encouragingly. "You have a talent for getting things organized, for making things better. You really should consider it."

"We'll see," I responded, pleased about Mark's confidence in me, but aware of some recently burned bridges as well. "But first, we need to move to our new office and successfully bring two new physicians on board."

We traded a few more compliments until we were both convinced we had violated too many rules from the unwritten Book of Guys concerning expressing either gratitude or emotions to other men. Then, I pulled out a framed photo of a man waving a conductor's baton from the Humor File. We both began laughing again. Mark had spent years caring for a seriously ill local artist who had achieved national notoriety. Mark had provided this somewhat eccentric gentleman with meticulous care and had genuinely admired his artwork. Shortly after his expected death, the patient's son came to the office to personally thank Mark for his excellent and compassionate care, and he told him how grateful the family had been. Mark also mentioned his admiration for the artist and his work.

The son, smiling broadly, said, "Well then, I have something very special for you!" He promised to return with a special gift "to help you remember my father by." Embarrassed, Mark didn't know what to say, other than to stammer, "Well, thank you, but, of course, that's not really necessary."

Despite his modesty, Mark became increasingly excited about the prospect, which, over the ensuing two weeks, became in his mind the certainty of receiving a signature piece of art created by his departed patient. I happened to be present the day Kathleen strolled into our cramped office quarters at noon with an elaborately wrapped gift box, about two by twelve by eighteen inches, announcing the gift was from the artist's son. Savoring the moment, Mark tilted it lightly to assess the weight of the contents, slowly unwrapped the paper, and gingerly opened the box.

"I think this is what I was hoping it might be," he said expectantly. We both knew the painting could be worth tens of thousands of dollars.

I was now standing behind him, eager to share the excitement of the moment. Inside the box was a smaller wrapped gift, this one about eight by ten by one-half inch. Now peeling the paper back more rapidly, he discovered a very grainy photograph of an older man with white hair, waving a baton. Squinting, I was trying to tell if this was an actual photo, or just a photocopy of one, in the $1.99 frame.

"Who is that, Mark?"

Mark let out a deep sigh. "That's my patient. He had a brief but unsuccessful foray into conducting after his paintings became popular."

"Well, that certainly will be something special to remember him by, won't it, Mark?"

Mark shook his head, and immediately opened the desk drawer, depositing the frame and its contents into the Humor File. Unlike most of the objects stored there, though, this one would not stay put. Somehow, the framed photo would appear on his desk just before an important meeting or a visit from a special guest. Each time, Mark would refile it at the earliest opportunity.

"Every time I see this picture, it reminds me to be humble. I worked so hard to provide him the best possible care, and when his son said he had something he wanted to give me to acknowledge all of my efforts, well…"

"You thought those efforts were worth more than $2.09, perhaps?" I said, finishing his sentence for him. We had determined the picture was a simple photocopy, worth about ten cents. The price tag was on still the frame when Mark opened the package.

"Well, I suppose each of our patients has something to teach us," Mark reflected.

"Yes, and the most important lessons seem to come from our most challenging teachers, don't they?"

Laughing, Mark summarized our first five years together well. "Before you joined me, Chuck Westerman told me, 'Being in a medical practice with someone is a lot like being married. You spend more time with him than your own family, you deal with life and death issues every day together, and you don't always agree. But if it's the right combination, it can work very well. If it is the wrong one, it will likely end in divorce.'"

We both fell silent. Nothing more needed to be said. We knew, between the two of us, we had what we needed to be successful in the practice of medicine. We could even add two new partners at one time, something unheard of at the time. In our total of fifteen years of practice together, we would grow to a group of fifteen internal medicine physicians.

It certainly wasn't our brilliant business acumen that would sustain us; we simply cared about our patients a great deal.

As Sir William Osler, considered by at least the two of us to be the father of modern medicine, had said, "Care more for the individual patient than for the special features of the disease... Put yourself in his place... The kindly word, the cheerful greeting, the sympathetic look – these the patient understands."

Somehow, through the caring we had provided each other through these five challenging years, we had also learned to truly care for each of our patients. No matter what new development health care financing would bring – be it HMO, PPO, or some other TLA (three letter acronym) – we both now knew with certainty that true caring would see us through.

ABOUT THE AUTHOR

The real Doctor Roberts (the author's name is a nom de plume) graduated from The University of Michigan Medical School in the 1970s and completed his Internal Medicine residency training in Ann Arbor, Michigan. He began in the private practice of Internal Medicine in 1981. The time period of this book is the first five years of his medical practice.

Since then, he has also received added certification in Geriatric Medicine, become an entertaining and sought after national public speaker, held several health care executive positions in Michigan and New Mexico (including the President of a one billion dollar health care company), and has been consistently named one of the Best Doctors in America for more than 15 years. In 2009, he happily returned to the practice of geriatric medicine and the art of writing, and has since been named every year as one of the Top Docs in Albuquerque.

He lives in an adobe home in the beautiful and sunny New Mexico desert south of Santa Fe.